POTASSIUM-ARGON DATING

A SERIES OF BOOKS IN GEOLOGY
Editors: James Gilluly and A. O. Woodford

POTASSIUM-ARGON DATING

Principles, Techniques
and
Applications to Geochronology

G. Brent Dalrymple and Marvin A. Lanphere
U. S. Geological Survey

W. H. FREEMAN AND COMPANY
San Francisco

Publication of this book has been authorized by
the Director of the U.S. Geological Survey.

Library of Congress Catalog Card Number: 71-84047
Standard Book Number: 7167 0241-X

1 2 3 4 5 6 7 8 9

To Sharon and Joyce

CONTENTS

Since 1905, when Rutherford first suggested that the transformation rates of radioactive nuclides might be used to determine the ages of rocks and minerals, nearly every naturally occurring radioisotope has been investigated for its possible use in geological age measurement. That the effort has been worthwhile is attested by the wide variety of radioactive dating methods now available to earth scientists. Of these, probably none has a wider range of applicability or has proven more useful than the potassium-argon method. Although first suggested as a "geological clock" about thirty years ago, the potassium-argon method has been in more or less routine use in geology for little more than a decade. Nevertheless, the growth of potassium-argon dating has been phenomenal, and in spite of its relative youth the technique is now widely used. Today literally thousands of potassium-argon age measurements are made each year by more than fifty laboratories throughout the world. More than ever, the earth scientist needs to understand the principles, the fundamental assumptions, the limitations, and the potential uses of this important method.

This book is an outgrowth of a pamphlet entitled *Potassium-Argon Dating: A Summary of Principles and Techniques*, written in 1965 and circulated within the Geologic Division of the U.S. Geological Survey. The pamphlet was written in response to requests from a number of our colleagues who desired to increase their knowledge of potassium-argon dating. What they needed was a brief and simple explanation of the principles and techniques of potassium-argon dating with emphasis on the practical questions of what the method can and cannot do. The pamphlet was our answer to that need. Since the pamphlet was distributed, we have been repeatedly urged to expand the work into publishable form and to add references, examples, and additional illustrations.

In writing this book, we have attempted to preserve the brevity and simplicity of the original pamphlet and yet make the book more nearly complete and, we hope, more useful. The book is not a scholarly or comprehensive review of potassium-argon dating, but rather an introduction to the principles, techniques, and applications of the method. Its length was dictated primarily by our view of a proper balance between an adequate amount of information and the time required to read it. We have placed special emphasis on explaining the fundamental assumptions that are made whenever analytical data are used to calculate a potassium-argon age—assumptions not only about the potassium-argon clock in particular but also about such things as the constancy of radioactive decay and the distribution of potassium and argon isotopes. We have also included a substantial amount of practical information that we feel will help earth scientists use potassium-argon dating and data to best advantage—among these, hints for sample preparation the amount of sample required for an analysis, a check list and discussion of the causes of anomalous ages, and an annotated list of the minerals and rocks that can be dated. It is our hope that both students and working earth scientists will find this book valuable not only as an introduction to potassium-argon dating but as a practical guide to its use.

Throughout the book we have used examples of age data to illustrate particular points. These examples, in the form of tables and figures, are not intended to be complete compilations, but to be representative of the available data. We have frequently cited our own data and referred to our own experience because that is the work with which we were the most familiar. Although the reference list is by no means complete, we have tried to include enough references so that readers can pursue subjects of particular interest further.

We have tried to organize the book in such a way that topics not of immediate interest to the reader may be skipped. Whenever information in one chapter is drawn from another chapter, we have tried to give cross-references to the particular page, figure, or formula. The first four chapters deal mainly with principles and theory. Much of this information, especially that in

Chapters 1 and 2, may already be familiar to many readers. Nevertheless, we hope that many will welcome, as we did when we wrote it, the opportunity to review the historical development of some of the fundamentals of physics and chemistry upon which all radioactive clocks depend. Chapters 3 and 4 are discussions of the discovery and distribution of the potassium and argon isotopes and of the way in which they interact to produce a successful geologic chronometer.

Chapters 5 and 6 are descriptions of the techniques commonly used to measure the amounts of argon and potassium in rocks and minerals. Mostly, we have described the methods and equipment used by the U.S. Geological Survey. The procedures used by other laboratories differ only in detail; the principles and goals are the same. We have described the methods for measuring argon in much greater detail than the methods for measuring potassium. This does not imply that the argon analysis is more important, for each element contributes equally to a potassium-argon age. Methods of potassium measurement, however, are adequately described in books on analytical chemistry and elsewhere in the literature, but very few complete descriptions of the methods of analyzing argon are available. All isotopic dating methods rely heavily upon the mass spectrometer, and for this reason we have included a somewhat detailed discussion of this analytical tool in Chapter 5.

Chapters 7 through 11 are concerned with applications, problems, and the practical limitations of potassium-argon dating. Chapter 7 is a discussion of accuracy and precision—an aspect of dating that is all too often treated lightly or ignored. Chapters 8 and 9 concern two of the most important problems with the potassium-argon clock: extraneous argon and argon loss. Chapter 10 is primarily an annotated list of the minerals that have and have not been found amenable to potassium-argon dating, but also contains some suggestions about sample preparation. The last chapter includes suggestions about ways in which age data can be evaluated and examples of the way in which the potassium-argon method has been used in several actual dating problems. We have included four brief appendices that we hope will be helpful. Appendix A includes a list of the constants that are necessary for the calculation of a potassium-argon age and a table of conversion factors; the latter is included because the way in which analytical data are reported has not been standardized, and there is little hope that it will be. Appendix B is a nomogram that can be used to calculate an age quickly from analytical data. A sample age calculation, with explanation, is given in Appendix C. Appendix D contains derivations of isotope-dilution formulae.

We would like to thank Allan Cox, Richard R. Doell, Ian McDougall, L. J. Patrick Muffler, Thomas W. Stern, and Robert E. Zartman, who read the manuscript and contributed many helpful suggestions. We are also grateful to Richard L. Hay, C. Oliver Ingamells, Ronald W. Kistler, Alan E.

Mussett, and Dallas L. Peck for reviewing particular sections or chapters, and to Frances M. Pickthorn, Patricia H. Jenkins, and Bessie S. Hayashida for their tireless typing, retyping, and preparation of the manuscript. We owe a special debt of gratitude to those of our colleagues who needled us into writing this book, for it has been a worthwhile and enjoyable experience. Finally, "Thanks anyway" to our five little daughters who wanted to help but couldn't.

Menlo Park, California   G. BRENT DALRYMPLE

January 1969   MARVIN A. LANPHERE

1

ATOMS, ELEMENTS, AND ISOTOPES

The origin of the idea that all matter is composed of some elementary substance or substances is not known, although the general concept can be traced as far into history as the ancient Greek philosophers. Thales believed that water was the basis of all things, and Heraclitus considered fire the "first principle." The concept of atomism, which eventually led to modern atomic theory, is generally attributed to Leucippus, who lived in the fifth century B.C. His ideas were expanded by his student Democritus, who believed that all that existed was composed of atoms and empty space. Democritus' ever-moving atoms had no qualities but position, shape, size, and impenetrability. Unfortunately, the concept of atoms ("indivisibles") was not accepted by Aristotle, whose teachings that matter consisted of earth, air, fire, and water dominated science for nearly two millennia. As a result, atomism languished until well after the Renaissance.

DEVELOPMENT OF ATOMIC THEORY

The Revival of Atomism

Although during the seventeenth and eighteenth centuries men like Robert Boyle, Sir Isaac Newton, and Antoine Lavoisier used forms of atomic theory in their writings about chemistry and physics, the concept did not truly dominate scientific thought until the time of John Dalton. In 1803 Dalton, whose ideas about the building blocks of nature were to revolutionize chemistry, arrived at his theory of the atom. From the study of gases, he reasoned that any element could be reduced to atoms—tiny indivisible spheres that for one element were alike in every way and were different from the atoms of any other element. In 1808 he announced his "Law of Multiple Proportions," which stated that elements that combine to form compounds do so in fixed mass ratios. To Dalton, compounds were formed by the joining of two or more atoms in proportions that were characteristic of the nature of the compound and the atomic weight of the elements. Thus, 16 grams of oxygen would combine with 2 grams of hydrogen to form 18 grams of water. Using this concept, Dalton was actually able to tabulate atomic weights (or atomic numbers, for at that time the difference was not recognized) for many of the elements.

In 1897 J. J. Thomson of the Cavendish Laboratory at Cambridge, England, discovered the electron. This important finding, along with the discovery of X-rays by Roentgen in 1895 and of radioactivity by Becquerel in 1896, soon led to the abandonment of the concept of the indivisible atom. Thomson proposed a new model in which an atom was composed of electrical "charges." According to Thomson an atom was a sphere of uniformly distributed positive electricity within which were embedded negatively charged electrons

Hydrogen   Oxygen

FIGURE 1-1

Examples of Thomson's concept of atoms, showing negative electrons distributed within a positively charged "fluid."

(Fig. 1-1). Thomson's atoms have been described as being similar to tiny plum puddings studded with raisins.

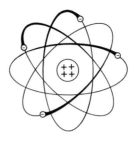

Hydrogen   Beryllium

FIGURE 1-2
Examples of Rutherford's concept of atoms. The nuclei and electrons are drawn more than 1,000 times too large relative to the size of the atoms.

The next major step in unraveling the mysteries of the atom was taken by Ernest Rutherford, also of the Cavendish Laboratory. In order to account for the manner in which some alpha particles (helium nuclei) were scattered by the atoms in foil targets, Rutherford (1911) proposed that all of the positive charges were concentrated in a tiny nucleus and that the electrons were distributed over a sphere of radius comparable to the atomic radius (Fig. 1-2). Rutherford's calculations and subsequent experiments showed that atomic nuclei were tiny indeed, having diameters on the order of only 10^{-12} centimeter as compared with atomic diameters of about 10^{-8} centimeter. Rutherford's work not only led to the concept of the atomic nucleus but also resulted in the very important discovery that the number of positive charges in the nucleus of an atom is exactly equal to the atomic number, Z. In a neutral atom, therefore, the atomic number also represents the number of electrons rotating about the nucleus. Thus was developed a theory that pictured atoms as consisting of a tiny nucleus composed of Z positive charges (protons) around which swarmed a "cloud" of Z negative charges (electrons) at distances that defined the atomic radius. Every element was composed of atoms that contained a like number of protons, and this number was unique for the atoms of a given element. We shall see how Rutherford's picture of the nucleus had to be modified later, but first let us examine an important revision of Rutherford's electron cloud.

The Bohr Atom

In 1900 Max Planck formulated his quantum theory, which states that radiation, such as light, travels as neither wave nor particle, but as small packets of energy (quanta) that display some of the properties of both wave and particle. Thirteen years later, Neils Bohr applied this revolutionary idea

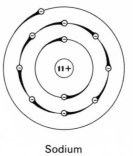

Carbon   Sodium

FIGURE 1-3
Two-dimensional views of atoms according to Bohr's concept.

to Rutherford's nuclear atom and developed a theory that is still embodied in the basic "picture" of the atom used today (Bohr, 1913).

Bohr proposed his atomic model to explain certain aspects of the emission and absorption of light, for which Rutherford's model could not account. His notion, like Rutherford's, was that an atom consists of a nucleus with Z positive protons surrounded by Z negative electrons. The important difference was that the electrons rotate in circular orbits around the nucleus and that their energy is quantized, or to put it another way, comes only in discrete packages. Thus arose the idea of electron shells, or orbits of distinct radius, to which the electrons were confined (Fig. 1-3). These shells are denoted, from the innermost one outward, by the letters K, L, M, N, ... It was possible, in Bohr's model, for an electron to jump from one orbit to another, but only under certain conditions, one of which was that the electron must either absorb or emit a specific quantity of radiation, depending, respectively, on whether it jumped to a higher or a lower orbit. We shall see one of the ways in which this phenomenon is put to practical use in Chapter 6, which describes methods of potassium measurement.

Bohr's atomic model not only accounted for the emission and absorption of light by atoms but, with some refinement, helped clarify certain aspects of chemical behavior. The addition, by Wolfgang Pauli in 1925, of the exclusion principle* to Bohr's theory explained chemical valency. Not only were the electrons confined to rotation in specific paths of fixed radius, but each path could accommodate only $2n^2$ electrons, where $n = 1, 2, 3, . . .$ is the position of the electron shell outward from the nucleus (Fig. 1-4). Thus

_____

*The Pauli exclusion principle states that no two electrons in an atom can exist in the same state. The electrons in a given shell do not all follow exactly the same path, but are distributed in pairs and occupy orbitals. The electrons in an orbital must spin in opposite directions in order to satisfy the exclusion principle. Orbitals are discussed further on page 7.

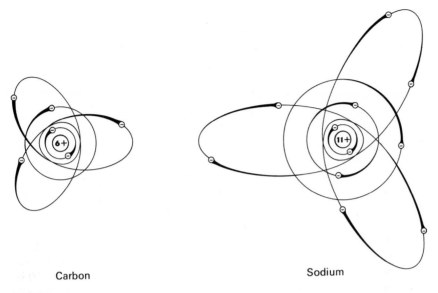

Carbon   Sodium

FIGURE 1-4
Two-dimensional views of Bohr's concept of atomic structure, showing the modified electron configuration required by the Pauli exclusion principle.

the first, or K, shell could have only $2(1)^2=2$ electrons, the L shell could have only $2(2)^2=8$ electrons, and so forth. The chemical inactivity of the inert gases could be accounted for easily by the fact that the outer shells of their atoms are completely filled with electrons and, therefore, chemical combination with another element is virtually impossible. This explanation is slightly oversimplified, for a quick calculation will show that the outer shell of an argon atom ($Z=18$) is not filled. The discrepancy arises because we have not considered the question of subshells, which are discussed briefly on page 7.

Still later developments in quantum mechanics forced abandonment of most of the details of the Bohr theory. Nevertheless, we still use the Bohr "picture" of the atom today, because these later developments really do not allow us to have a "picture" of the atom at all—at least not one that can be drawn on paper.

DISCOVERY OF ISOTOPES

As early as 1886, it was suggested by W. Crookes that atoms of an element might have several different whole-number weights. The discovery of radioactivity by Becquerel a decade later, and the research on radioactive substances that rapidly followed, soon made it apparent that there were at least some elements whose atoms had identical chemical properties but differed in atomic weight. This was a considerable departure from Dalton's original concept of what constituted an element, for Dalton's atoms were identical in every respect, including weight.

In 1910 Frederick Soddy proposed the name "isotope" (meaning "same place") for atoms with different atomic weights but identical atomic numbers. Three years later, Thomson (1914), using a prototype of the mass spectrograph, discovered two isotopes of neon of mass 20 and 22. His experiment was not sensitive enough to measure the relative proportions of the two isotopes, but the 10 percent difference between their masses made them easily detectable. Almost immediately, F. W. Aston, working in Thomson's laboratory, redesigned Thomson's apparatus and using this first quantitative mass spectrograph,* verified Thomson's result and discovered yet a third isotope of neon (Ne^{21}) (Aston, 1920a). The search for isotopes began. Work progressed rapidly, and only 10 years after the first isotope was discovered, 70 isotopes of 29 elements had been identified (Aston, 1923). Among the 104 elements so far discovered, nearly 300 stable isotopes are known. In addition, there are about 1,000 unstable isotopic species, most of which must be manufactured, so to speak, in the laboratory.

It was well known in the 1920's that the chemical properties of an atom depended only on its atomic number. How then could the difference in the masses of the isotopes of an element be explained within the framework of the atomic theory of that time? This problem was solved by hypothetically increasing the number of protons in the nucleus enough to account for the atomic mass, A, and then neutralizing the excess positive charge by adding $A - Z$ electrons to the nucleus. Thus, electrons were required both in the nucleus and in the electron shells. In 1932 Chadwick discovered the neutron, an uncharged particle with about the same mass as a proton, and the hypothetical dual role of the electron was no longer required (Chadwick, 1932).

THE MODERN VIEW OF THE ATOM

Let us briefly summarize all of these ideas on the nature of the atom as they have been incorporated into modern atomic theory. Each element consists of atoms that are characterized mainly by their atomic number, Z. An atom of atomic number Z has Z protons in its nucleus and, if electrically neutral, Z electrons distributed about the nucleus in *electron shells*. In general, electrons are added to shells from the innermost, or K, shell out-

---

*The principle of operation of the mass spectrograph is virtually the same as that of the mass spectrometer, which is described in Chapter 5.

wards* (*L*, *M*, *N*, and so forth), and a shell can contain no more than $2n^2$ electrons, where $n = 1, 2, 3, \ldots$ is the relative position of the shell from the nucleus. Each shell except the *K* shell is divided into *subshells*. These subshells are the reason that argon is an inert gas in spite of the fact that its outer electron shell is incompletely filled. Atoms with certain of their subshells filled are stable and form the inert gas elements. Electrons are distributed in pairs and occupy *orbitals*. The word "orbital" is used because the electrons actually do not occupy specific orbits but instead move in a rather random manner. The orbitals are merely the most probable positions of the electrons. Each orbital may contain only two electrons, and these must spin in opposite directions to satisfy the exclusion principle.

As the electron shells are filled, the inner shells decrease in radius because of the repulsive forces of the outer electrons and the attraction of the nucleus. This explains why atomic radii of all atoms differ from one another by less than a factor of three, instead of in proportion to the number of electron shells and subshells. An electron may jump from a higher orbit to a lower one if there is a vacancy, and in the process the atom emits a quantum of radiation. In fact, in some special atoms, an electron may even fall from an orbit into the nucleus. This phenomenon, discussed in some detail in the next two chapters, is the *basis* of the potassium-argon dating method.

If one or more electrons are removed from the outer shell of an atom, the atom becomes a positively charged *ion*; if electrons are added to the outer shell, it becomes a negatively charged ion. In this state the atom, or ion, can be influenced by electrical or magnetic fields. The chemical behavior of the elements is controlled almost entirely by the configuration of the electrons.

The nucleus of an atom occupies only about 10^{-14} of the volume of an atom and yet contains nearly all of the mass. For example, the density of a single neutral hydrogen atom of mass 1 is about 8 grams per cubic centimeter, whereas the density of its nucleus alone is 2×10^{14} grams per cubic centimeter. A thimble-full of these nuclei would weigh about 40 million tons! All known elements have two or more isotopes that are chemically identical in every way but differ in the number of neutrons in the nucleus. Some isotopes, however, are unstable, and don't occur naturally. Ordinary hydrogen consists of a nucleus of one proton and one orbiting electron. Deuterium, a second isotope of hydrogen, has one proton and one neutron in its nucleus; this neutron doubles the mass number but leaves the atomic number unchanged. A third isotope of hydrogen, tritium, has one proton and two neutrons in the nucleus and is radioactive (Fig. 1-5). The naturally occurring, stable isotopes of some of the most common rock-forming elements are given in Table 1-1.

---

*This is true up through titanium ($Z = 22$), whereupon electrons begin to be added to some of the inner shells once more.

 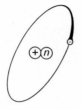 

Protium, H^1 Deuterium, H^2 Tritium, H^3

FIGURE 1-5
The isotopes of hydrogen. Tritium is radioactive.

TABLE 1-1
Naturally occurring stable isotopes of some of the elements
commonly found in rocks.

Element	Atomic no. (Z)	Mass no. (A)	Symbol	Relative abundance (percent)
Hydrogen	1	1	$_1H^1$	99.98
		2	$_1H^2$	0.02
Oxygen	8	16	$_8O^{16}$	99.76
		17	$_8O^{17}$	0.04
		18	$_8O^{18}$	0.20
Sodium	11	23	$_{11}Na^{23}$	100.00
Magnesium	12	24	$_{12}Mg^{24}$	78.70
		25	$_{12}Mg^{25}$	10.13
		26	$_{12}Mg^{26}$	11.17
Aluminum	13	27	$_{13}Al^{27}$	100.00
Silicon	14	28	$_{14}Si^{28}$	92.21
		29	$_{14}Si^{29}$	4.70
		30	$_{14}Si^{30}$	3.09
Calcium	20	40	$_{20}Ca^{40}$	96.97
		42	$_{20}Ca^{42}$	0.64
		43	$_{20}Ca^{43}$	0.14
		44	$_{20}Ca^{44}$	2.06
		46	$_{20}Ca^{46}$	<0.01
		48	$_{20}Ca^{48}$	0.18
Iron	26	54	$_{26}Fe^{54}$	5.82
		56	$_{26}Fe^{56}$	91.66
		57	$_{26}Fe^{57}$	2.19
		58	$_{26}Fe^{58}$	0.33

TABLE 1-2
Masses of the principal subatomic particles.

Particle	Mass
Electron	$(9.1085 \pm 0.0006) \times 10^{-28}$ gram
Proton	$(1.6724 \pm 0.0001) \times 10^{-24}$ gram
Neutron	$(1.6747 \pm 0.0001) \times 10^{-24}$ gram

A proton weighs 1,836 times more than an electron (Table 1-2), and its mass is very nearly equal to one atomic mass unit (1 amu $= 1.6597 \times 10^{-24}$ gram), which is defined as one-sixteenth of the weight of the isotope O^{16}. There is very little difference between the masses of the proton and the neutron. It is sometimes convenient to think of a neutron as the combination of a proton and an electron. In fact, a free neutron has a mean life of only about 17 minutes and will spontaneously decay into a proton and an electron. Likewise, the collision of a proton and an electron may result in the formation of a neutron.

The mass number, A, of an isotope is the mass of the atom, in amu, expressed to the nearest whole number. It is also the number of protons plus neutrons in the nucleus, because the weight of each of these two nucleons* is almost identical to one atomic mass unit. An atom with 2 neutrons and 2 protons (helium) has an atomic mass number of 4, one with 18 neutrons and 17 protons (chlorine) has a mass number of 35, and so forth. The mass number and atomic number generally are represented by superscripts and subscripts, respectively. Carbon of mass 12 is $_6C^{12}$, oxygen of mass 17 is $_8O^{17}$, and so forth. The international convention is to use a left-hand superscript for the mass number and reserve the right-hand superscript for valency, but many workers in the United States use the right-hand superscript for mass number, as will be done in this book.

Just as the word "element" is used for atoms with like atomic number, the word "nuclide" is used to characterize atomic species with a unique number of protons and neutrons in the nucleus. Thus each isotope of any element is called a *nuclide*.

It might appear that an unlimited number of isotopes of any one element could be made merely by adding neutrons to the nucleus, but this is not the case. The nucleus is held together by what might be described as a sort of nuclear "glue" that is not well understood but apparently consists of particles called mesons. If a nucleus contains too many neutrons the repulsive forces overcome the forces binding the nucleus together and it becomes unstable. When this happens, the isotope is said to be radioactive. Nuclear stability and radioactivity will be treated in more detail in the next chapter.

---

*Protons and neutrons in the nucleus are collectively called *nucleons*.

UNITS OF MEASUREMENT

In the same year that Dalton announced his "Law of Multiple Proportions," the French physicist and chemist J. L. Gay-Lussac published evidence showing that gases also combine chemically in fixed proportions. Gay-Lussac discovered that these proportions were by volume, which immediately suggested to the Italian physicist Amedeo Avogadro that equal volumes of gases contain equal numbers of molecules and that for any given pressure and temperature the volume of a gas depends only upon the number of molecules present. This is known as *Avogadro's Law*.

Today, the amount of a chemical compound or element usually is expressed in terms of the *gram-molecular weight*, usually called *mole* and abbreviated *mol*, which is the molecular weight of the compound expressed in grams. The concept of the mole is valid whether we are considering an element, a compound, or an isotope. For an isotope, a mole is its atomic mass expressed in grams. For an element it is the atomic weight expressed in grams,* and for a compound it is the sum of the atomic weights of the constituent elements expressed in grams (Table 1-3).

TABLE 1-3
Gram-molecular weights of some isotopes, elements, and compounds.

Substance	Symbol	Atomic weight(s)	Gram-molecular weight (grams)
Argon	Ar	39.94	39.94
Argon-40	Ar^{40}	40.00	40.00
Potassium	K	39.10	39.10
Carbon	C	12.01	12.01
Carbon-14	C^{14}	14.00	14.00
Oxygen	O_2	2(16.00)	32.00
Silicon	Si	28.06	28.06
Potassium oxide	K_2O	2(39.10) + (16.00)	94.20
Carbon dioxide	CO_2	(12.01) + 2(16.00)	44.01
Silicon dioxide	SiO_2	(28.06) + 2(16.00)	60.06

One mole of a compound contains 6.0225×10^{23} molecules. Likewise a mole of a single element or a single isotope contains 6.0225×10^{23} atoms. This number is known as *Avogadro's Number*. Even if we are working with a fraction of a gram of an element, we are still dealing with huge numbers

---

*Actually, for an element the correct term is "gram-atomic weight," but mole is commonly used anyway.

of atoms. For example, in one million-billionth (10^{-15}) of a mole there are nearly one billion (10^9) molecules!

For gases at 0° centigrade and one atmosphere of pressure, a mole occupies a volume of 22.41 liters, which is known as a *molar volume*. For a gas like nitrogen, which forms diatomic molecules (N_2), 22.41 liters contain 6.0225×10^{23} molecules and (2) $(6.0225 \times 10^{23}) = 1.2045 \times 10^{24}$ atoms. For the inert gases, however, a mole contains only Avogadro's Number of atoms because they are monatomic and do not form molecules.

The amount of a gas also can be expressed in terms of the volume that it would occupy at standard temperature and pressure (STP),* which is 0°C and 760 mm of mercury (one atmosphere). When this is done, the standard unit is the cubic centimeter (cc STP), of which there are 2.241×10^4 in a mole of gas at STP.

Measured quantities frequently are expressed in percent. This is almost always true of the elements and their oxides whenever an analysis of a rock is presented, and unless otherwise specified, this always means weight percent. Another measure sometimes used is parts per million (ppm); that it is by weight is also understood. Only infrequently is the amount of gas in a substance expressed in ppm.

All of these units are valid measures of quantity, and their use is mainly a matter of preference. We will follow the convention of using weight percent for the solid elements and their oxides, and moles for gas. Conversion factors are given in Appendix A.

---

*NTP, or normal temperature and pressure, and SC, which stands for standard conditions, mean the same thing as STP.

2

RADIOACTIVITY

The dream of the medieval alchemists was to change lead into gold, but they were never able to accomplish this transformation of elements. Although no one has been able to change base metals into gold, transformation of some elements into others occurs commonly in nature. This phenomenon is known as radioactivity and is the basis of the modern physical dating methods.

DISCOVERY OF RADIOACTIVITY

The starting point in the sequence of events that led to the development of radioactive dating methods was the discovery, by Wilhelm Roentgen in 1895, of X-rays, which are produced when a beam of cathode rays (electrons) strikes a solid target. It was thought that the emission of X-rays might be related to the phosphorescence produced by cathode rays on the walls of a vacuum tube, and this speculation stimulated research on the phosphorescence of certain minerals. In 1896 Henri Becquerel, while studying phosphorescence, discovered that uranium salts emitted radiation that had properties similar to X-rays. This radiation could penetrate matter that was either transparent or opaque to light, could darken a photographic plate, and could induce electrical conductivity in gases. This property of matter, the spontaneous emission of radiation, was termed "radioactivity," and the term "activity" was used to describe the intensity of the radiation of a substance compared to that of a standard substance, usually uranium.

Shortly after Becquerel's discovery of radioactivity, Marie Curie systematically examined different substances for natural radiation, and found that thorium also was radioactive. She also discovered that the radioactivity of uranium was an atomic property; that is, the observed activity depended only on the amount of uranium present and not on the chemical compound in which the uranium occurred. Moreover, she found that some minerals known to contain uranium and thorium were several times more radioactive than pure uranium or thorium, and she deduced that the large activity must be caused by an unknown substance. This led to the famous experiment in which Madame Curie chemically separated the source of the unknown radioactivity from uranium ore (pitchblende from Joachimsthal, Czechoslovakia). She discovered, in the various chemical fractions, not one but two active substances, which were identified later as the elements radium and polonium.

The discovery of radium caused a great deal of interest in the chemical examination of radioactive minerals in order to see if other radioactive substances could be found. By 1902, many different radioactive substances had been discovered, and it became obvious that the radioactivity of uranium and thorium was a composite effect produced by several different radioactive elements.

Between 1900 and 1902, experiments by Crookes, Becquerel, and Rutherford and Soddy provided evidence on the manner in which one radioactive substance is produced from another. Crookes found that a highly radioactive substance could be separated chemically from uranium salts; the active substance (named uranium X, or UX) produced nearly all of the observed activity whereas the uranium itself had very little activity. In subsequent experiments, Becquerel found that if the uranium X were separated from the uranium, and the fractions allowed to stand separately for some time, the activity of the uranium X fraction decreased whereas the activity of the uranium fraction increased. Rutherford and Soddy obtained similar results with thorium salts, and in addition, they were able to make quantitative measurements that enabled them to propose a general theory to explain radioactivity.

THE LAWS OF RADIOACTIVITY

Rutherford and Soddy (1902a, 1902b, 1902c, 1902d) carried out a series of important experiments beginning with an investigation of the radioactive gas or "emanation" emitted by thorium compounds. They found that the gas, if separated from a thorium compound and left to itself, lost its activity

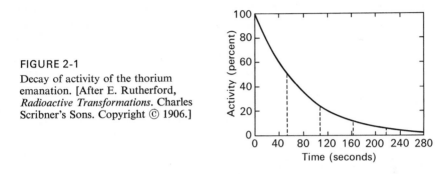

FIGURE 2-1

Decay of activity of the thorium emanation. [After E. Rutherford, *Radioactive Transformations*. Charles Scribner's Sons. Copyright © 1906.]

as shown in Figure 2-1. After 54.5 seconds the activity was only one-half of its initial value, after 109 seconds the activity was only one-quarter of its initial value, after 163.5 seconds the activity was only one-eighth of its initial value, and so on. They had discovered that the decay of activity of the thorium emanation was exponential. It was subsequently demonstrated that the property of exponential decay is characteristic of all radioactive substances.

Next, Rutherford and Soddy investigated the source of the thorium emanation. They dissolved some thorium nitrate in water and then precipitated the thorium as the hydroxide. The filtrate was evaporated to dryness, leaving a small, highly active residue that Rutherford and Soddy called thorium X (later shown to be radium^{224}). The activity of the thorium X

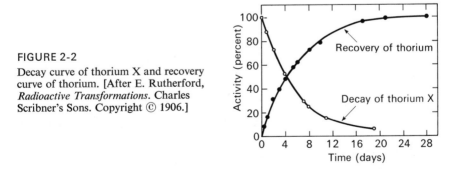

FIGURE 2-2

Decay curve of thorium X and recovery curve of thorium. [After E. Rutherford, *Radioactive Transformations*. Charles Scribner's Sons. Copyright © 1906.]

decreased with time, and the activity of the thorium, which had been removed, increased with time. The activity curves plotted in Figure 2-2 show that the thorium activity recovered steadily and reached a constant value in about a month, whereas during the same interval of time the thorium X activity decayed to essentially nothing.

On the basis of these observations, Rutherford and Soddy proposed a theory to explain radioactive change or transformation. It had already been shown that radioactivity is an atomic property. Rutherford and Soddy suggested that the atoms of radioactive elements are unstable and that within a given period of time a fixed proportion of the atoms spontaneously disintegrate to form atoms of a new element. They further proposed that this disintegration is accompanied by emission of alpha or beta particles* and that the activity or intensity of radioactivity is proportional to the number of atoms that disintegrate per unit time. Because radioactivity is a property of the atom, Rutherford and Soddy concluded that the activity of a substance is directly proportional to the number of atoms of the substance present. That is, radioactive decay is a statistical process in which the number of atoms that disintegrate per unit time, $-dN/dt$, is proportional to the number of atoms present, N. Thus

$$-\frac{dN}{dt} = \lambda N, \tag{2-1}$$

where λ, the *decay constant*, represents the probability that an atom will decay in unit time.

If equation (2-1) is integrated between $N = N_0$ at $t = 0$ and $N = N$ at $t = t$ we get

$$\int_{N_0}^{N} \frac{dN}{N} = -\int_{0}^{t} \lambda \, dt, \tag{2-2}$$

$$\log_e \frac{N}{N_0} = -\lambda t, \tag{2-3}$$

$$N = N_0 e^{-\lambda t}, \tag{2-4}$$

which is the basic radioactive decay formula; N_0 is the initial number of atoms present and N is the number of atoms at time t.

Egon von Schweidler independently deduced the exponential law of decay in 1905 without making any assumptions about the structure of the radio-

---

*Alpha and beta particles are discussed on pages 19–20.

active atoms or about the mechanism of disintegration. He assumed only that the disintegration of an atom of a radioactive element is subject to the laws of chance and that the probability for an atom to disintegrate in any given time interval is independent of the past history of the atom and is the same for all atoms of the same type (Meyer and Schweidler, 1927).

At first it may seem contradictory to say that the number of decaying atoms depends on the number of atoms present and yet to claim that the probability that an atom will disintegrate is always the same. However, there is no conflict. Imagine a box containing a number of radioactive atoms, all with the same probability of decay. Let us say that the probability is 50 percent that any given atom will decay in 10 minutes. Then, in 10 minutes we can expect one-half of the atoms to undergo decay (provided that the number of atoms is large enough to be treated statistically). This will be true regardless of the number of atoms present in the box, but at the same time the number that decay will depend on the number of atoms present.

A radioactive nuclide is characterized by the rate at which it disintegrates, and three different quantities—the decay constant, the half-life, and the mean life—are used as a measure of this rate. The decay constant already has been introduced. The *half-life*, $t_{1/2}$, is the time required for half of a given quantity of radioactive atoms to decay. The relation between the half-life and the decay constant is obtained by setting $N/N_0 = 1/2$ in equation (2-3) and solving for t,

$$t_{1/2} = \frac{\log_e 2}{\lambda} = \frac{0.693}{\lambda}. \tag{2-5}$$

The *mean life*, τ, is the average life expectancy of a radioactive atom, and is simply the reciprocal of the decay constant. The mean life is used commonly in describing short-lived radioactive nuclides, but for the long-lived nuclides used for radiometric dating the decay constant and the half-life generally are used.

EARLY ATTEMPTS TO DATE RADIOACTIVE MINERALS

The first suggestion that the rate of transformation of radioactive nuclides might be used to determine the age of geologic materials was made less than ten years after the discovery of radioactivity. Rutherford, who as we have seen was a central figure in many of the fundamental studies of the process of radioactivity, suggested during a series of lectures delivered at Yale University in 1905 that the time of formation of uranium minerals might be determined by measuring the amount of helium that had accumulated in these minerals.

The helium observed in the radioactive minerals is almost certainly due to its production from the radium and other radioactive substances contained therein. If the rate of production of helium from known weights of the different radio-elements were experimentally known, it should thus be possible to determine the interval required for the production of the amount of helium observed in radioactive minerals, or, in other words, to determine the age of the minerals. This deduction is based on the assumption that some of the denser and more compact of the radioactive minerals are able to retain indefinitely a large proportion of the helium imprisoned in their mass. In many cases the minerals are not compact but porous, and under such conditions most of the helium will escape from its mass. Even supposing that some of the helium has been lost from the denser materials, we should be able to fix with some certainty a minimum limit for the age of the mineral.*

Thus Rutherford not only suggested using radioactivity to date minerals but also recognized the phenomenon of inert gas loss that is a problem in both potassium-argon dating and uranium-helium dating. This was only three years after Rutherford and Soddy suggested that helium might be a disintegration product of radioactive elements and two years after Ramsey and Soddy (1903) proved that helium was produced during the radioactive decay of radium.

The first mineral ages were determined by Rutherford (1906); using the uranium and helium contents of the minerals and the disintegration rate of radium, and making the assumption that the radium and uranium were in radioactive equilibrium, he calculated an age of 500 million years for a sample of the uranium-bearing oxide fergusonite, and for a sample of an unspecified uranium mineral from Glastonbury, Connecticut. He suggested that these be considered minimum ages because some of the helium may have escaped. Rutherford's calculations spurred interest in developing the uranium-helium method of age determination, and this method was used to determine the ages of a number of rocks and minerals. It has since been found, however, that most uranium-helium ages are in fact minimum ages, because the crystal structure of most minerals is damaged by the formation of alpha particles during the decay of uranium or thorium, so that some of the helium produced in the mineral is not retained but escapes even at relatively low temperatures.

At the same time that U/He ratios were being used to calculate ages, the uranium-lead dating method was being developed. In 1905, Bertram Boltwood suggested that lead was the final (nonradioactive) product of the radioactive decay of uranium. Shortly thereafter, Rutherford stated,

---

*Rutherford, E., *Radioactive Transformations*, New York: Charles Scribner's Sons, p. 187–188, 1906.

If the production of lead from radium is well established, the percentage of lead in radioactive minerals should be a far more accurate method of deducing the age of the mineral than the calculation based on the volume of helium, for the lead formed in a compact mineral has no possibility of escape.*

Boltwood (1907) published uranium-lead ages ranging from 410 to 2,200 million years for several minerals. These ages, commonly called "chemical lead ages," were calculated before isotopes were discovered, before the disintegration rate of uranium was known accurately, and before it was discovered that lead is also a product of the radioactive decay of thorium. All three factors combined to produce chemical lead ages that were usually too high (Table 2-1).

TABLE 2-1
Comparison of three of Boltwood's (1907) chemical uranium-lead ages of uraninite with modern isotopic age determinations of uraninite from the same (or nearby) locality.

Locality	Boltwood's U-Pb ages (10^6 years)	Modern ages (10^6 years)	
		U^{238}-Pb^{206}	U^{235}-Pb^{207}
Portland, Conn.	410	268	266
Branchville, Conn.	535	367	365
Spruce Pine, N.C.	510	344–385	346–390

Source: Modern data are from the compilation by Wetherill and others (1965).

Although these initial uranium-helium and uranium-lead ages had several inherent uncertainties, they demonstrated two very important facts: (1) in many places the rocks and minerals in the earth's crust were very old, as geologists had believed for many years; and (2) the phenomenon of natural radioactivity offered great potential in constructing a quantitative scale of geologic time.

PROCESSES OF RADIOACTIVE DECAY

When a radioactive element decays spontaneously to produce another element, various atomic particles and radiations are emitted. Most nuclear transformations involve emission of three principal particles or rays—alpha particles (α particles), beta particles (β^- particles), and gamma rays (γ rays).

---

*Rutherford, E., *Radioactive Transformations,* New York: Charles Scribner's Sons, p. 192, 1906.

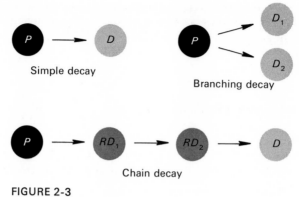

FIGURE 2-3

Three processes of radioactive decay. P=radioactive parent, RD=radioactive daughter, D=stable daughter. In branching decay, either daughter nuclide (but not both) may be produced by a given parent nuclide.

Alpha particles are doubly ionized helium nuclei, beta particles are electrons, and gamma rays are similar to X-rays except that they come from the nucleus whereas X-rays come from the electron shells. Some elements emit α particles, other elements emit β^- particles; γ rays sometimes accompany α particles and sometimes accompany β^- particles. But no radioactive substance undergoes all three modes of decay simultaneously. Another mode of decay, called *electron capture*, occurs when a proton in the nucleus of an atom captures an orbiting electron.

The processes of radioactive decay that are most important in the various physical dating methods are simple decay, chain decay, and branching decay. These three processes are shown diagramatically in Figure 2-3.

When a radioactive parent nuclide decays to produce a stable daughter nuclide, the process is known as *simple decay*. The process is called "unsupported" if the radioactive parent nuclide is itself not a product of radioactive decay. An example of simple, unsupported decay is the transformation of Rb^{87} to Sr^{87}, which is the basis of the rubidium-strontium dating method.

If a radioactive parent nuclide decays to produce a radioactive daughter nuclide that, in turn, also decays (and so forth), the process is known as *chain decay*. This process is "supported," because each radioactive daughter nuclide is itself produced by radioactive decay. Examples of chain decay are the decay series of U^{238}, U^{235}, and Th^{232}. All three decay series are utilized in the uranium-lead and thorium-lead dating methods, and some of the intermediate daughter products are utilized in dating methods based on radioactive disequilibrium.

If a radioactive parent nuclide decays to produce either of two different daughter nuclides, the process is known as *branching decay*. The decay of

K^{40} is branching: most K^{40} decays by β^- emission to Ca^{40}; the rest decays by electron capture to Ar^{40}. The K^{40}–Ar^{40} branch is the basis for the potassium-argon dating method. The decay of K^{40} is discussed in more detail in the next chapter.

THE GENERAL AGE EQUATION

The decay of a radioactive parent ultimately will result in the production of one or more stable nuclides. Most of the geologic dating methods are based on the relationship between the remaining radioactive parent nuclide and the stable daughter nuclide that has been produced.

It already has been shown (equation 2-4) that the number of parent atoms, N, remaining at any time, t, is a function of the initial number of parent atoms present, N_0:

$$N = N_0 e^{-\lambda t}. \tag{2-4}$$

As it stands, this equation is not very useful for calculating ages because it is not possible to determine N_0 without first knowing t. This difficulty can easily be overcome, however, by recognizing that if neither parent nor daughter atoms are lost or gained by a particular system (for example, a rock sample) except by radioactive decay, the decrease in the number of parent nuclides must be equal to the increase in the number of daughter nuclides, D:

$$\frac{dD}{dt} = -\frac{dN}{dt}. \tag{2-6}$$

Moreover, at any given time,

$$N_0 = N + D. \tag{2-7}$$

Substituting equation (2-7) into (2-4) we obtain

$$D = N(e^{\lambda t} - 1). \tag{2-8}$$

Thus it is not necessary to know the initial number of parent nuclides, but only the numbers of the parent and daughter nuclides present in the system today.

In order to calculate ages, equation (2-8) may be solved for t,

$$t = \frac{1}{\lambda} \log_e\left(\frac{D}{N} + 1\right). \tag{2-9}$$

This equation is valid only if all daughter atoms, D_t, are due entirely to radioactive decay of the parent since the system formed—that is, if

$$D_t = D. \tag{2-10}$$

This is generally a valid assumption in potassium-argon dating because argon does not occur as a chemical constituent in minerals. In many other dating methods, however, a correction must be made for the number of daughter atoms initially present, D_0. An example is the rubidium-strontium method, in which a correction is made for initial Sr^{87}. In this method,

$$D_t = D_0 + D, \tag{2-11}$$

and equation (2-9) becomes

$$t = \frac{1}{\lambda} \log_e \left(\frac{D_t - D_0}{N} + 1 \right). \tag{2-12}$$

Equation (2-12) is called the *general age equation* for simple, unsupported decay. It must be modified slightly when used for branching decay. The development of the age equation for the branching decay of K^{40} will be discussed in Chapters 3 and 4.

CONSTANCY OF DECAY

The changes that take place because of radioactive decay are quite different from ordinary chemical changes because radioactive decay occurs in the nucleus of an atom whereas chemical changes involve the electrons surrounding the nucleus. Furthermore, radioactive decay is spontaneous and is unaffected by physical or chemical conditions. This means that the decay constant, or the rate of transformation of a radioactive substance, should be the same at any temperature or pressure or in any chemical state. The constancy of decay is the backbone of all radioactive dating methods. Although there are exceptions, which will be discussed later, the hypothesis of constant decay is generally true. For example, it has been found that decay constants are the same at a temperature of 2,000°C or at a temperature of −186°C, and the same in a vacuum or under a pressure of several thousand atmospheres. The reasons why the decay constant is not affected by physical or chemical environment are that the distances over which nuclear forces act are much smaller than the distances between nuclei, and that the amounts of energy involved in nuclear transformations are much greater than the amounts of energy involved in normal chemical reactions.

Decay by electron capture, however, involves interaction between the nucleus of an atom and an orbital electron, and the decay rate may be affected by variations in the electron density near the nucleus of the atom. In Be^7, an artificially radioactive isotope of beryllium that decays by electron capture, the electron density is influenced by the chemical environment. Segre and Wiegand (1949) and Kraushaar and others (1953) measured differences of up to 0.07 percent between the decay constant of Be^7 in beryllium metal and the decay constant of Be^7 in BeO and BeF_2.

Chemical environment also may affect the constancy of decay for certain elements that undergo isomeric transition.* Bainbridge and others (1951) measured λ for Tc^{99m}, an isomer of the element technetium, in different chemical compounds. They found that λ for Tc^{99m} in $KTcO_4$ was 0.3 percent greater than λ for Tc^{99m} in technetium metal, and that λ for Tc^{99m} in Tc_2S_7 was 0.03 percent greater than λ for Tc^{99m} in technetium metal.

Although the decay constant for Be^7 and Tc^{99m} can be changed slightly by varying the chemical environment, measurements of the decay rate of K^{40} in different compounds indicate that varying the chemical environment of K^{40} has no significant effect on its electron-capture decay constant. Therefore, we can safely assume that the decay rate of K^{40} is constant no matter in which rock, mineral, or chemical compound it occurs.

STABILITY OF NUCLIDES

In addition to the more than 270 known stable nuclides, more than 1,000 naturally and artificially radioactive nuclides have been identified. Why are some nuclides stable and others unstable? The answer to this question is incompletely known, but a few aspects are worth mentioning.

In the most general terms a nucleus is unstable when the repulsive forces within the nucleus are greater than the attractive forces. At relatively large distances from a nucleus (more than approximately 10^{-13} centimeters) protons are acted upon only by ordinary electrostatic forces; neutrons are not appreciably affected by these forces. At shorter distances, however, protons and neutrons are both strongly attracted by short-range, or nuclear, forces. These forces are much different and much stronger than any that could arise from magnetic, electrostatic, or gravitational causes, and are unique to nuclei. The exact reason for this powerful nuclear attraction is not known, but it is thought to be due at least partly to a family of nuclear particles called *mesons*, which can be positive, negative, or neutral, and have masses

---

*Usually nuclides in an excited state release their excess energy quickly by emitting γ rays. If, however, the transition from an excited state to a lower energy state is delayed, it is known as an *isomeric transition*. It involves no change in the atomic or mass numbers. A letter "*m*" in the mass number indicates the high-energy member of the isomeric pair.

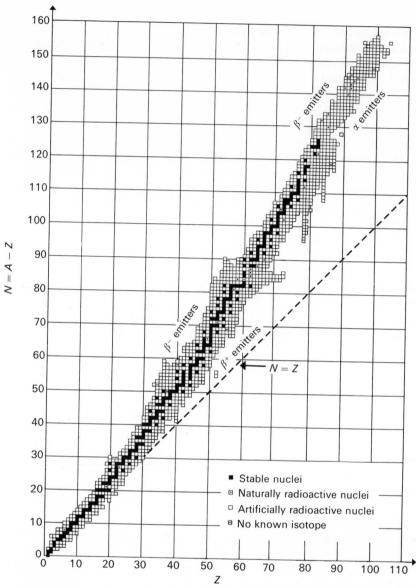

FIGURE 2-4

Chart of known nuclei. [From *Chemical Systems—Energetics, Dynamics, Structure*, by J. A. Campbell. W. H. Freeman and Company. Copyright © 1969.]

ranging from about 200 to 1,000 times the mass of the electron. These particles apparently overcome the electrostatic repulsion between protons in the nucleus.

Nuclear forces show saturation effects, which account for the fact that stable nuclides with unlimited numbers of protons and neutrons do not exist. When nuclear forces are oversaturated, nuclides become radioactive and eject "unwanted" particles. In a graph in which the number of neutrons ($N = A - Z$) is plotted against the number of protons (Z), the radioactive nuclides lie above and below a "curve" formed by the stable nuclides (Fig. 2-4). In addition, all isotopes with Z greater than 83 are radioactive. Except in $_1H^1$ and $_2He^3$, the number of neutrons in the nucleus always equals or exceeds the number of protons. Elements lighter than argon have nearly equal numbers of neutrons and protons. In the elements heavier than argon, the number of neutrons increases more rapidly than does the number of protons, but the neutron/proton ratio seldom exceeds 1.5. For example, Pb^{208} contains 82 protons and 126 neutrons.

The unstable nuclides tend to become stable through a number of different nuclear reactions, all of which depend partly upon the number of neutrons and protons in their nucleus. For example, nuclides that lie above the stable-nuclide curve in Figure 2-4 have too many neutrons and tend to increase their nuclear charge (number of protons) whereas nuclides that lie below the curve have too many protons and tend to decrease their nuclear charge. Electron emission (β^- decay) is one way in which the nuclear charge can be increased, and positron emission (β^+ decay)* and electron capture (e.c. or K capture) are ways in which the nuclear charge can be decreased. These modes of decay are especially common among the lighter elements. Among the heavier elements, α-particle emission and spontaneous fission (splitting of the nucleus) are the common modes of decay.

Even though a large amount of experimental data about the nature of nuclear forces has been acquired, knowledge remains incomplete, and no detailed theories of nuclear structure and radioactivity can yet be developed. For the purpose of geological dating, however, the natural radioactivity of certain elements is an empirical fact. Thus we can utilize the phenomenon even in the absence of a theory to explain it.

---

*A positron (β^+) is the antimatter counterpart of the electron (β^-). Discovered by C. D. Anderson in 1932, it has the same mass as an electron but is positively charged.

3

THE ISOTOPES OF
POTASSIUM AND ARGON

The salts of sodium and potassium, obtained by leaching the ashes of certain plants, sometimes were used as seasoning by primitive people, and several compounds of potassium have been known since the time of Nero. The use of potassium carbonate (potash) in the manufacture of glass, to give strength and flexibility, was described in a seventeenth-century book entitled *The Art of Glass*. It was not until 1807, however, that Sir Humphrey Davy succeeded in isolating the pure metal by electrochemical methods. Because Davy had obtained the metal from potash, he named it potassium (Weeks, 1956).

Because argon does not form compounds in nature, one might suspect that its discovery and isolation would be more recent, and this is so. Argon, the first of the inert gases to be identified, was discovered in 1894 by Sir William Ramsay and Lord Rayleigh. Upon passing what they thought was pure nitrogen from the atmosphere over hot magnesium, Ramsay and Rayleigh observed that not all of the gas was absorbed by the metal. The residual gas produced an optical spectrum that was unknown. Ramsay and Rayleigh observed that there was room on the periodic chart for an element with the peculiar properties of their unknown gas when they announced their finding. Because it showed a reluctance to form compounds, this new element was called argon, "the lazy one."

DISCOVERY OF RADIOACTIVE POTASSIUM

In 1905 J. J. Thomson found that several of the alkali metals emitted radiation. In his classic experiments, Thomson (1905) used a gold-leaf electroscope suspended above an alloy of sodium and potassium metals. Both the alloy and the electroscope were housed within a glass bulb that was shielded from light and from which the air had been evacuated. He found that when the electroscope was charged with positive electricity there was a slow but definite "leak"; that is, the positive charge on the gold leaves was neutralized and they slowly came back together again. When charged with negative electricity, however, there was no such leak. Thomson concluded from this that the sodium-potassium alloy was emitting negative particles. He found a similar emission from rubidium and showed how the radiation he observed from the alkali metals could be an important source of heat within the earth.

Although Thomson's experiment proved that some alkali metals gave off radiation, it did not show whether sodium or potassium or both metals were radioactive. Soon after, however, Campbell and Wood (1906) and Campbell (1908) showed that a number of potassium salts emitted radiation, that this radiation was due to β^- particles, that it was always a function of the amount of potassium present, and that the radiation was independent of the chemical state of the potassium. They used fractional crystallization to try to eliminate impurities, for it was thought that the radiation might be due to an impurity associated with potassium.

Although it was known that several of the heavy elements, such as uranium and radium, were radioactive, the emission of radiation by any of the lighter elements was surprising. Numerous attempts were made to explain the radioactivity of potassium by the presence of a universally associated impurity of heavier mass. This line of reasoning led Dobrosserdow (1925) to propose the existence of a new and widespread heavy element, "ekacaesium," to explain the apparent radioactivity of potassium. All efforts to separate this impurity ended in failure, and the idea was abandoned by the mid-1930's.

Aston (1921), who during the 1920's was discovering new isotopes at a remarkable rate, turned his mass spectrograph on natural potassium and learned that it was composed of a minimum of two isotopes with masses of 39 and 41. As more became known about nuclear theory, it became apparent that neither K^{39} nor K^{41} was capable of emitting β^- particles. This led

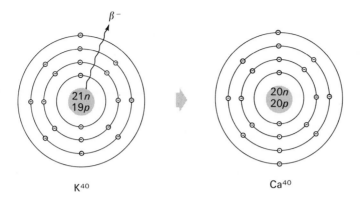

FIGURE 3-1
The decay of K^{40} to Ca^{40} occurs by the emission of a beta particle
from the nucleus, which results in the conversion of a neutron to a
proton. The atomic number is increased by one, but the mass number
is unchanged.

Klemperer (1935) and Newman and Walke (1935) to propose the existence
of an isotope of mass 40 to account for the observed β^- radiation from
potassium. According to their hypothesis, K^{40} would decay to Ca^{40} by the
emission of a β^- particle from the nucleus. This emission would result in
the conversion of a neutron to a proton, thereby raising the atomic number
by one but leaving the mass number the same (Fig. 3-1). Shortly thereafter
Nier (1935), using a much more sensitive instrument for mass analysis than
was available to Aston fifteen years before, presented conclusive evidence

FIGURE 3-2
Nier's evidence for the existence of the isotope
K^{40}. Mass 40 appears in the potassium spectrum
as a small bump on the "tails" of the K^{41} and
K^{39} peaks. [After Nier (1935).]

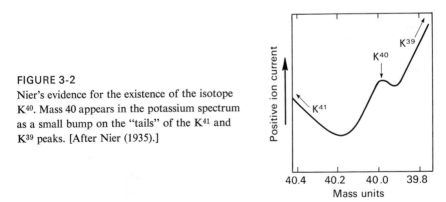

for the existence of K^{40} (Fig. 3-2). Nier calculated that K^{40} was only about
1/8,600 as abundant as K^{39}. Nier's work was almost immediately substantiated by Brewer (1935), and two years later Smythe and Hemmendinger

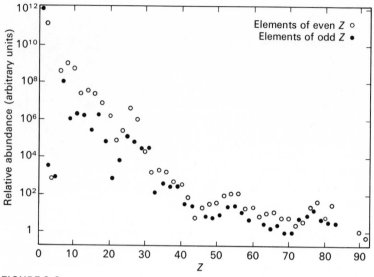

FIGURE 3-3

Abundance of elements in the solar system ("cosmic abundance"). [Data from Aller (1961).]

(1937) were able to demonstrate that all of the radiation from potassium was indeed due to the rare isotope K^{40}.

Thus by the late 1930's it was known that potassium consisted of the isotopes K^{39}, K^{40}, and K^{41}. Of these, K^{40} was the least abundant and was radioactive, undergoing a transmutation to Ca^{40} by the emission of a β^- particle from the nucleus. To these facts should be added the observation by Köhlhorster (1930) that potassium also emitted gamma radiation. Although Köhlhorster's discovery went largely unnoticed for several years, it was the first hint that potassium might be capable of dual decay.

DUAL DECAY OF POTASSIUM

Surprisingly, the first suggestion that K^{40} underwent radioactive decay to Ar^{40} came not from Köhlhorster's discovery of gamma radiation from potassium, but from an entirely different and more subtle line of reasoning that involved arguments about the relative abundances of the elements. The story is an excellent example of first-rate scientific sleuthing, and the credit is largely due the German physicist C. F. Von Weizsäcker (1937).

The two most abundant isotopes of argon, Ar^{40} and Ar^{36}, were discovered by Aston (1920b) one year before his work on potassium. By the late 1930's, it was known that argon had three natural isotopes, Ar^{36}, Ar^{38}, and Ar^{40}. It was also clear that of these, Ar^{40} was by far the most abundant and

accounted for more than 99 percent of all argon, which in turn made up
about one percent of the atmosphere.

Von Weizsäcker began his argument by recalling several well-known facts
about the abundance of elements. As a general rule, the abundance of the
elements in the solar system (the so-called "cosmic" abundance) varies
rather smoothly with atomic number (Fig. 3-3). The most abundant elements
are those with small atomic numbers. With increasing Z, the relative abundance decreases rather steadily up to the elements with Z of about 40 or 50,
whereupon the relationship between abundance and atomic number becomes
less regular. This rule of thumb is also true for the inert gases: the decrease
in abundance with increasing atomic number is remarkably systematic
(Fig. 3-4).

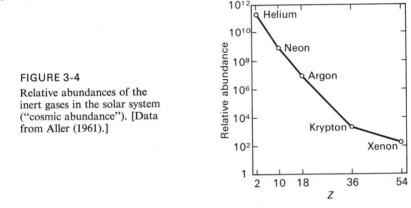

FIGURE 3-4

Relative abundances of the
inert gases in the solar system
("cosmic abundance"). [Data
from Aller (1961).]

In the earth's atmosphere, the inert gases are about a thousand times less
abundant than they are in the solar system. In addition, there are several
important departures from the general rule of decreasing abundance with
increasing atomic number. Helium is about a hundred times less abundant
in the earth's atmosphere, and argon about a thousand times more abundant, than expected (Fig. 3-5). The helium anomaly is not surprising, for

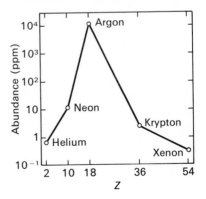

FIGURE 3-5

Abundance of the inert gases in the
earth's atmosphere. [Data from
Mason (1958).]

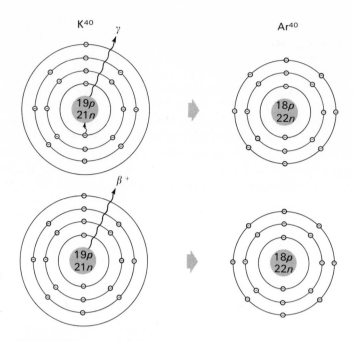

FIGURE 3-6

Two mechanisms for the decay of K^{40} to Ar^{40}. (Top) Electron capture, in which an extranuclear electron, usually from the K shell, falls into the nucleus and a proton is converted into a neutron. (Bottom) Positron emission, which also results in the creation of a neutron from a proton. This mechanism is rare.

helium is light enough to overcome the earth's gravitational attraction and escape into space. But the anomalous excess of argon in the atmosphere cannot be explained so easily. Von Weizsäcker observed that nearly all of this "excess" argon could be attributed to argon of mass 40, which, he hypothesized, could be formed from the decay of K^{40} in rocks. He proposed that this decay might take place either by electron capture or by positron emission (Fig. 3-6). For theoretical reasons, and because positron emission had not been observed from potassium, he concluded that electron capture was the more likely mechanism even though electron capture never before had been observed in any element. As a test of his hypothesis, Von Weizsäcker suggested that it should be possible to find an excess of argon in old potassium-bearing minerals. Von Weizsäcker's arguments were strengthened later in the same year by Bramley (1937), who showed that the abundance of Ar^{40} and Köhlhorster's observation of gamma radiation from potassium were, when taken together, strong evidence for the dual decay of K^{40}.

In 1943 F. C. Thompson and S. Rowlands, of the George Holt Physics Laboratory in Liverpool, England, reported the results of the first experiment that confirmed that Ar^{40} formed from K^{40} by electron capture. They stated that they were unable to continue this line of research because of England's involvement in World War II, but suggested that it would be interesting to measure the argon contents of old potassium-bearing minerals to see if there was any variation of argon content with age (Thompson and Rowlands, 1943). During the next few years, several workers followed this suggestion, but all of them concluded that there was no variation of argon content with the age of potassium minerals. In these first attempts to find such a correlation, however, the argon measurements were made without analyzing the isotopic composition of the argon and, hence, without making a correction for the atmospheric argon present.

The first to find an excess of Ar^{40} in old potassium-bearing minerals were L. T. Aldrich and A. O. Nier (1948a). Using mass spectrometric techniques, they found that the ratio Ar^{40}/Ar^{36} in four geologically old minerals (orthoclase, microcline, sylvite, and langbeinite) was higher than in the atmosphere (Fig. 3-7). From their data they confirmed that K^{40} did, in fact, undergo

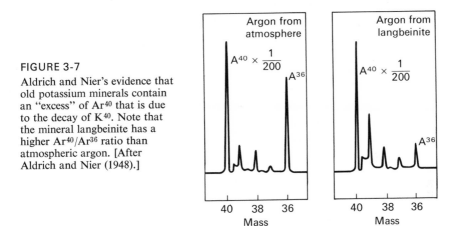

FIGURE 3-7

Aldrich and Nier's evidence that old potassium minerals contain an "excess" of Ar^{40} that is due to the decay of K^{40}. Note that the mineral langbeinite has a higher Ar^{40}/Ar^{36} ratio than atmospheric argon. [After Aldrich and Nier (1948).]

dual decay and that the decay of K^{40} to Ar^{40} was a potentially useful dating tool for the earth sciences.

Thus, by 1948, the foundations for the successful development of the potassium-argon method into a useful geologic tool had been laid. It was known that K^{40} underwent a dual decay, by β^- emission to Ca^{40} and by electron capture to Ar^{40}. In addition, Aldrich and Nier had demonstrated that at least some of the argon generated within potassium-bearing minerals was retained within the mineral structure. This made the transformation of potassium to argon potentially useful as a geologic dating tool. From this time on, work proceeded rapidly, and by the mid-1950's potassium-argon dating was being used widely to help solve geologic problems.

ISOTOPE ABUNDANCES
OF POTASSIUM AND ARGON

For several reasons, knowledge of the relative abundances of the isotopes of potassium and argon is a necessary prerequisite to the successful use of the potassium-argon transformation as a geologic dating tool. First, the determination of radiogenic argon requires a correction for contamination by atmospheric argon. This cannot be done without knowing the composition of the argon in the atmosphere. Second, the common method of calibrating the Ar^{38} tracers that are used in argon analysis (discussed in Chapter 5) requires that the isotopic composition of atmospheric argon be known. Third, the determination of K^{40} (discussed in Chapter 6) is greatly simplified if it can be assumed that (1) the fraction of potassium of mass 40 is constant in all materials today, and (2) this fraction is known. With these two prerequisites satisfied, it is possible to measure potassium by any one of a number of standard analytical techniques and then merely calculate the amount of K^{40} present.

It should be emphasized at this point that what is meant here by the isotopic composition of potassium is the composition of potassium wherever it may occur. In contrast, the discussion about the isotopic composition of natural argon is concerned only with the composition of argon in the atmosphere. The distinction is important, for, as will be shown, there are good reasons to believe that the isotopic composition of potassium is relatively uniform regardless of its location, whereas the isotopic composition of argon varies considerably (if it did not there would be no basis for potassium-argon dating!). The reasons for this difference are easy to see. $Potassium^{40}$ is continually decaying at a steady rate regardless of its physical or chemical environment. Thus the proportion of K^{40} in ordinary potassium today should be constant everywhere unless potassium isotopes are fractionated by some naturally selective physical or chemical process. In contrast, the concentration of Ar^{40} depends on its rate of production from K^{40}, the amount of potassium present, and the degree to which Ar^{40} is retained by a particular system. Moreover, the percentage of Ar^{40} in the atmosphere depends upon the rate at which Ar^{40} escapes from rocks and minerals.

Potassium

The isotopic abundances of potassium and atmospheric argon that are used today in potassium-argon dating are those determined by the careful work of A. O. Nier of the University of Minnesota. Nier (1950) has determined that the present-day atomic abundance ratio of K^{40} to total potassium is 1.19×10^{-4} (Table 3-1). This value was determined by measuring the composition of pure potassium metal that had been prepared from the mineral

TABLE 3-1
Isotopic abundances of atmospheric
argon and potassium.

Isotope	Relative atomic abundance (percent)
Ar^{40}	99.600
Ar^{38}	0.063
Ar^{36}	0.337
K^{41}	6.91 ± 0.04
K^{40}	0.0119 ± 0.0001
K^{39}	93.08 ± 0.04

Source: Data from Nier (1950).

sylvite. The abundance of K^{40} is known to within a probable error* of slightly less than one percent. Because K^{40} is continually decaying, this abundance ratio has decreased through time (Fig. 3-8). As shown by equation (2-8),

FIGURE 3-8

Change in the abundance of K^{40} relative to total potassium with time.

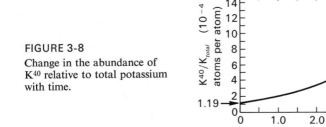

however, it is only necessary to know the amount of K^{40} present in the rock or mineral today; the changing abundance ratio does not enter into the calculations for potassium-argon age determinations. But because the amount of K^{40} is usually calculated from a determination of total potassium, it is necessary to assume that at any time in the past the ratio of K^{40} to total potassium was constant in all materials. How safe is this assumption?

The chemical behavior of an atom is controlled by several factors, the most important of which are the configuration of its electrons and its ionic radius. Because the isotopes of potassium are virtually identical in both of these respects, it might be suspected that normal chemical processes would not separate potassium isotopes. This appears to be correct.

*The *probable error* in statistics is defined as the 50-percent confidence level.

The problem of possible isotopic fractionation of potassium has attracted a great deal of attention because of the importance of radioactive potassium as a source of heat and radiation both in the earth and in living things. Consequently, the isotopic composition of potassium from a great variety of materials has been measured. In some of the early work on this problem, significant fractionation of potassium isotopes was reported. For example, Brewer (1938), who made mass spectrographic measurements of the ratio K^{39}/K^{40} in rocks, minerals, plants, and animal tissue, concluded that although the variation in potassium from minerals was slight, the variation in potassium from plants and animals was considerable.

Other experiments, especially the more recent ones, have not supported the idea that potassium isotopes are fractionated in nature. Laznitski and Oeser (1937), using a Geiger-Müller counter, compared potassium from the muscle tissue of three adult rabbits with potassium from reagent-grade potassium chloride and found, within two percent, no difference in radio-activity, and hence no difference in the ratio K^{40}/K_{total}. Schumb and others (1941) found no difference, within 2.9 percent, in the radioactivity of potassium from the Pultusk meteorite and potassium from reagent-grade KCl. In a very carefully done and important experiment with a double-focusing mass spectrograph, Cook (1943) compared the ratio K^{39}/K^{40} in Pacific kelp (11 samples, 8 species), fossil cryptozöoan (3 samples, 2 species), perthite (7 samples), microcline-antiperthite (5 samples), plagioclase (2 samples), leucite (2 samples), muscovite (3 samples), granite (2 samples), basalt from the Columbia River Group (one sample), and Triassic diabase (one sample). Cook's rock and mineral samples ranged in age from Precambrian to Tertiary. He was unable to detect any difference to within 1 percent and stated that his measurements might be accurate to within 0.5 percent. Mullins and Zerahn (1948) measured the radioactivity of potassium from beech trees, the longbones of cows and horses, Vesuvius lava, and commercial KCl and could find no difference to within 0.5 percent. Mullins and Zerahn give a good review of previous claims of differences in potassium isotopic composition from different materials, but conclude that none of the claims are above criticism and that there is no evidence of fractionation of potassium isotopes in nature.

Kendall (1960) made mass spectrometric measurements of the ratio K^{39}/K^{41} in 27 samples and K^{41}/K^{40} in 15 samples of various materials, including minerals, normal and cancerous human tissues, embryonic tissue, Indian Ocean water, tektites, and a plant specimen. His measurements had probable errors of 0.3 percent for K^{39}/K^{41} and 0.7 percent for K^{41}/K^{40}, and within these limits he detected no variations in the isotopic composition of potassium. From these data, Kendall concluded that, for the purpose of potassium-argon dating, the usual assumption that the abundance of K^{40} is constant is valid within small limits for terrestrial samples.

Burnett and others (1966) examined the isotopic ratio K^{41}/K^{40} in 11 meteorites and four terrestrial samples (plagioclase, olivine-hornblende, basalt, and a potassium salt). In three of the meteorites, they detected K^{40} enrichments of as much as several percent; apparently these enrichments were caused by the production of K^{40} from Ca^{40} by cosmic rays. Otherwise, they concluded that there were no differences in the isotopic abundance of K^{40} in terrestrial and meteoritic samples.

Although the weight of the evidence seems skewed in favor of a uniform distribution of potassium isotopes, the question is not completely closed. Taylor and Urey (1938) passed solutions of potassium salts through zeolites and found that the ratio K^{39}/K^{41} could be increased or decreased by as much as 10 percent from the normal abundance ratio. In addition, D. M. Douglas, G. A. Elliott, W. R. Ellis, and R. H. Lee were able to reduce the K^{40} content of potassium salts by cation exchange with a natural zeolite (Rankama, 1954). Verbeek and Schreiner (1967) studied the distribution of K^{39} and K^{41} near the sharp contact between a granite and an amphibolite. They found anomalously high values for K^{39}/K^{41} in the amphibolite within 3 centimeters of the contact. Within less than 1 centimeter from the granite, enrichment in K^{39} of up to about 3 percent was observed. They concluded that this localized enrichment was due to diffusion of potassium from the granite into the amphibolite.

Thus it is clear that though detectable variations in the isotopic composition of potassium are rare in nature, they can occur under special conditions. Moreover, fractionations of as much as 10 percent have been produced in the laboratory. It is therefore possible that the natural ratio K^{40}/K_{total} may be different from the value 1.19×10^{-4} under some circumstances, especially in those aqueous environments where cation exchange might be operative. The isotopic composition of potassium in natural zeolites especially should be determined using modern, mass-spectrometric techniques. The present distribution of potassium isotopes, however, suggests that it is probably safe to assume that the isotopic composition of potassium is constant in most, if not all, materials used in potassium-argon dating. Because this seems to be true today, it is reasonable to assume that it has been true throughout geologic time.

Finally, it might be of interest to ask how long the abundance of K^{40} relative to K_{total} will be 1.19×10^{-4}? The answer is, practically forever when compared to the span of a human life. Although the amount of K^{40} is steadily decreasing, this decrease is so slow that it will take 16 million years for the ratio to decrease by one percent!

Argon

Nier's values for the composition of argon in the atmosphere are given in Table 3-1. They were determined to within a probable error of less than 0.5 percent. One of the constants commonly used in potassium-argon dating is the ratio of Ar^{40}/Ar^{36} in the atmosphere, which from Nier's data is 295.5. This constant will be referred to frequently in some of the later chapters.

As is the case with potassium, the cosmic composition of argon is continually changing in a regular fashion because of the slow but steady creation of Ar^{40} from K^{40}. On any scale less than cosmic, however, the isotopic composition of argon is not necessarily uniform. Although Ar^{40} is being created continually wherever there is potassium, its abundance relative to the other argon isotopes depends greatly on the amount of potassium present, and accumulation of argon depends on the environment. Recall that Aldrich and Nier found a significantly higher ratio of Ar^{40}/Ar^{36} in old minerals than in the atmosphere. Fortunately, neither the cosmic nor the "earthly" composition of argon enters into the calculations for potassium-argon dating. The only quantities needed for the calculations are the isotopic compositions of argon in the present atmosphere and, of course, in individual rock and mineral samples. Because of the rapidity of atmospheric mixing, it is reasonable to assume that the atmospheric composition of argon is constant everywhere on earth at any given time even though Ar^{40} probably is being released from the crust of the earth at different rates in different places.

Although the relative proportion of argon isotopes in the atmosphere can be considered uniform at any given time, it is not possible to determine what this proportion was at any time in the geologic past, because the potassium contents of the mantle and the crust are poorly known and because much of the Ar^{40} generated is retained within both crust and mantle. This poses an interesting question. In the argon analysis, a correction must be made for atmospheric argon that is present as a contaminant in the sample and in the equipment. What if some of the atmospheric argon in the sample was incorporated at the time of formation of the sample? The answer is simple. The correction for atmospheric argon, and hence the calculated age, would be incorrect. Even for rocks a few hundred million years old, the error would probably be negligible, because the composition of the atmosphere changes very slowly, but for very old rocks this could be an important source of error. At present, there is no way to determine whether any given rock contains a bit of ancient atmosphere, and even if this could be determined, there would be no way to apply a proper correction, because of lack of knowledge about the composition of the ancient atmosphere. Fortunately, the problem probably is not serious, otherwise the potassium-argon method would not work as well as it obviously does, even on quite old rocks. Most rocks old enough to be subject to this kind of potential error did not crystallize in contact with the atmosphere. Furthermore, only a small correction for atmospheric argon is usually necessary in dating old rocks, and this lessens the error considerably. Finally, most, and perhaps all, of the contamination by atmospheric argon comes from gas adsorbed onto the sur-

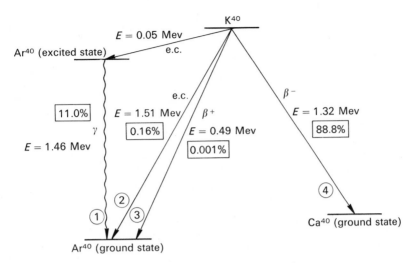

FIGURE 3-9

Decay scheme of K^{40}. The four branches are: (1) electron capture accompanied by the emission of a γ ray, (2) electron capture without γ ray emission, (3) positron emission, and (4) beta, or electron, emission. Also indicated are the energy, E, released in each mode of decay and the percentage of K^{40} that decays by each mode.

faces of samples and equipment or from gas embedded in minerals after contact with the present-day atmosphere. Thus it is almost certain that this factor does not contribute significantly to errors in potassium-argon dating.

DECAY OF K^{40}

As has been discussed, the decay of K^{40} is a branching process. The decay to Ca^{40} occurs by the emission of a β^- particle from the nucleus and the conversion of a neutron to a proton (Fig. 3-1). The decay to Ar^{40} takes place when an electron, usually from the K-shell, is captured by the nucleus and a neutron is created at the expense of a proton (Fig. 3-6, top). When this happens the argon atom is in an energetically excited state and quickly decays to its stable ground state by emitting a gamma-ray. As will be discussed later, a small percentage of the argon that decays by electron capture goes directly to the ground state without the emission of a gamma-ray. The decay scheme of K^{40} is shown in Figure 3-9.

Several attempts have been made to utilize the decay to Ca^{40} as a geological dating tool, but these efforts have not been successful. The problem is that Ca^{40} is the most abundant of the calcium isotopes and is so ubiquitous that it is difficult to tell the Ca^{40} atoms produced by the decay of K^{40} from those that were present at the time of formation of the rock or mineral. In other words, the value of D_0 in equation (2-12) is very large. As a result, the potassium-calcium method is subject to very large errors and consequently is not used. As will be discussed in the next chapter, the problem of "original" argon does not enter into the potassium-argon method except for rather rare instances.

It was shown in Chapter 2 that the general formula for radioactive decay could be expressed in terms of the present-day amounts of the parent and daughter atoms,

$$D = N(e^{\lambda t} - 1). \qquad (2\text{-}8)$$

For branching decay with daughter products D_1 and D_2, the formula becomes

$$D_1 + D_2 = N[e^{(\lambda_1 + \lambda_2)t} - 1]. \qquad (3\text{-}1)$$

For the specific case of the decay of K^{40} this is written

$$\mathrm{Ar}_{rad}^{40} + \mathrm{Ca}_{rad}^{40} = K^{40}[e^{(\lambda_\epsilon + \lambda_\beta)t} - 1], \qquad (3\text{-}2)$$

where λ_ϵ and λ_β are the decay constants for the branches K^{40}–Ar^{40} and K^{40}–Ca^{40}, respectively. Note that Ar_{rad}^{40} and Ca_{rad}^{40} represent only the radiogenic daughter products, and not any Ar^{40} or Ca^{40} present initially.

No attempt will be made here to recount the numerous attempts to determine the values of the decay constants, λ_ϵ and λ_β, or to recount the difficulties encountered in doing so. For this information the reader is referred to reviews by Wetherill (1957, 1966), Aldrich and Wetherill (1958), and Hamilton (1965). The usual procedure is to determine the gamma and beta activities of natural potassium by scintillation counting. The activities of K^{40} then are calculated from the known isotopic composition of natural potassium. It is also possible to use potassium that has been artificially enriched in K^{40}. This has the advantage that the activities can be measured more precisely. But if this is done, it is necessary to determine the exact isotopic composition of the enriched potassium with a mass spectrometer before the activities of K^{40} can be calculated. Once the gamma and beta activities of K^{40} have been found, it is possible to calculate the decay constants λ_ϵ and λ_β. A rather complete table summarizing the many determinations of the gamma and beta activities of K^{40}, with references, is given by Houtermans (1966).

The decay constants used today by most workers in potassium-argon dating are those suggested by Aldrich and Wetherill (1958). They correspond to activities of natural potassium of 3.4γ/gram sec and $27.6\beta^-$/gram sec and are

$$\lambda_\epsilon = 0.585 \times 10^{-10}/\mathrm{yr}$$

and

$$\lambda_\beta = 4.72 \times 10^{-10}/\mathrm{yr}.$$

The total decay constant is

$$\lambda = \lambda_\epsilon + \lambda_\beta = 5.305 \times 10^{-10}/\text{yr}.$$

Although the uncertainties are somewhat difficult to evaluate, the value of λ_β is probably known to within about one percent. The determination of the gamma activity of K^{40} is more difficult, however, and the uncertainty in λ_ϵ is probably nearer 3 percent. The effects of these uncertainties on the calculation of ages are discussed in Chapter 7.

The ratio of Ar^{40} to Ca^{40} produced by the decay of K^{40} is called the *branching ratio*,

$$R = \frac{\lambda_\epsilon}{\lambda_\beta} = 0.124. \tag{3-3}$$

This means that $1/0.124$ or 8.06 times as many Ca^{40} atoms are generated as Ar^{40} atoms. Putting it another way, 88.8 percent of the K^{40} atoms decay to Ca^{40} whereas only 11.2 percent decay to Ar^{40}. By using the decay constants, the half-life of K^{40} can be calculated from equation (2-5),

$$\text{Half-life of K}^{40} = \frac{\log_e 2}{\lambda} = \frac{0.693}{\lambda_\epsilon + \lambda_\beta} = 1.31 \times 10^9 \text{ yr.}$$

It was mentioned previously that Ar^{40} can be produced from K^{40} by positron emission as well as by electron capture with the emission of γ rays (Fig. 3-6). A third mode by which K^{40} decays to Ar^{40} is by electron capture without the emission of γ rays. Because the commonly used decay constant for the decay to argon was determined from the gamma activity, the decay constant would be in error if either positron emission or electron capture without γ-ray emission were common. Tilley and Madansky (1959) searched for positron emission from natural potassium using sensitive counting techniques but detected none. They set an upper limit of $(1.3 \pm 0.7) \times 10^{-5}$ on the ratio β^+/β^-, which corresponds to an upper limit for positron activity of $(3.6 \pm 1.8) \times 10^{-4}\beta^+/\text{gram sec}$ for natural potassium. The gamma activity of natural potassium is $3.4\gamma/\text{gram sec}$ so their experiment suggested that decay by positron emission amounts to much less than 0.1 percent. More recently, Engelkemeir and others (1962) repeated this experiment using potassium enriched in K^{40} and found that positrons actually were emitted. They found a β^+/β^- ratio of $(1.12 \pm 0.14) \times 10^{-5}$, which confirmed that the formation of Ar^{40} by positron emission was quantitatively negligible. Having confirmed positron emission, they were then able to calculate, from energy considerations, that 1.4 percent of the potassium that decays by electron capture goes directly to the Ar^{40} ground state without gamma-ray emission (Fig. 3-9). This means that the value of λ_ϵ given on page 40 is not exactly correct. Nevertheless, most workers agree that a small change in the decay constants would not be worth the resulting confusion, especially in comparison with the experimental errors in the measurement of λ_ϵ.

4

THE POTASSIUM-ARGON CLOCK—
HOW IT WORKS

The potassium-argon method of age determination was first suggested in 1940 by the M.I.T. physicist Robley D. Evans, even before it was proved that Ar^{40} was a decay product of K^{40} (Goodman and Evans, 1941). Evans concluded, however, that because of the abundance of Ar^{40} in the earth's atmosphere and the difficulty of making a correction for "nonradiogenic" argon, it did not appear likely that this method of age determination would be capable of extensive application.

During the five years after Aldrich and Nier (1948a) demonstrated that Ar^{40} from the decay of K^{40} was trapped in geologically old minerals and that this Ar^{40} could be distinguished from atmospheric argon by a careful determination of isotopic composition, numerous attempts were made to utilize the potassium-argon method to determine geologic ages. A table of some of these early age determinations is presented by Rankama (1954).

One of the earliest and most frequently quoted age determinations was made by F. Smits and W. Gentner (1950), both of the University of Freiburg.

TABLE 4-1
Some early potassium-argon ages in millions of years.

Material used for K-Ar age determination	Geologic period	U-He or U-Pb	K-Ar	
			Without atmospheric Ar correction	With atmospheric Ar correction
Amazonite (microcline)	Jurassic	130	147	—
Nordmarkite (alkali syenite)	Carboniferous or Permian	—	227	—
Amazonite (microcline)	Carboniferous	250	240	—
Lepidolite	Carboniferous or Permian	230	275	228
Amazonite (microcline)	Precambrian	—	1,330	—
Amazonite (microcline)	Precambrian	—	1,260	1,190
Microcline	Precambrian	—	1,490	—
Microcline	Precambrian	1,420	1,510	—
Microcline	Precambrian	1,720	1,514	1,485

Source: Data from Gerling and others (1952).

They chose samples of coarse- and fine-grained sylvite from the Buggingen salt deposits (Oligocene) of the Upper Rhine Valley. They determined the amount of radiogenic Ar^{40} in their sample by dissolving the salt in water, removing the reactive components from the released gases, and measuring the volume of argon with a McLeod gauge.* An isotopic analysis for the ratio Ar^{40}/Ar^{36} enabled Smits and Gentner to subtract the Ar^{40} due to atmospheric contamination. Their calculated age for the Buggingen deposits was 20 million years. Some of their samples gave considerably lower results, which they attributed to argon leakage. In the same paper, they gave an age of 200 million years for sylvite of Permian age from Friedrichshall I, near Hanover.

Another example of early potassium-argon age determinations is provided by the work of Gerling and others (1952). They selected potassium-bearing minerals that ranged in age from Precambrian to Jurassic and compared the results with previously determined uranium-helium and uranium-lead ages.

---

*A McLeod gauge is a manometric device that can be calibrated from its dimensions to give a direct reading of pressure.

A summary of the results of this important experiment is given in Table 4-1. Argon was released from the samples by prolonged heating to 1,250°C in a quartz tube, and the liberated gas was purified. Like Smits and Gentner, Gerling and his colleagues measured the amount of argon with a McLeod gauge. For three of the samples, they determined the amount of atmospheric argon contamination by measuring the amount of Ar^{36} with a mass spectrometer. But because only a small fraction of the argon was atmospheric, the corrected ages differ little from the uncorrected ones.

ADVANTAGES AND LIMITATIONS OF THE METHOD

In the span of two decades, the potassium-argon method has been developed to the stage where it is now one of the most useful dating techniques available to geologists. At the present time, thousands of potassium-argon ages have been published—the product of more than fifty laboratories throughout the world.

The principle advantages of the potassium-argon method are:

1. Potassium is the seventh most abundant element in the earth's crust (about 2.6 percent by weight) and is found in most rock-forming minerals. Even in many of the minerals in which potassium is not an essential cation, it is often present in amounts greater than 0.1 percent.

2. The half-life of K^{40}, 1.31×10^9 years, is such that measurable quantities of argon have accumulated in potassium-bearing minerals of nearly all ages. Because of this, the potassium-argon method has perhaps the widest range of applicability of any of the radiometric dating tools and can be used on rocks as young as 10^4 years as well as on the oldest rocks known.

3. Because argon is an inert gas, it can be measured easily and accurately, even in small quantities.

4. Because no naturally occurring compounds of argon are known, the argon present in any mineral can only come from atmospheric contamination, for which a correction can be made, or from the decay of K^{40}. There are some exceptions to this, and they will be discussed in Chapter 8.

The disadvantages, more appropriately called limitations, are:

1. Not all geologic materials will retain argon completely. Most minerals will lose argon when heated to several hundred degrees centigrade,

and some will not retain argon under any circumstances. This handicap usually can be overcome by careful sample selection procedures.

2. The method cannot be applied to sedimentary rocks except in a few rare instances. About the only sedimentary mineral that can be dated successfully is glauconite. Thus the method is limited almost entirely to igneous and metamorphic rocks.

3. The method is expensive because it requires a highly specialized laboratory and a scientist trained in its use. This, however, is true of many modern analytical techniques.

HOW THE CLOCK WORKS

The potassium-argon clock is an accumulation clock. That is, in contrast to the C^{14} method and some other dating methods that require measuring the *disappearance* of the radioactive parent atoms, the potassium-argon method relies on the *accumulation* of radiogenic daughter atoms. When a K^{40} atom in a mineral decays to Ar^{40}, the Ar^{40} is trapped within the mineral lattice. There are few minerals whose lattice structures allow an argon atom (atomic radius $= 1.9$ Å) to pass through; thus the Ar^{40} is trapped and can escape only if the mineral is melted, recrystallized, or heated to a temperature that will allow the Ar^{40} to diffuse through the mineral lattice. In "retentive" minerals (those that are considered satisfactory for age determination purposes), the temperatures at which appreciable diffusion will take place is usually above several hundred degrees centigrade. Although K^{40} is constantly decaying, a silicate melt usually will not retain the Ar^{40} that is produced, and thus the potassium-argon clock is not "set" until the mineral solidifies and cools sufficiently to allow the Ar^{40} to accumulate in the mineral lattice. Minerals undergoing complete metamorphism or other types of recrystallization likewise will not accumulate Ar^{40} until the recrystallization stops and the rock has cooled. If a rock that has accumulated Ar^{40} for a time is melted, reheated, or recrystallized, the Ar^{40} escapes and the clock is ready to be set again by subsequent cooling.

The time at which the potassium-argon clock is set, called time-zero (t_0), is not a single moment in time but is instead some interval of time that may be anywhere from a few hours to millions of years in duration. For an extrusive rock such as a lava flow, the potassium-argon clock measures the time that has elapsed since the rock solidified. This is because lava flows cool quickly—that is, within a few months or a few years. For an intrusive igneous rock, which would cool considerably slower than an extrusive rock, the age determined by this method is somewhere between the time of solidification and the time when the rock reached a temperature low enough to prevent any significant argon loss by diffusion (Fig. 4-1). In a metamorphic

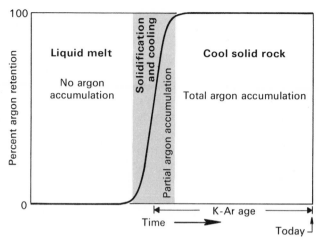

FIGURE 4-1

Accumulation of argon in an igneous rock.

rock, the age roughly represents the time that the mineral formed in its stability field. This also applies to authigenic minerals in sedimentary rocks.

If any of the rocks in the above examples were reheated later by the intrusion of a nearby batholith, mild metamorphism, or deep burial, then the measured age could be anywhere between the time of solidification or metamorphism and the time of completion of the heating event, depending on the extent of argon loss caused by the heating (Fig. 4-2). In general, anything that will affect the physical or chemical state of a rock, including

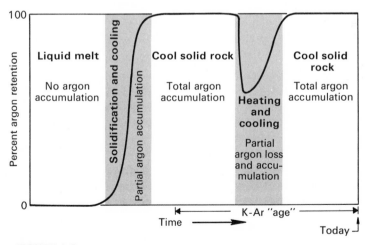

FIGURE 4-2

Accumulation of argon in an igneous rock subjected to a superimposed heating event.

heating, metamorphism, weathering, and alteration, also will reset, at least partially, the potassium-argon clock.

In the absence of a later and distinctly separate thermal event, potassium-argon ages usually approximate crystallization ages, but this is not always true. For example, intrusive or metamorphic rocks may remain at elevated temperatures long after the minerals have formed and the rocks have solidified, in which case a potassium-argon age would record the time of final cooling. If high post-crystallization temperatures are maintained by deep burial, then potassium-argon ages may represent the time of uplift rather than the time of crystallization.

The usefulness of a potassium-argon age determination depends not only on the heating and cooling history of the rock, but also on the effectiveness of the mineral(s) as an argon trap. The usefulness of various rock-forming minerals for potassium-argon dating is discussed in Chapter 10.

As a geologic tool, the potassium-argon method is used in three principal ways: (1) for correlation and age assignment, (2) for determining the rates of geologic processes, and (3) as an indicator of geologic conditions. Potassium-argon dates have been used to determine the age and duration of the geologic eras, periods, and epochs; to assign formations to the classic geologic time-scale in the absence of fossils; to establish correlations over both short and long distances; and to determine the ages of meteorites and the solar system. The method also has contributed valuable information about the rate of evolution of extinct forms of life preserved as fossils, about the length of time required for a batholith to cool, and about the history and rate of fluctuation of the earth's magnetic field. These are just a few examples. As an indicator of geologic conditions, potassium-argon data have been used to calculate the depth of emplacement of batholiths, to infer some of the properties of the earth's primitive atmosphere, to aid in determining the provenance of sedimentary rocks, and to recognize otherwise obscure metamorphic events. Several specific examples of the use of the potassium-argon method are described in Chapter 11.

THE K-Ar AGE EQUATION

It was shown in Chapter 3 that the formula for the branching decay of K^{40} is

$$\text{Ar}_{rad}^{40} + \text{Ca}_{rad}^{40} = K^{40}[e^{(\lambda_\epsilon + \lambda_\beta)t} - 1]. \tag{3-2}$$

For calculating geologic ages, equation (3-2) is written

$$\text{Ar}_{rad}^{40} = K^{40} \frac{\lambda_\epsilon}{\lambda_\epsilon + \lambda_\beta} [e^{(\lambda_\epsilon + \lambda_\beta)t} - 1], \tag{4-1}$$

where K^{40} and Ar_{rad}^{40} are the amounts of these nuclides present in the rock today. Note that the quantity Ar_{rad}^{40} is only the number of daughter atoms produced by radioactive decay of K^{40} and not the total number of atoms of that isotope. Equation (4-1) can be solved for t,

$$t = \frac{1}{\lambda_\epsilon + \lambda_\beta} \log_e \left[\frac{Ar_{rad}^{40}}{K^{40}} \left(\frac{\lambda_\epsilon + \lambda_\beta}{\lambda_\epsilon} \right) + 1 \right],$$ (4-2)

which is the *potassium-argon age equation.*

Substituting the values given in Chapter 3 for λ_ϵ and λ_β, equation (4-2) becomes

$$t = 1.885 \times 10^9 \log_e \left[9.068 \frac{Ar_{rad}^{40}}{K^{40}} + 1 \right].$$ (4-3)

For small values of Ar_{rad}^{40}/K^{40}, that is, for young rocks,

$$\log_e \left[9.068 \frac{Ar_{rad}^{40}}{K^{40}} + 1 \right] \simeq 9.068 \frac{Ar_{rad}^{40}}{K^{40}}.$$

Thus for late Cenozoic age calculations equation (4-3) can be simplified to

$$t = 1.885 \times 10^9 \left[9.068 \frac{Ar_{rad}^{40}}{K^{40}} \right]$$

or

$$t = 1.709 \times 10^{10} \frac{Ar_{rad}^{40}}{K^{40}},$$ (4-4)

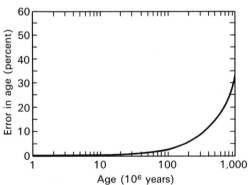

FIGURE 4-3
Error in the calculated age as a result of using the simplified age equation (equation 4-4).

which is the *simplified potassium-argon age equation*. As shown in Figure 4-3, the error in the calculated age introduced by using this simplified age equation is negligible for late Tertiary and Pleistocene rocks and only reaches 1 percent at about 40 million years.

FUNDAMENTAL ASSUMPTIONS

There are five assumptions made whenever equation (4-3) is used to calculate the geologic age of a rock or mineral. Some of these have already been discussed in previous chapters, but they will all be mentioned here for the sake of completeness.

1. The decay of K^{40} takes place at a constant rate, regardless of its chemical or physical environment. The evidence for the validity of this assumption was presented in Chapter 2.

2. The present-day proportion of K^{40} to K_{total} is the same in all materials to which the potassium-argon method is applied. This was discussed in Chapter 3, where it was shown that it is unlikely that natural chemical or physical processes fractionate the potassium isotopes.

3. All argon in the rock or mineral is either radiogenic or atmospheric; that is, there is no extraneous argon. Atmospheric argon is present as a contaminant in the minerals and in the equipment used for the argon analyses. Fortunately, it is possible to identify the fraction of Ar^{40} that is atmospheric contamination, Ar_A^{40}, and to subtract it from the total amount of Ar^{40} to find the radiogenic Ar^{40},

$$Ar_{rad}^{40} = Ar_{total}^{40} - Ar_A^{40}. \tag{4-5}$$

The way in which this atmospheric correction is made is explained in the next chapter. It is assumed that the Ar^{40} generated from the decay of K^{40} escapes continually until the rock solidifies and cools. If this does not happen, however, and for some reason the sample incorporates Ar^{40} at the time of formation, then the calculated age will be too old. This problem of extraneous argon is a fundamental one and is the subject of Chapter 8.

4. The rock or mineral has been a closed system since t_0; that is, there has been no loss or gain of K^{40} or Ar^{40} except for that which results from the radioactive decay of K^{40}. The validity of this assumption depends strongly on the geologic conditions and each case must be decided separately. Argon loss can be a serious problem in potassium-

argon dating and is the subject of Chapter 9. Argon gain would lead to the same result as the presence of extraneous argon and is discussed briefly in Chapter 8. Potassium migration probably is not a serious problem except possibly under certain conditions of metamorphism or hydrothermal alteration, both of which might be expected to cause other changes in the rock that could be recognized by careful petrographic examination. Moreover, the gain or loss of potassium from a mineral lattice probably would lead to at least temporary disruption of the mineral structure, which, in turn, would result in argon loss. In this connection, it is of interest to note that Kulp and Engels (1963) were able to remove nearly 80 percent of the potassium from biotite by base exchange without seriously affecting the potassium-argon age (Fig. 4-4). This supports the observation that badly altered and weathered biotites often give reasonable potassium-argon ages. Apparently the loss of potassium is a layer-by-layer process that also results in loss of argon.

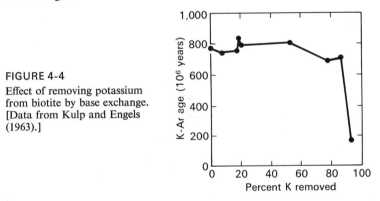

FIGURE 4-4

Effect of removing potassium from biotite by base exchange. [Data from Kulp and Engels (1963).]

5. The time of formation of the rock or mineral is short compared to its age. If this is not true, then the concept of time-zero loses its meaning. This assumption is almost always true, because rocks that take a geologically long time to form and cool usually do so deep within the earth. As a consequence, it is generally a long time before the processes of uplift and erosion expose these rocks.

5

ARGON MEASUREMENT

Several different methods of argon analysis have been developed, but each of these methods can be divided into two essential parts: (1) extraction and purification of argon from a rock or mineral sample, and (2) measurement of the amount of radiogenic Ar^{40} that is present in the extracted gas sample. The argon is extracted from a rock or mineral sample by fusing or decomposing it, either with or without a flux, in a high-vacuum system. The gases that are released from the sample are purified by separating the inert gases, including argon, from the reactive gases. Argon may or may not have to be separated from the other inert gases, depending on which technique is used to measure the quantity of argon in the gas sample.

Three fundamentally different techniques—stable-isotope dilution, direct-volume measurement, and neutron activation—have been used to measure argon. Isotope dilution is the most widely used and is the most satisfactory method. We will describe the isotope dilution method first in some detail and compare it with the other methods later in this chapter. Descriptions of the various methods of argon analysis also are included in a recent review by Kirsten (1966).

ISOTOPE DILUTION

Stable-isotope dilution is a very sensitive analytical method in which a known quantity of *tracer*, or *spike*, which has an isotopic composition different from that of the natural element, is mixed with the sample being analyzed. The isotopic composition of the mixture is measured on a mass spectrometer, and the amount of the natural element in the sample is calculated. A simple analogy to isotope dilution can be drawn using the classic standbys, apples and oranges. Suppose you had an unknown number of oranges and wanted to find out how many you had. You could mix a known number of apples with the oranges, take a representative sample of the mixture, determine the ratio of oranges to apples in the representative sample, and then easily calculate the number of oranges.

Isotope dilution was used by biochemists before 1940 to determine the concentration of hydrogen, carbon, and nitrogen in organic molecules and to determine the rates of chemical reactions (Rittenberg, 1942). The extension of the method to other elements was delayed, however, until about 1945, because until that time hydrogen, carbon, and nitrogen were the only elements for which tracers were available. Separated stable isotopes of many elements have been available since 1945, with the result that isotope dilution can now be used to analyze for a majority of the elements. The method can be applied to any element that has more than one isotope. More than 80 percent of the known elements can now be analyzed in this way (Inghram, 1954). For several of the elements that have only one natural isotope, a long-lived radioactive isotope produced in a nuclear reactor can be used in the same way as a second stable isotope.

Isotope dilution is simplest when an element, A, has only one natural isotope, A_1. If an unknown number of atoms, x, of element A is mixed with a known quantity, y, of a second, artificially produced isotope, A_2, then the ratio of the two isotopes in the mixture would be

$$(A_1/A_2)_M = \frac{x}{y}. \tag{5-1}$$

The amount of the natural element present can be calculated from

$$x = y(A_1/A_2)_M \tag{5-2}$$

after measuring $(A_1/A_2)_M$ with a mass spectrometer.

In practice, situations this simple are seldom encountered, and the degree of complexity of the formula for isotope dilution increases with the number of isotopes. For example, suppose that element A consists of two isotopes, A_1 and A_2, whose natural proportions are $(A_1/A_2)_N$. It would be possible to determine some unknown quantity, x, of the element by mixing with it y atoms of a tracer whose composition is $(A_1/A_2)_T$. The resulting ratio of the two isotopes in the mixture would then be

$$(A_1/A_2)_M = \frac{x(A_1/A_2)_N[1+(A_1/A_2)_T]+y(A_1/A_2)_T[1+(A_1/A_2)_N]}{x[1+(A_1/A_2)_T]+y[1+(A_1/A_2)_N]}, \quad (5\text{-}3)$$

and x could be determined from

$$x = \frac{y[1+(A_1/A_2)_N][(A_1/A_2)_T-(A_1/A_2)_M]}{[1+(A_1/A_2)_T][(A_1/A_2)_M-(A_1/A_2)_N]}. \quad (5\text{-}4)$$

This is the general isotope-dilution equation for an element with two natural isotopes (see derivation in Appendix D). Because the ratio $(A_1/A_2)_N$ is known, the amount of A_1 and A_2 in the natural sample can be calculated.

For an element having more than two isotopes equation (5-4) can still be used. In this case A_1 and A_2 are chosen to be any two of the isotopes of the element.

Isotope dilution is an extremely powerful analytical technique, because after the tracer is mixed with the sample it is only necessary to determine the isotope ratios of a representative sample of the mixture. Note that in equation (5-4) the only measurement required is the ratio $(A_1/A_2)_M$. The composition and amount of the tracer, and the natural composition of the element, are determined beforehand in separate experiments. Thus, after the sample and tracer are mixed, it is not necessary to obtain complete chemical yield as in most other analytical techniques. This is important, because the quantities involved in most radiometric age-dating techniques are so small that they cannot be handled by ordinary methods, and mass spectrometers are best for measuring ratios, not absolute amounts. The optimum sensitivity in isotope dilution is obtained when the isotopic composition of the tracer is significantly different from the natural isotopic composition of the element. Matters would be greatly simplified if an entirely separate element could be used for a tracer, but unfortunately this is not possible. As will be discussed later, material analyzed with a mass spectrometer must be ionized in order for the mass spectrometer to work. Because different elements have different ionization potentials, the ratios measured on the mass spectrometer would not be correct.

Argon analysis is complicated by the fact that the straightforward application of equation (5-4) breaks down when either A_1 or A_2 is a radiogenic daughter product. In equation (5-4) the quantity $(A_1/A_2)_N$ is measurable and constant only for an element with two *stable* isotopes. If either A_1 or A_2 is a radiogenic daughter, $(A_1/A_2)_N$ will not be constant but instead will be an unknown quantity for every sample. This problem can be overcome either by measuring $(A_1/A_2)_N$ in a sample to which no tracer has been added or employing a more complex expression than equation (5-4) if the daughter element has a third, nonradiogenic isotope. Fortunately, argon has three isotopes, so the second alternative, which is easier, can be used, as will be shown later in this chapter.

The sample of argon gas that is analyzed with the mass spectrometer consists of three components—radiogenic argon, the tracer, and atmospheric argon. The radiogenic argon consists only of Ar^{40}, whose amount is to be determined. The tracer is prepared in the laboratory, and its isotopic composition and concentration are known. Most argon tracers today are nearly pure Ar^{38} with only minor amounts of Ar^{36} and Ar^{40}. The composition of atmospheric argon, which has been carefully determined by analyzing air from different locations, is constant. It consists of 99.600 percent Ar^{40}, 0.063 percent Ar^{38}, and 0.337 percent Ar^{36} (Table 3-1), and is present as a contaminant in the gas extracted from the rock or mineral sample. This atmospheric contaminant, whose amount must be determined, comes from several different sources: (1) it is adsorbed onto the surface of mineral grains during sample preparation, (2) it is present in the extraction apparatus both as part of the air adsorbed on equipment surfaces and as part of the air in the crucibles used in fusing the mineral sample, and (3) in volcanic rocks, some atmospheric argon may even be incorporated at the time of crystallization.

The amount of radiogenic argon in a sample can be calculated because the composition of atmospheric argon is known, and the composition and amount of the tracer as well as the composition of the mixture of these gases can be measured. An argon sample consists of a mixture of the three isotopes contributed from the sources indicated in Figure 5-1 and in the following series of equations:

$$Ar_M^{40} = Ar_{rad}^{40} + Ar_A^{40} + Ar_T^{40},$$
$$Ar_M^{38} = Ar_A^{38} + Ar_T^{38},$$
$$Ar_M^{36} = Ar_A^{36} + Ar_T^{36},$$

(5-5)

where

Ar_M^i = no. of atoms of isotope i in the mixture,

Ar_A^i = no. of atoms of isotope i in the atmospheric contaminant,

Ar_T^i = no. of atoms of isotope i in the tracer, and

Ar_{rad}^{40} = no. of atoms of radiogenic Ar^{40}.

If, for the moment, we neglect the small amount of Ar^{36} in the tracer, the way in which Ar_{rad}^{40} is calculated can be explained quite simply. The fraction of Ar^{38} that is due to atmospheric contamination can be determined from

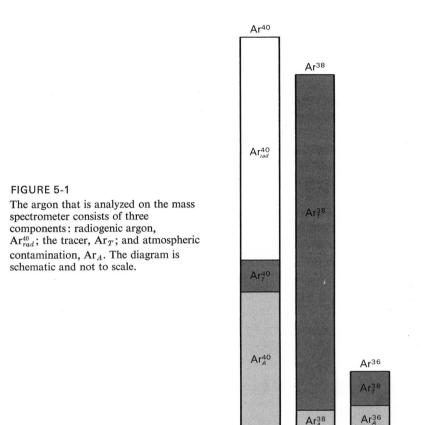

FIGURE 5-1

The argon that is analyzed on the mass spectrometer consists of three components: radiogenic argon, Ar_{rad}^{40}; the tracer, Ar_T; and atmospheric contamination, Ar_A. The diagram is schematic and not to scale.

the known ratio of Ar^{36} to Ar^{38} in the atmosphere. In a similar manner, the fraction of Ar^{40} that is due to atmospheric contamination can be determined from the ratio of Ar^{40} to Ar^{36} in the atmosphere. The remaining fraction of Ar^{38} comes from the tracer, and the known Ar^{40}/Ar^{38} ratio in the tracer can be used to determine the fractional amount of Ar^{40} that is from the tracer. Finally, because the amount of Ar^{38} in the tracer is known, the exact amount of Ar_{rad}^{40} can be calculated from the ratio Ar_{rad}^{40}/Ar_T^{38}. In actual practice, this is done algebraically, and the small amount of Ar^{36} in the tracer also is taken into account.

Equations (5-5) can be expressed in terms of isotope ratios and combined to give the following relationship:

$$Ar_{rad}^{40} = Ar_T^{38} \left\{ (Ar^{40}/Ar^{38})_M - (Ar^{40}/Ar^{38})_T \right.$$

$$\left. - \left[\frac{1 - (Ar^{38}/Ar^{36})_M (Ar^{36}/Ar^{38})_T}{(Ar^{38}/Ar^{36})_M (Ar^{36}/Ar^{38})_A - 1} \right] \left[(Ar^{40}/Ar^{38})_A - (Ar^{40}/Ar^{38})_M \right] \right\}, \quad (5-6)$$

where Ar_{rad}^{40} = number of atoms of radiogenic Ar^{40} in the sample being analyzed, and Ar_T^{38} = number of atoms of Ar^{38} in the tracer. Equation (5-6) is an extension of the general isotope dilution formula (5-4); its derivation is given in Appendix D.

THE ARGON TRACER

The tracer used by most laboratories is nearly pure Ar^{38}, and contains only minor amounts of Ar^{36} and Ar^{40}. The Ar^{38} is available commercially and is produced either by passing atmospheric argon through diffusion columns or by irradiating a chlorine-containing compound (usually a salt) in a nuclear reactor. Some laboratories have used atmospheric argon as the tracer (Amirkhanoff and others, 1961), but this is successful only when the atmospheric argon correction can be ignored.

Naughton (1963) described experiments with a solid tracer that contained the isotope Ar^{39} and could be added to the mineral or rock sample as a powder. He used an artificial silicate glass that contained more than 10 percent potassium. The glass was placed in a reactor and subjected to neutron bombardment, which resulted in the production of Ar^{39} from K^{39}. After the amount of Ar^{39} per gram of glass had been determined, a portion of the solid tracer could be weighed and added to the sample to be analyzed. Although this solid-tracer technique is potentially useful, the difficulties in manufacturing and calibrating it outweigh its obvious advantages, hence it is not currently used.

Two quite different methods are commonly used to prepare argon tracers. In what is called a *bulb system*, tracers are prepared one at a time by a very simple method, whereas in what is called a *manifold*, or *batch*, *system*, as many as 600 tracers can be made at one time by a more difficult process.

Bulb System

In general, a bulb system consists of a gas pipette of known volume attached to a reservoir that has been evacuated, checked for leaks, and filled with tracer argon. Wasserburg and others (1962) described a bulb system in which mercury cutoffs were used to seal the ends of a glass pipette of known volume. Pipettes constructed entirely of metal also have been used (Bieri and Koide, 1967).

We have found that a somewhat simpler system is very satisfactory (Lanphere and Dalrymple, 1966). It will serve to illustrate the general principles of bulb systems. This system (Fig. 5-2) consists of three 2-mm-bore mercury-seal stopcocks connected to a 2-liter pyrex boiling flask, *E*. The gas pipette, *D*, is the piece of tubing of known volume located between control stopcocks

B and C. Stopcock A is a safety stopcock that allows the system to be removed from a vacuum line without exposing stopcock B to the atmosphere. The apparatus is constructed inside a wooden case so that the system can be moved or stored easily when it is not in use.

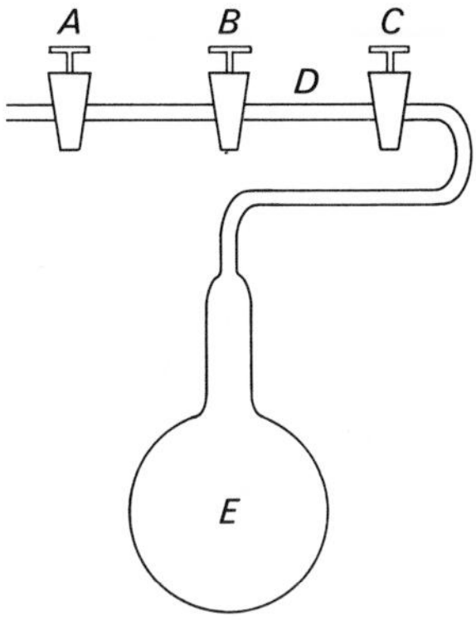

FIGURE 5-2
Schematic diagram of a simplified bulb system for preparing argon tracers: A=safety stopcock, B and C=control stopcocks, D=gas pipette, and E=gas reservoir. [After Lanphere and Dalrymple (1966).]

A tracer is extracted from the system by opening stopcock C with stopcock B closed and letting the gas equilibrate between the reservoir and the pipette. Stopcock C is then closed, and stopcock B is opened to release the tracer. The bulb system can be attached directly to an extraction line, or tracers can be collected in sample takeoff tubes for use at a later time.

The volumes of the flask, V_E, and of the pipette, V_D, are determined as precisely as possible. The uncertainty in these volume measurements generally is less than 0.1 percent standard deviation. Each time a tracer is taken from the bulb system, the gas in the bulb is depleted by a fractional amount

$$\delta = \frac{V_D}{V_D + V_E},$$
(5-7)

where δ is called the *depletion constant*. The amount of Ar^{38} in any given tracer, Ar_T^{38}, is found from

$$Ar_T^{38} = T_0 e^{-\delta X},$$
(5-8)

where T_0 is a constant and X is the tracer number. For example, if the tracer is the 145th taken from the bulb, $X = 145$. Equation (5-8) is used to calculate T_0 from experimentally determined values of Ar_T^{38}. These experimentally determined values of Ar_T^{38} are found by calibrating several individual tracers using methods described later.

In our experience, bulb systems generally are more precise than the manifold type described below. In addition, they are simple to construct

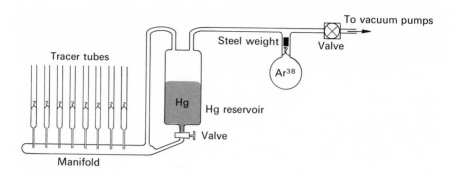

FIGURE 5-3

Simplified schematic diagram of a manifold system for preparing argon tracers. As many as 600 tracers may be made at the same time.

and easy to use. One disadvantage is that the entire bulb can be emptied accidentally by turning the wrong valve. Bulb systems in which greased stopcocks or mercury cutoffs are used eventually may build up a small amount of atmospheric argon because of gas contained in the grease or in incompletely degassed mercury. This is not a serious problem, however, because the atmospheric argon in the tracer is subtracted when the atmospheric argon correction is made, but it is a disadvantage in dating very young rocks, for it is necessary to keep the atmospheric argon contamination to a minimum. All-metal bulb systems do not have this drawback, but they are somewhat more difficult to construct than those made of glass.

Manifold System

A manifold system consists of a large number of individual, numbered tubes that are constructed with breakoff tips, weighed empty and full of mercury to determine the volume of each, and joined by capillary tubes to a manifold (Fig. 5-3). The manifold and the filling apparatus are evacuated and checked for leaks. Mercury is distilled into the mercury reservoir, and the system is then closed off from the pumps with a valve. The tracer argon is released by dropping the steel weight above the sealed argon container and is allowed to equilibrate throughout the system. After equilibration, the mercury is released from the reservoir and allowed to run into the manifold until it has risen high enough to seal off the capillary of every tracer tube. With the argon trapped within the individual tubes, each tracer tube is sealed off at a mark on its capillary with a glassblower's torch. A more detailed discussion of this method of tracer preparation is given by Reynolds and Spira (1966).

Because all tracer tubes on the manifold are filled at a constant pressure, each tube contains the same amount of argon per cubic centimeter of volume. The amount of Ar^{38} in any given tracer is found from

$$Ar^{38}_T = VC, \tag{5-9}$$

where V is the volume of the tracer tube and C, the *calibration constant*, is the amount of Ar^{38} per cubic centimeter. The calibration constant differs for each manifold of tracers.

The manifold system allows a large number of tracers to be prepared all at once. The disadvantages are that the system is difficult and expensive to construct. Entire manifolds of tracers have been lost during preparation because the weight of the mercury in the manifold caused the glass to break while the tracers were being filled. Manifold tracers are probably better and safer than bulb tracers, however, when a laboratory must be used by a large number of people.

Calibration

The amount of argon in the tracers must be measured; the procedure for doing this is called *tracer calibration*. Tracer calibration is the only absolute measurement made in argon analysis; every other measurement is relative. There are two ways in which tracer systems are calibrated: (1) by comparison with a known amount of atmospheric argon, and (2) by comparison with a mineral of known radiogenic argon content.

The tracer system is calibrated by mixing an individual tracer with a carefully measured volume of atmospheric argon* and measuring the composition of the mixture with a mass spectrometer. The amount of Ar^{38} in the individual tracer can then be calculated, and from this information the entire system is calibrated. One way to obtain the known amount of atmospheric argon is to measure a small amount of commercially purified atmospheric argon with a McLeod gauge. The amount of atmospheric argon must be 100 to 1,000 times larger than an individual tracer or else it cannot be measured precisely enough with the McLeod gauge. The entire amount of atmospheric argon that is measured with the McLeod gauge, or a known fraction of it (a system similar to a bulb-tracer system can be used to get the known fraction), can then be mixed with an individual tracer. The major disadvantage of using commercial atmospheric argon is that it may be fractionated and not have the isotopic composition of normal atmospheric argon; its composition must be measured carefully. Another way to obtain a known amount

---

*Any other gas of known composition could be used instead of atmospheric argon, but a correction would then have to be applied to take into account the difference in the ionization probability between the other gas and the tracer argon, and this is difficult to do accurately.

of atmospheric argon is to measure a quantity of air with a McLeod gauge and then remove the reactive gases, leaving only the one percent that is argon to be mixed with an individual tracer. This has the advantage that the removal process reduces the amount of gas by a factor of 100, but has two slight disadvantages. One disadvantage is that the partial pressure of water in the air must be precisely measured with a hygrometer in order to reduce the pressure measurements to those of dry air, in which the abundance of argon is known. The other disadvantage is the uncertainty in the concentration of argon in air, which results in a comparable uncertainty in the tracer calibration. This uncertainty is small—only about 0.1 percent.

In order to use an intra- or interlaboratory standard mineral for tracer calibration, an argon extraction is done on the mineral in the usual manner (described in the following section), and the known Ar_{rad}^{40} content of the mineral is then used to calculate the amount of Ar^{38} in the individual tracer. Although the easiest to do, this type of calibration is only secondary, and the ultimate calibration of any standard mineral still depends on an earlier tracer calibration using atmospheric argon.

In practice, the calibration measurements must be made on enough individual tracers to get statistically significant results; usually six or more calibrations are made. With the bulb system, the values obtained for the individual tracers are used to calculate values of T_0, the mean of which can then be used to calculate the amount of Ar_T^{38} in any given tracer. Calibrations are done periodically instead of all at once because the amount of argon per release decreases with the number of tracers taken from the bulb, and it is desirable to follow this depletion of the bulb with calibrations. With the manifold system, the values obtained for each individual tracer are used to calculate the calibration constant, C. The mean of all of the values of C is then used to calculate Ar_T^{38} for any given tracer.

The composition of the tracer argon in either a bulb or a manifold system is found by analyzing a number of individual tracers on the mass spectrometer and averaging the measured values of the Ar^{40}/Ar^{38} and Ar^{36}/Ar^{38} ratios.

EXTRACTION AND PURIFICATION

The argon is extracted from a sample, purified, and mixed with the tracer in a high-vacuum extraction line. The techniques and apparatus used in the extraction process vary somewhat from laboratory to laboratory but the principles and goals are identical. The objective of the process is to extract the argon from a sample so that the amount of argon can be determined.

Two basically different methods have been used to decompose the sample and free the argon. In one of these methods the sample is decomposed by chemical reaction with a flux at temperatures less than 1,000°C. In the other

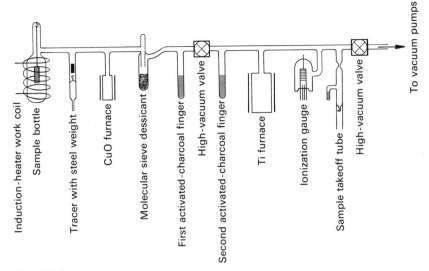

FIGURE 5-4

Schematic diagram of an argon extraction system. The system is constructed of pyrex glass except for the valves and the CuO and Ti furnaces, which are stainless steel.

method the sample is fused without a flux at temperatures as high as 1,800°C.

The flux method was developed first and was widely used until about ten or fifteen years ago, but since then fusion systems that do not employ fluxes have been more widely used. A nickel furnace containing NaOH as the flux was the most common apparatus. The main advantage of the flux method is that an external resistance furnace can be employed because the temperature required for decomposition of the sample is relatively low. This makes the procedure relatively inexpensive. Disadvantages of the flux method include chemical reaction between the flux and the reaction vessel and difficulty in controlling the reaction between the flux and the mineral sample. The most serious disadvantage, however, is that degassing of the flux and the resulting high atmospheric argon correction make the flux method less sensitive, particularly for young samples.

In extraction systems that do not use fluxes, the samples are fused either with an external induction heater or a resistance furnace located inside of a high-vacuum system. Internal resistance furnaces have been used extensively in meteorite studies and for other special uses, but induction heaters have been found to be more satisfactory for standard potassium-argon dating studies.

A typical argon extraction system is shown in Figure 5-4. This is the type used in the U.S. Geological Survey and is essentially the same as the one developed at the University of California, Berkeley, by J. H. Reynolds, J. Lipson, J. F. Evernden, and G. H. Curtis (Evernden and Curtis, 1965a).

The sample to be analyzed is weighed and placed in a molybdenum crucible that is then suspended in a pyrex sample bottle; the bottle is sealed and joined to the extraction line. A pyrex sample bottle with a vycor* liner is used for refractory minerals such as pyroxene and calcic plagioclase, which must be fused at high temperatures (greater than 1,300°C). A tracer and a sample takeoff tube also are joined to the apparatus. The extraction line and sample are then evacuated and baked overnight (generally at 300°C) to facilitate the removal of adsorbed air and water vapor and to increase the pumping speed of the vacuum pumps. The sample bottle may be baked at a different temperature than the rest of the system if necessary. The next day the system is cooled, the pressure is checked with an ionization gauge (a device for measuring pressures in the high to ultrahigh range of vacuum)† and the system is checked for leaks. After an overnight bakeout, the pressure in the extraction line generally is less than 10^{-7} torr and may be as low as 10^{-11} torr.

The extraction line is isolated from the pumping system by closing the valves, the work coil of an induction heater is placed around the sample bottle, and the sample is melted. The radio frequency field from the work coil induces a current flow in the molybdenum crucible, which is thus heated without heating the glass sample bottle. There is some heating of the sample bottle by radiation from the crucible, so the bottle is often cooled with forced air. Some laboratories employ a water jacket around the sample bottle for cooling purposes. While the sample is being fused, the tracer is introduced by lifting the steel weight with a magnet and letting it drop on the breakoff tip. During the fusion process the gas that is evolved is constantly collected on the first activated-charcoal finger, which is immersed in liquid nitrogen.‡ This keeps the pressure in the system low, and the low pressure prevents gas ionization and discharge in the sample bottle due to the high-frequency field inside the work coil. Such a discharge may drive a small fraction of the ionized gas into the walls of the glass sample bottle and is thus undesirable. After the sample has been fused and cooled to room temperature, the charcoal finger is warmed and the gas is released and exposed to a mixture of copper and copper oxide held at a temperature of about 450° to 550°C. Hydrogen is oxidized to H_2O, and hydrocarbons are oxidized or ignited. Water is absorbed by the synthetic molecular sieve.

---

*Vycor is a type of SiO_2 glass.

†*High vacuum* is a pressure of less than 10^{-3} torr, *very high vacuum* is a pressure of less than 10^{-6} torr, and *ultrahigh vacuum* is a pressure of less than 10^{-8} torr. One torr is a pressure of 1 mm of mercury and is the common unit used in vacuum measurements. For comparison, 1 atmosphere is 760 mm of mercury.

‡Activated charcoal is a highly efficient absorber of most gases, including argon, when cooled to the temperature of liquid nitrogen (-196°C), but argon is not absorbed on activated charcoal at room temperature.

The gas is then transferred to the portion of the extraction line between the valves, using the second activated-charcoal finger immersed in liquid nitrogen. The high-vacuum valve is closed, the charcoal finger is warmed, and the gas is exposed to titanium metal at 800°C. The titanium removes all of the reactive gases (O_2, N_2, and so forth). After the titanium is cooled to room temperature, the remaining gas, which is almost pure argon but contains small amounts of some of the other inert gases, is collected in the sample takeoff tube using liquid nitrogen around the small charcoal finger on the takeoff tube. The takeoff tube is removed at the constriction with a glassblower's torch. The gas is then analyzed with the mass spectrometer.

MASS SPECTROMETERS

The mass spectrometer is an instrument in which substances are analyzed according to the mass of the elements or molecules present in the sample. It is probably the most sensitive modern analytical instrument available. The design and applications of the many types of sensitive mass spectrometers are the subject of the field known as mass spectroscopy. This field is much too broad to cover here, and we will briefly describe only the principles of mass analysis and the types of mass spectrometers used in most age-dating laboratories for argon analysis. For further details about mass spectroscopy the reader is referred to review papers and monographs, such as those by Inghram and Hayden (1954), Duckworth (1960), and Hintenberger (1962).

The development of mass spectroscopy was another facet of the explosive growth of physics during the early part of the twentieth century. The evolution of mass spectroscopy closely paralleled investigations into the nature of radioactivity that led to the development of radioactive dating methods. The present-day mass spectrometer evolved from the apparatus used by Thomson (1921) to study the behavior of positive rays. In this apparatus, called a parabola mass analyzer, positive ions were produced by an electrical discharge in a tube filled with gas at reduced pressure. The beam of positive ions was collimated and passed through a narrow tube into a region where the ions were acted upon by parallel electric and magnetic fields that analyzed the beam—that is, separated it into components of various charge-to-mass (e/M) values.* After passing through the electric and magnetic fields the positive ions formed a pattern of parabolas on a photographic plate, each parabola having a different value of e/M. Soddy had previously introduced the concept of isotopy to explain certain chemical properties of radioactive

---

*Charged particles entering an electrical field are deflected in the direction of the applied potential. Those entering a magnetic field are deflected in a direction perpendicular to both the field and their direction of travel.

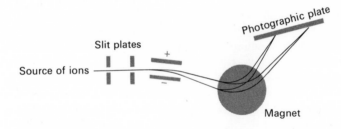

FIGURE 5-5
Schematic diagram of Aston's mass spectograph. [After F. W.
Aston, A positive ray spectograph, Philosophical Magazine, v. 38,
p. 707-714, 1919.]

elements, and with the parabola mass analyzer Thomson made the important
discovery that isotopes also existed among the stable elements (see Chapter 1).

Thomson's work on positive rays was extended by Aston (1919), who
developed a new instrument which he called a *mass spectrograph*. Aston's
spectrograph (Fig. 5-5) had the property of focusing the beam of positive
ions as well as analyzing it into components of different values of e/M.
The collimated beam of positive ions, produced in a discharge tube, was
deflected first in one direction by a uniform electric field and then in the
opposite direction by a uniform circular magnetic field. This arrangement
allowed ions with the same value of e/M to be brought to a single focus—a
line on a photographic plate. Aston's spectrograph possessed the property
of *velocity focusing*; that is, ions of the same e/M ratio were focused at the
same place regardless of their initial energies. Aston's spectrograph had a
resolution of 130, which means that it was capable of separating ions that
differed in e/M ratio by 1 part in 130.

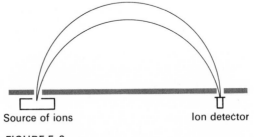

FIGURE 5-6
Schematic diagram of Dempster's mass spectograph.
[After Errock (1965).]

At approximately the same time, Dempster (1918) introduced a completely
different type of mass spectrograph. Ions produced in a monoenergetic
source were accelerated through a potential, collimated by a system of slits,

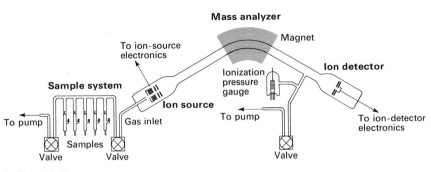

FIGURE 5-7
Schematic diagram of a mass spectrometer for argon analysis.

and deflected through 180° by a uniform magnetic field (Fig. 5-6). This arrangement possesses the property of *direction focusing*; that is, mono-energetic ions of the same e/M ratio are focused after passing through the semicircular magnetic field. In Dempster's first instrument the magnetic field was fixed, the detector was a photographic plate, and the different ions characteristic of the sample material were portrayed as a series of images of the source slit, with each image corresponding to a particular e/M ratio. The resolution of this instrument was 1 part in 100; in other words, it was capable of distinguishing between masses that differed by one percent. Dempster subsequently substituted a simple electrical ion detector for the photographic plate, and this instrument became the first in a long and complex series of *mass spectrometers*.

During the 1920's workers in mass spectroscopy determined the isotopic composition of most of the elements and made systematic measurements of isotopic masses using either velocity-focusing or direction-focusing instru-ments. In the late 1920's and early 1930's, advances in the understanding of the focusing properties of magnetic and electrical fields led to the develop-ment of double-focusing instruments. Many different types of double-focusing instruments have been designed, some with resolutions as great as 1 part in 900,000. But because double-focusing instruments have never been used widely for the mass analyses involved in age measurements, we will concentrate on the details of the single-focusing spectrometers used for argon analysis. A quite different type of mass spectrometer that is sometimes used for argon measurements, the omegatron, is described later in the chapter.

The mass spectrometers used for argon analysis, shown schematically in Figure 5-7, consist of four major parts—the sample system, the ion source, the mass analyzer, and the ion detector. A pumping system capable of obtaining an ultrahigh vacuum in the spectrometer, an oven in which the spectrometer can be baked at relatively high temperatures, and various electronic components also are required.

Sample System

The sample system is simply the apparatus used to introduce the gas sample into the source region where the sample is ionized. In some laboratories the spectrometer is attached directly to the extraction line, and each argon sample is introduced into the spectrometer after the gas extracted from a mineral sample is purified. In other laboratories the sample system consists of a manifold to which purified argon samples in breakseal tubes are attached and analyzed one by one.

The mass analysis of a gas sample may be made using either of two basic methods, and the sample systems used differ from one method to the other. In the *dynamic method* the gas to be analyzed is placed in a storage reservoir and slowly leaked into the source region of the spectrometer. After the sample has passed through the ionization chamber it is pumped out the other end of the spectrometer. In the *static method* the spectrometer is isolated from its pumping system, and the entire gas sample is introduced into the spectrometer tube at one time. Each method has certain advantages and certain disadvantages, and the choice of which method to use usually is made on the basis of the size of the gas sample that is available. Some spectrometers are equipped with a system of valves that allow the instrument to be operated in either the dynamic or static mode, but most spectrometers used for argon analysis in the United States are operated in only one of the two modes.

The pressure in the sample reservoir of a spectrometer operated in the dynamic mode may range from 10^{-2} torr to several torr. Typical pressures in other parts of the spectrometer are 10^{-4} torr in the ionization chamber, 10^{-6} torr in the analyzer region, and 10^{-8} torr in the pumping system. The design of the leak system for dynamic operation is very important, and an ideal leak system should have the following characteristics:

1. The composition of the gas mixture in the ionization chamber should be identical with the composition of the sample.

2. The concentration of the gas mixture being analyzed should not change with time.

3. A change in the concentration of one substance in a gas mixture should not affect the ion beam intensity due to the other substances.

4. The gas flow rate should remain essentially constant during the period of the analysis.

Inghram and Hayden (1954) have presented a detailed discussion about how well various types of leak systems satisfy certain of the requirements for an ideal leak.

The way in which a sample is introduced into a spectrometer operated in the static mode is extremely simple compared to the complex leak systems used in the dynamic mode. A valve between the sample system and the rest of the spectrometer is opened and the entire sample is admitted into the spectrometer, or more precisely, the gas sample is allowed to equilibrate between the sample system and the spectrometer. Because the volume of the spectrometer is generally about 10 times as large as the volume of the sample system, nearly all of the sample gets into the spectrometer. Since isotopic equilibration is maintained, there is no problem with sample fractionation, as there is in the leak systems of spectrometers operated in the dynamic mode. Equilibration of the sample generally takes less than 1 minute, after which the valve to the sample system is closed. Mass analysis of the sample isolated in the spectrometer is then made.

A spectrometer operated in the static mode is much more sensitive than one operated in the dynamic mode, because in the dynamic mode most of the sample is pumped away without being ionized. Thus, for the same type of ion-detection system, the sensitivity of a static analysis probably is a hundred times greater than the sensitivity of a dynamic analysis. The sensitivity of an instrument operated in either mode can be increased by employing an electron multiplier for the ion detector, as will be described later.

Ion Source

The ion source is the part of the mass spectrometer where ions are formed, accelerated, and focused into a narrow beam. All spectrometers used for argon analysis employ an electron-bombardment ion source to produce positive ions that are characteristic of the gas sample. In the ion source the

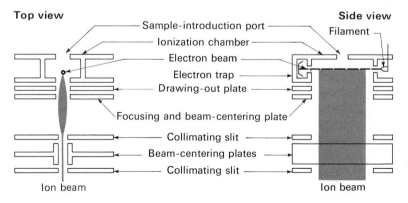

FIGURE 5-8

Electron-bombardment ion source. [After M. G. Inghram and R. J. Hayden, *A Handbook on Mass Spectroscopy*, Publication 311, Committee on Nuclear Science, National Academy of Sciences-National Research Council, Washington, D.C., 1954.]

gas sample is passed through an ionization chamber that is traversed by a beam of electrons. This type of ion source was first introduced by Dempster and was subsequently refined and modified by many workers. A typical electron-bombardment ion source is shown in Figure 5-8.

In an electron-bombardment ion source electrons are produced by a filament, which generally is a tungsten ribbon or wire. The electrons emitted by the filament are accelerated across the ionization chamber by a small potential between the filament and the chamber. Some of the gas atoms that enter the ionization chamber collide with electrons and are ionized, and these positive ions are then drawn out of the ionization chamber by the weak field produced between the drawing-out plate and the ionization chamber. The ions are further accelerated through a potential difference of several thousand volts developed between the ionization chamber and the final collimating, or source-object, slit. The slit system of the ion source is an electrostatic lens that focuses and collimates the ion beam before it enters the analyzer region of the spectrometer.

The energy of electrons used for ionization generally is about 50 to 70 volts. The reason for choosing this energy is shown by the ionization-efficiency curve for argon (Fig. 5-9). This range of energy maximizes the efficiency of single ionization, thus increasing the sensitivity of the spectrometer; at the same time this energy is too low to produce a significant number of multiply charged ions.

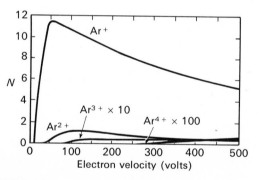

FIGURE 5-9

Ionization-efficiency curve, showing number of argon ions, N, formed per centimeter path at a pressure of one millimeter of mercury as a function of the energy of the impinging electrons. [After Bleakney (1930).]

The current of the ionizing-electron beam must be constant in order for the source to give constant sensitivity for a particular gas. If the ionizing current varies during the analysis of a sample, the variation will contribute a comparable uncertainty to the analytical result. A key element in regulating the ionizing current is the electron trap (Fig. 5-8). The trap is held at a potential about 20 volts more positive than the ionization chamber in order to prevent escape of secondary electrons. The difference between the electron current actually flowing to the trap and the desired current is measured by a feedback amplifier system, and the power to the filament is automatically varied in order to reduce this difference. With this type of circuit the ionizing current can be regulated to about 1 part in 10^4.

The principal advantage of an electron-bombardment ion source is the stability of the resulting ion beam. In a carefully designed source the variation in intensity of the ion beam is no more than ± 0.05 percent, and the spread in energy of the ion beam can be held to ± 0.05 volts (Inghram and Hayden, 1954). The principal disadvantage of the electron-bombardment ion source is that the vacuum system must be extremely clean, because the electrons ionize all gases present in the ionization chamber.

Mass Analyzer

The analyzer portion of a mass spectrometer separates the ion beam emerging from the ion source into its component e/M beams. There are many possible analyzer configurations, but only one basic type is used widely for argon analysis—the first-order direction-focusing mass analyzer. The basic principle of this type of mass analyzer is simple. The ions that emerge from the source are traveling in a narrow beam at high velocity. This beam contains ions of all e/M values. As the ion beam passes through the magnetic field the ions are deflected into circular paths, the radii of which are inversely proportional to the square root of e/M. Thus the ions are separated into beams, each with a particular value of e/M.

The instrument introduced by Dempster (1918) was the first mass analyzer that incorporated any focusing properties. Dempster's original machine employed a magnetic field that deflected the ions through an angle of 180°. As a result of the development of the theory of mass analyzers during the 1930's, it was found that a sector-shaped (pie-shaped) magnetic field produced the same effect as a semicircular magnetic field. A sector magnet has certain advantages in design, though it must be designed to eliminate the effects of fringing magnetic fields on the ion beam. Most of the modern spectrometers have a sector magnet that produces an ion deflection of about 60 degrees. The direction-focusing mass analyzer is sensitive to ion momentum; therefore, the spectrometer must use an ion source that produces ions that are approximately monoenergetic. As was discussed earlier, the electron-bombardment ion source can produce essentially monoenergetic ions.

The focusing properties of magnetic fields were developed by several workers, but the terminology of Herzog (1934) is usually employed. For the arrangement shown in Figure 5-10, let us suppose that ions of mass M_0

Mass analyzer (magnet)

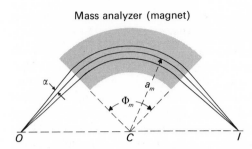

FIGURE 5-10

Focusing properties of a homogeneous magnetic field. [After H. E. Duckworth, *Mass Spectroscopy*, Cambridge Univ. Press, 206 p., 1960.]

and velocity v_0 are introduced into the mass analyzer from the ion source. The object point, O, is the object slit (that is, the exit slit from the source region), and α is the half-angular spread of the ion beam. Ions moving along the median of the ion beam, which is called the optic axis, enter the magnetic field perpendicularly, are deflected along a circular path of radius a_m through an angle Φ_m, and then leave the field perpendicularly. Those ions that diverged with angle α from the optic axis at O are refocused by the magnetic field at the image point, I. If S_0 is the width of the object slit at O, the resolution, $\Delta M/M$, for a monoenergetic ion beam in a symmetrical arrangement like that shown in Figure 5-10 is

$$\Delta M/M = S_0 a_m. \tag{5-10}$$

But since most spectrometers have an image slit of width S_i at I, the resolution for a symmetrical arrangement of an instrument that has perfect focusing is

$$\Delta M/M = (S_0 + S_i)/a_m. \tag{5-11}$$

The theory outlined in this section assumes that the angular spread and the velocity spread of the ion beam are small. For high-resolution instruments this assumption is invalid, but for argon analyses the first-order mass analyzer has adequate resolution.

The deflection of ions in the mass analyzer depends not only on the strength of the magnetic field but also on the momentum of the ions, which is a function of the accelerating voltage in the ion source.

The gain in kinetic energy of ions leaving the source is equal to the potential energy through which the ions fall in the source. That is,

$$eV = 1/2\ Mv^2, \tag{5-12}$$

where e is the charge of the ion, V is the accelerating voltage, M is the mass of the ion, and v is the velocity of the ion. In the mass analyzer the ions will be forced to move along a circular path defined by the relationship

$$Hev = Mv^2/R, \tag{5-13}$$

where R is the radius of the circular path and H is the strength of the magnetic field. Combining equations (5-12) and (5-13) gives the basic mass-spectrometer equation, which is

$$e/M = 2V/H^2R^2. \tag{5-14}$$

It is clear that ions having a particular e/M value will generate a unique circular path for a given combination of accelerating voltage and magnetic field. Thus, in order to collect and measure ions having other e/M values, either the accelerating voltage or the magnetic field must be changed. Instruments designed for both types of scanning options are used for argon analysis, but magnetic scanning is the more popular because with high-voltage scanning the energy of the ion beam changes with mass and the current of the ion beam is therefore not proportional to the amount of the various ions present.

It should now be clear that mass spectrometers do not actually separate ions by mass alone but by both their mass and their charge. In an argon analysis, the beam with e/M equal to $+1/40$ will contain not only ions with e/M values of $+1/40$ but also ions of other elements (if they are present) with values of $+2/80$, $+3/120$, and so forth. Another beam contains ions whose e/M ratios are $+1/38$, $+2/76$, $+3/114$, and so forth. Furthermore, a small percentage of the argon atoms are doubly ionized and appear in the same e/M beam as the singly charged masses 18, 19, and 20 (corresponding, for example, to O^{18}, F^{19}, and Ne^{20}). Because the ionization potentials of the three argon isotopes are essentially the same, the same percentage of each isotope is doubly charged, and this double ionization does not affect the ratios that are measured. Any slight differences would be corrected by the discrimination correction described in a later section. The amount of multiply charged isotopes of higher mass that might appear in the same e/M beams as the argon isotopes is generally negligible, because the energy of the ionizing electrons is considerably lower than the third, fourth, and fifth ionization potentials of most atoms.

Mass spectrometers used for argon analysis are usually not used to analyze elements other than the inert gases. It is very important to exclude from the spectrometer those materials that might interfere with the argon measurements. For example, chlorine has two natural isotopes, Cl^{35} and Cl^{37}. If these combine with hydrogen to form HCl, a common compound, the result is molecules that have the same mass as Ar^{36} and Ar^{38}. For this reason normal cutting oils, which contain HCl, must not be used to machine mass spectrometers used for argon analyses.

Ion Detector

In the first instruments employed in the study of positive ions, fluorescent screens were used as ion detectors. About 1910, fluorescent screens were

74

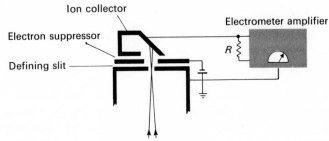

Ion collector

Electron suppressor

Defining slit

Electrometer amplifier

R

Resolved ion beam

FIGURE 5-11

Schematic diagram of a simple electrical ion detector. [After M. G.
Inghram and R. J. Hayden, *A Handbook on Mass Spectroscopy*,
Publication 311, Committee on Nuclear Science, National Academy of
Sciences-National Research Council, Washington, D.C., 1954.]

largely superseded by photographic plates, which have been used widely
in spectroscopic studies where the accurate measurement of ion current
intensities is of secondary importance. In argon analysis, however, the
accurate measurement of ion currents is of primary importance; thus all
instruments used for argon analysis have some type of electrical ion detector.

Two basically different types of ion detectors, *simple collectors* and *electron
multipliers*, are used in argon spectrometers. Simple collectors have sufficient
sensitivity to measure the quantity of argon in most rock or mineral samples,
and, for the most part, electron multipliers are used only for very small
gas samples, which require a high-sensitivity ion detector.

A simple electrical ion detector consists of three major parts: a defining
slit, an electron suppressor, and a cage-type ion collector (Fig. 5-11). The
function of the electron suppressor, or repeller, as it is often called, is to
suppress the secondary electrons that are formed when the ion beam strikes
a surface. The number of secondary electrons produced is a function of the
mass and energy of the ions, so the secondary electrons must be suppressed
or else the behavior of the collector will not be linear. Secondary ion sup-
pression is generally accomplished by applying a potential of approximately
-90 volts to the suppressor plate. The use of an electron suppressor in
combination with a cage-type collector will reduce the nonlinear effects of
the ion detector to less than 0.5 percent (Inghram and Hayden, 1954).

The cage-type ion collector (also called a Faraday cup) is connected to
an amplifier that is, in turn, connected to an output device such as a meter
or a strip-chart recorder. In the United States, commercial amplifiers known
as vibrating-reed electrometers are used in most spectrometers. These
electrometers are extremely stable and can detect an ion current as low as
10^{-17} amperes.

An electron-multiplier collector is advantageous when extreme sensitivity is required, but, since a multiplier is nonlinear with mass, with energy, and with stray magnetic field, this collection system is not used unless absolutely necessary. In argon analyses for geochronology, electron multipliers are generally not required on a spectrometer operated in the static mode, but on an instrument operated in the dynamic mode a multiplier may be required in order to obtain sufficient sensitivity to date young rocks.

In an electron-multiplier collector, the positive ions impinge on the first plate of the multiplier, which is called the conversion dynode. Conversion dynodes are commonly made of copper-beryllium or silver-magnesium alloys, but other materials also have been used. The positive ions liberate secondary electrons from the conversion dynode, and these electrons are accelerated and focused on a second dynode to produce more secondary electrons. These secondary electrons are, in turn, accelerated and focused on another dynode, and so on. The result is an ever-increasing cascade of electrons. In an electron multiplier containing 10 to 20 dynodes, or stages of multiplication, a gain of 10^6 can be obtained. There are, however, many variables involved in the process of converting an ion beam to an electron beam, and all of these variables introduce discrimination effects. A comprehensive description of multiplier effects is given by Inghram and Hayden (1954).

The principal advantages of an electron multiplier are its extreme sensitivity and its fast response compared to a vibrating-reed electrometer. But most spectrometers used for argon analysis have ample sensitivity with simple collectors. The many problems associated with multipliers make them less desirable than simple collectors for most applications.

TYPES OF MASS SPECTROMETERS
USED FOR ARGON ANALYSIS

A mass spectrometer used for argon analysis must meet three basic requirements: (1) it must have adequate sensitivity, (2) it must have a low argon background, and (3) it must be able to resolve the argon masses.

Sensitivity of mass spectrometers is generally no longer a problem in argon analysis. Most laboratories are equipped with instruments that are capable of measuring the argon in extremely young rocks even though they currently may not be used for this purpose. Occasionally, one still reads about potassium-argon ages being determined with "a mass spectrometer with very high sensitivity," but one should not be unduly impressed, for most modern argon spectrometers fit this description. Few dating laboratories, even those that routinely date young rocks, find an electron multiplier necessary. Most mass spectrometers used in analyzing argon have sensitivities on the order of 10^{-14} to 10^{-15} mole of argon per millivolt of output signal and require approximately 10^{-10} mole of argon for an analysis. A sensitivity greater than this is necessary only if very small gas samples are available. The primary limiting factor in dating young rocks is the atmospheric argon correction, not the sensitivity of the mass spectrometer.

It is important that the argon background be low; unless the amount of the background is negligible compared to the amount of the sample, a correction must be made. Moreover, it is important to minimize the amounts of other compounds and elements whose e/M values are the same as those of the argon isotopes. Modern mass spectrometers used for argon analysis are usually baked at temperatures of about 300° to 450°C in order to reduce background, which in most laboratories is negligible.

The resolution of a mass spectrometer used for argon analysis must be sufficient to separate completely the isotopes Ar^{36}, Ar^{38}, and Ar^{40}. Because these isotopes are two mass units apart, it might appear that a resolution of 1 part in 20 would be adequate, but this is not so. An ion beam is not perfectly shaped but has "tails" that extend out to its low-mass and high-

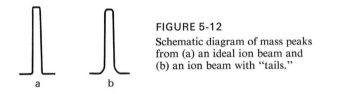

FIGURE 5-12
Schematic diagram of mass peaks from (a) an ideal ion beam and (b) an ion beam with "tails."

a   b

mass sides (Fig. 5-12). If these tails interfere to any significant degree with the adjacent peaks, the resolution may not be adequate. For this reason, all mass spectrometers used in argon analysis have resolutions much higher than 20. Resolutions of 100 to 150 are typical. Note that the Ar^{36} peak in Figure 5-14 is resting on a very slight tail (the sloping baseline) from the adjacent Ar^{38} peak, even though the analysis was made on a mass spectrometer with a resolution of about 100.

Four somewhat different types of mass spectrometers are used for argon analysis. Since they are usually referred to by name in publications on isotope dating, they deserve a brief description. Three, the *Nier-type*, the *Reynolds-type*, and the *MS-10*, are first-order direction-focusing instruments. The fourth, the *omegatron*, works on an entirely different principle. Of the four types of spectrometers, the Nier-type and Reynolds-type are the most commonly used.

First-order Direction-focusing Types

Nier-type instruments are 60-degree magnetic deflection analyzers with a 6-inch radius of curvature and are modifications of a design introduced by Nier (1947). They are constructed of stainless steel and can be baked. These instruments may be operated in either the static or the dynamic mode. Their resolution is usually about 150 to 200.

Reynolds-type mass spectrometers are very much like the Nier-type except that they have a $4\frac{1}{2}$-inch radius of curvature and are usually constructed of pyrex glass. The first instrument of this type was designed by J. H. Reynolds (Reynolds, 1956) at a time when good, bakeable, metal vacuum flanges were unavailable. At that time, glass instruments could be baked at higher temperatures than metal machines and hence had a lower inert gas background. Developments in vacuum technology during the late 1950's resulted in construction of metal spectrometers that also can be baked at high temperatures, and the Reynolds-type spectrometer no longer has this advantage. Reynolds-type machines may be operated either statically or dynamically. Their resolution is about 100.

The *MS-10* utilizes a 180-degree magnetic deflection with a 2-inch radius of curvature and is patterned after the design introduced by Dempster (1918). This instrument was designed originally as a vacuum leak testing device but has been used successfully for argon analysis (Farrar and others, 1964). Because of its small radius, it has a resolution of only about 50. The instrument usually has a permanent magnet, and the ion beam is scanned electrostatically by varying the ion accelerating voltage. Generally it is operated in the static mode. One of its main advantages is its low cost compared to the larger Nier- and Reynolds-type machines.

The resolution of all three types of spectrometers is adequate for argon analysis, but the low resolution of the MS-10 will not permit its use for the analysis of the heavier inert gases, krypton and xenon. A troublesome problem with spectrometers operated in the static mode is the "memory effect"—that is, contamination of the gas sample being analyzed by residues from previous analyses. The memory effect apparently is caused by exchange with ions from previous samples that were driven into metal or glass surfaces by the high-energy ion beam (Reynolds, 1956). Baking the spectrometer can decrease, but not entirely eliminate, the memory effect; besides, it is not practical to bake before every analysis. The procedure generally used to minimize the memory effect is to schedule the analyses so that the argon ratios of the sample being analyzed are as similar as possible to the ratios of the preceding sample. The larger, 60-degree spectrometers exhibit a memory effect, because of the high ion-accelerating voltages used (about 2,000 to 5,000 volts). The MS-10, which employs an accelerating voltage of only 100 volts, exhibits no memory effect according to Farrar and others (1964).

The Omegatron

The omegatron is a mass spectrometer that is used primarily for measuring the partial pressures of various gases in an ultrahigh-vacuum system, but it

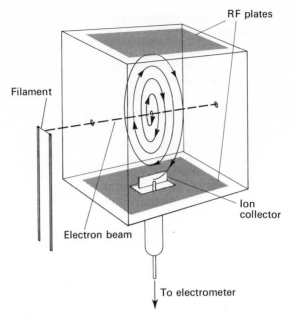

FIGURE 5-13

Diagram of the analyzer of an omegatron. [After Alpert and Buritz (1954).]

also has been used for argon analysis in a few laboratories. The principle of operation of an omegatron is more like that of a cyclotron rather than that of the magnetic-deflection instruments described previously.

Electrons emitted from a hot filament produce ions in a gas sample by electron bombardment in the center of the omegatron chamber, which is a metal box about 2 cm on an edge (Fig. 5-13). These ions are caused to spiral around the magnetic lines of force produced by a homogeneous magnetic field of strength H. The radii of these spirals are very small, and the frequency of revolution is given by the cyclotron frequency

$$\omega = \frac{eH}{M}, \tag{5-15}$$

where e is the electronic charge. The cyclotron frequency, ω, is independent of velocity, but is a linear function of mass. Very few ions would escape from the electron beam because of their own initial energies. However, the application of a radiofrequency (RF) field causes ions whose cyclotron frequency is the same as the frequency of the applied RF voltage to be accelerated in orbits that resemble Archimedes spirals. The spiral orbits of these ions, which are called resonant ions, eventually terminate at an ion collector, and the ion current generated at the collector is measured with a vibrating-reed electrometer or some other type of detector. The nonresonant ions are held within the central spiral orbits. Scanning of the mass spectrum is produced by varying either the RF or the magnetic field, although usually the RF is varied.

The omegatron possesses high resolution for low masses; a resolution of 1 part in 10,000 is possible for low masses (Duckworth, 1960). The resolution can be increased by increasing the number of revolutions between the ion source and the ion collector. But collisions between the ions and other particles become more numerous as the path length is increased, and this tends to decrease the resolution. Nevertheless, the instrument has adequate resolution up to at least mass 40 (Dushman, 1962) and can be used for argon analysis.

Grasty and Miller (1965) have described an omegatron used for argon measurements. Even though their instrument has a resolution of only 1 part in 30, the effect of the tail of the mass 38 peak on the mass 36 peak is still undetectable.

The volume of an omegatron is less than 10 cc, and hence it has extremely high sensitivity compared to magnetic-deflection instruments, which have volumes of 1,000 cc or so. A gas sample of about 10^{-10} cc (about 4.5×10^{-15} mole) is used by Grasty and Miller (1965) for an argon analysis. For comparison, a gas sample of about 6×10^{-6} cc (about 3×10^{-10} mole) is used for an argon analysis on the standard magnetic-deflection instrument.

Like the MS-10, the omegatron does not appear to have a memory effect. Grasty and Miller (1965) suggest that this may be because resonant ions are completely collected, leaving none to be driven into the walls of the tube. They note that the background can be restored to its original state within only a few minutes after a sample is analyzed.

ANALYSIS WITH THE MASS SPECTROMETER

In this section we will briefly describe the procedure used in making a static argon analysis on a Nier-type or Reynolds-type mass spectrometer, the instrumental corrections that must be applied, and the way in which the argon ratios are measured. The procedures used for a dynamic analysis are similar, and the main differences will be pointed out.

In practice, the gas from the sample system is admitted to the mass spectrometer tube through a valve and allowed to equilibrate, which usually takes less than a minute. If the gas sample is too large, then only a fraction of it may be admitted by closing the valve before the sample has had time to equilibrate. In this case an *orifice correction*, which takes into account the resulting mass fractionation, must be applied to the measured mass ratios. The orifice correction depends on the fraction of gas admitted and may be as much as about 2.5 percent. The operator scans, or "sweeps," back and forth over masses 40, 38, and 36 by varying the magnet current. This can be done semiautomatically or manually. The recorder runs continuously at a constant speed, usually about two inches or so per minute, and records the mass peaks as they occur. The operator also must change scales on the vibrating-reed electrometer in order to keep all of the peaks on the chart. One typical pair of "sweeps" from an actual mass analysis is shown in Figure 5-14. Data from this analysis are also used in Figure 5-15 and in the sample age calculation in Appendix C. Five or six such sweep pairs are sufficient for an analysis. The procedure for a dynamic run is essentially the same except that the sample is leaked slowly into the spectrometer tube and continuously pumped out the other end as the analysis is made.

The vibrating-reed electrometer has a number of different scales, each expressed in terms of a voltage, which allows signals of widely differing strengths to be put on the same chart. The precision of these scales is checked regularly by feeding in a precisely known voltage and measuring the resulting "peak height" on the chart. This results in a correction factor for each scale, by which all data recorded on that scale must be multiplied. Usually these corrections are negligible. The procedure is part of the calibration of any mass spectrometer, and the purpose of it is to be sure that a 1-volt signal would be read as 1 volt not only on the 1-volt scale, but also on all other scales on which this signal might, in practice, be recorded. Because the mass spectrometer is used only for determining ratios and not absolute amounts, it is not essential that this hypothetical 1-volt signal read exactly 1 volt, or anywhere near 1 volt. It must, however, read the same on all scales. For example, if a 1-volt signal were 20.0 cm high on the 1-volt scale, it should be $20.0/3 = 6.67$ cm high on the 3-volt scale; if not, a correction must be applied.

Another correction that must be applied to data from the mass spectrometer is the *discrimination correction*, which must be determined periodically. A mass spectrometer may not give exactly the true ratio of the masses present in the tube. This is caused by the slight differences in physical properties of the isotopes and by the spectrometer itself. The discrimination correction is found by analyzing a small sample of argon from the atmosphere. The sample is usually obtained by "cleaning" a small amount of air—that is, removing the reactive gases—on the extraction line. The ratio of Ar^{40} to Ar^{36} that is determined in the sample is compared with the true Ar^{40}/Ar^{36} ratio in air (295.5), and the appropriate correction factor is calculated. This correction is then applied to all ratios determined on the mass spectrometer. Although the discrimination correction is nearly always less than 1 percent, and generally influences the age by a similar amount, it may make a difference of as much as 10 percent or more in the age if the atmospheric argon correction is large.

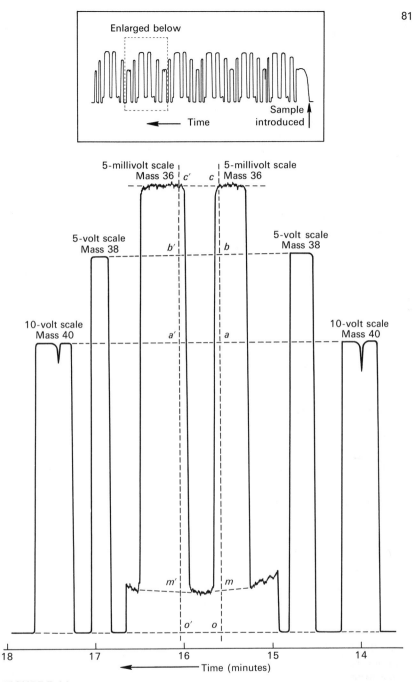

FIGURE 5-14

One pair of "sweeps" from a typical mass spectrometer chart. The recorder scale (full-scale value) is indicated above each mass peak. Inset shows the entire mass spectrometer chart. The sweeps are from the actual mass spectrometer chart of hornblende sample 7G013. See also Figure 5-15 and Appendix C.

The chart from the mass spectrometer must be measured to find the appropriate argon ratios. There are a number of equally good ways to do this; we will describe only the way it is done in our laboratory. Lines are drawn to connect the baselines between peaks and to connect the tops of peaks of the same mass (broken lines in Fig. 5-14). A vertical line is then drawn through the mass 36 peaks, avoiding, as much as possible, the tail from the mass 38 peak, if there is any. The height of each mass peak is then measured with a ruler along this line. For example, the heights of the mass 40, 38, and 36 peaks at 15.6 minutes (Fig. 5-14) would be *oa*, *ob*, and *mc*, respectively; the corresponding values at 16.0 minutes would be *o'a'*, *o'b'*, and *m'c'*. The final result is a series of peak-height values at various times since the sample was first let into the mass spectrometer. From these peak heights the ratios Ar^{40}/Ar^{38} and Ar^{38}/Ar^{36} are calculated for each time.

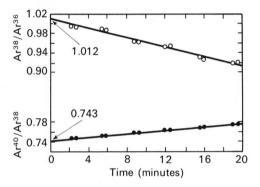

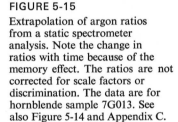

FIGURE 5-15

Extrapolation of argon ratios from a static spectrometer analysis. Note the change in ratios with time because of the memory effect. The ratios are not corrected for scale factors or discrimination. The data are for hornblende sample 7G013. See also Figure 5-14 and Appendix C.

In a dynamic analysis the ratios are merely averaged, but in a static analysis the ratios must be plotted versus time and extrapolated back to zero time (Fig. 5-15) because the composition of the argon changes with time due to the memory effect discussed on page 77. These extrapolated values of Ar^{40}/Ar^{38} and Ar^{38}/Ar^{36} are then corrected for discrimination and scale factors, and used in the age calculation as shown in Appendix C.

OTHER METHODS OF ARGON ANALYSIS

In addition to isotope dilution, two other techniques—the volumetric method and neutron activation—have been used to determine the quantity of radiogenic argon in rock and mineral samples. But since these techniques have neither the precision nor the versatility of isotope dilution, they are not used in many laboratories at the present time.

The Volumetric Method

The volumetric method is primarily of historical interest. It was used widely before enriched Ar^{38} tracers were available. In the volumetric method the rock or mineral sample is fused as described previously, and the reactive gases are removed. In addition, the argon must be separated from the other inert gases. This is done by taking advantage of the fact that each of the inert gases condenses at a different temperature. Xenon and krypton are condensed in a pyrex cold trap cooled with liquid nitrogen. Argon, helium, and neon are transferred to another part of the system, where the argon is absorbed on an activated-charcoal finger immersed in liquid nitrogen, and helium and neon are pumped away. The argon is then introduced into a part of the vacuum system that contains a McLeod gauge. The quantity of argon can be calculated from the known volume of this part of the system and the pressure measured with the McLeod gauge. This method requires that a 100-percent yield of argon be obtained from the sample and measured with the McLeod gauge or else the calculated age will be low.

After the total quantity of argon is determined volumetrically, a mass spectrometric analysis of the argon must be made in order to correct for atmospheric argon. The quantity of radiogenic argon in the rock or mineral sample can be calculated from the measured isotopic composition of the argon, the known isotopic composition of atmospheric argon (Table 3-1), and the total quantity of argon.

The volumetric method is not applicable to young samples because about 10^{-4} cc of Ar (4.5×10^{-9} mole Ar) is needed for a reasonably precise volumetric measurement. For example, a 350-million-year-old biotite that has a K_2O content of 8 percent contains approximately 10^{-4} cc of Ar_{rad}^{40} per gram. Thus, for young rocks the volumetric method requires an inordinately large sample. Of course, the atmospheric contamination is in some ways a help because it adds to the total quantity of argon available for measurement.

Neutron Activation

Neutron-activation analysis for argon has been carried out in several laboratories. The most systematic application of activation analysis to potassium-argon dating was done by Armstrong (1966). But at the present time, the precision, accuracy, and sensitivity of argon analyses made by isotope dilution are better than those made by neutron activation.

When argon is irradiated with thermal neutrons,* Ar^{41} and Ar^{37}, both of which are radioactive, are produced from Ar^{40} and Ar^{36}, respectively. Ar^{41}

Thermal neutrons are low-energy neutrons. They usually are made by slowing down high-energy, or *fast*, neutrons.

decays by β^- emission to K^{41} and has a half-life of 110 minutes, and Ar^{37} decays by electron capture to Cl^{37} and has a half-life of 35 days.

If a rock or mineral sample could be irradiated without previous processing, neutron activation for argon would be a very rapid and relatively inexpensive technique. But because the neutrons also react with calcium and potassium to produce appreciable quantities of Ar^{37} and Ar^{41}, the sample first must be fused and the purified inert gas fraction must be separated as described previously. The inert gas fraction is then irradiated and the activities of Ar^{37} and Ar^{41} measured. This requires that 100-percent yields of argon be obtained or else the measured argon content, and hence the calculated age, will be low. Armstrong (1966) reported difficulty in maintaining consistent 100-percent yields of argon because glass in the extraction system became dirty with use and resulted in low argon yields.

In an isotope-dilution analysis the concentration of Ar^{36} is used to make the correction for atmospheric argon. In Armstrong's activation technique the measured activity of Ar^{37} in the irradiated sample is used in a comparable way to make the correction for atmospheric argon. The total quantity of Ar^{40} is calculated from the Ar^{41} activity. After the correction for atmospheric argon is made, on the basis of the Ar^{37}/Ar^{41} ratio, the quantity of radiogenic Ar^{40} in the original sample can be calculated. Standard samples of atmospheric argon of known volume are irradiated along with the inert-gas fraction from the rock or mineral sample so that a correction for the effect of variation in neutron flux can be made.

On the basis of replicate analyses of gas standards, Armstrong (1966) reported the precision of his neutron-activation analysis for argon as 4 percent ("coefficient of variation", which is the ratio of the standard deviation to the mean, expressed in percent). Because the blank correction and the correction for atmospheric argon in an activation analysis are somewhat larger than in an isotope-dilution analysis, the precision of an activation analysis is less than the precision attainable by isotope dilution. For example, Armstrong's blank correction averaged about 0.8×10^{-6} cc STP Ar^{40} per analysis, and for most of his experiments the blank correction was less than 10 percent of the radiogenic Ar^{40}. For comparison, Dalrymple (1968) reported a blank correction that averages 2×10^{-11} mole per analysis (equivalent to about 0.4×10^{-6} cc STP per analysis) for isotope dilution analyses. The atmospheric argon corrections reported by Armstrong are several times larger than are obtained in the completely bakeable extraction system described earlier in this chapter. The effects of larger blank and atmospheric argon corrections can be decreased in part by fusing larger samples so that the amount of argon handled per experiment is larger. After evaluating his analytical procedure and results, Armstrong (1966) reported a precision of $+15$ percent, -5 percent for a potassium-argon age of a sample that contains more than 5 percent potassium. These precision estimates are for the 80-percent confidence level.

Armstrong analyzed several mineral standards by neutron activation that have been analyzed in other laboratories by isotope dilution. The radiogenic argon content of these standards determined by the two different methods agree within the limits of experimental error. This is very important, because the two methods are completely independent except for primary calibration involving volumetric measurement of samples of atmospheric argon. Thus these results substantiate the basic principles of both methods.

A rather ingenious activation technique has been suggested by Mitchell (1968), who called it the Ar^{40}/Ar^{39} method for potassium-argon age determination. In this method the argon analysis and the measurement of potassium are both done on the same portion of the sample. The mineral sample itself is irradiated with fast neutrons. Ideally the only reaction that occurs is the production of Ar^{39} from K^{39}. After irradiation, the sample is fused in a vacuum system, and the isotopic composition of the argon is measured on a mass spectrometer. If no other reactions except the production of Ar^{39} from K^{39} occur, Ar^{36} can be used to make the atmospheric correction, and the age can be calculated directly from the Ar_{rad}^{40}/Ar^{39} ratio. It is only necessary to measure argon isotopic ratios, and it is not necessary to determine the concentration of either radiogenic argon or potassium.

In this technique, the principle source of interference is argon produced by neutron interactions with isotopes of calcium. For example, any Ar^{36} produced through neutron reactions with Ca^{40} will make the atmospheric argon correction too high, and thus the radiogenic argon and the age will be low. Some Ar^{39} is produced from a neutron reaction with Ca^{42}, but if the potassium/calcium ratio of the sample is greater than 0.1, this reaction will contribute less than one percent of the total Ar^{39}. Since Ar^{40} is produced by neutron interactions with K^{40} and Ca^{43}, any Ar^{40} produced by these interactions will make the apparent age too high. For a 1-million-year-old sample with a potassium/calcium ratio of 1, the neutron-induced Ar^{40} will be approximately 10 percent of the radiogenic Ar^{40}.

Using this Ar^{40}/Ar^{39} method, Mitchell (1968) analyzed an assortment of biotite and muscovite samples whose ages, determined by conventional isotope dilution, range from 5 to 850 million years. For most of the minerals the difference in ages determined by the two different methods was less than 5 percent. Although all of the interferences have not been completely evaluated, the Ar^{40}/Ar^{39} method seems promising for those minerals, biotite and muscovite in particular, that have high potassium/calcium ratios.

6

POTASSIUM MEASUREMENT

Many different methods have been used to determine the amount of potassium in rocks and minerals. These include gravimetric methods; instrumental methods, such as flame photometry and atomic-absorption spectroscopy; and physical methods, such as X-ray fluorescence, isotope dilution, and neutron activation. Numerous articles and books have been published that describe these methods in detail (see, for example, Müller (1966)). We will summarize only briefly some of the methods of measuring potassium that commonly are used in geochronology and evaluate their usefulness for potassium-argon dating.

GRAVIMETRIC METHODS

The classical chemical methods for measuring the amount of potassium in a rock or mineral involve the precipitation and weighing of an insoluble potassium compound. There are numerous ways to do this, but all require that the alkali metals (potassium, sodium, lithium, rubidium, and cesium) first be separated from the other elements in the rock or mineral. The decomposition of the mineral(s) and separation of the alkalis usually is done by one of two well-known techniques, both of which start with grinding the sample to a fine powder and result in precipitation of the alkalis as chlorides. The oldest of these, the *Berzelius method*, was devised by J. J. Berzelius in 1824 and begins with the attack of the rock or mineral by hydrofluoric and sulfuric acids. Silicon and fluorine are evaporated, and other undesired elements are precipitated as insoluble oxides or salts. Finally, the alkalis are converted to chlorides. In the *J. Lawrence Smith method*, which dates from 1871, the mineral or rock is decomposed by heating with ammonium chloride and calcium carbonate. The resulting sinter cake is leached with water and the alkali earths, magnesium, and any sulphates present are precipitated. The final solution contains the alkali chlorides.

After the alkalis have been separated from the rock as chlorides by one of these two methods, potassium must be separated from the other alkali metals and its amount determined. This may be done by several gravimetric techniques, including precipitation as potassium hexachloroplatinate (K_2PtCl_6), potassium perchlorate ($KClO_4$), potassium tetraphenylboron ((C_6H_5)$_4$BK), and potassium silvercobaltinitrite ($K_2Ag(Co(NO_2)_6)$).

The *chloroplatinate method*, based on the insolubility of potassium chloroplatinate in ethanol, is one of the most satisfactory techniques. Because the chloroplatinates of lithium, sodium, and the alkali earth elements are soluble in ethanol, they can be removed from solution. Potassium chloroplatinate is, ideally, a stochiometric compound, so the amount of potassium in the sample can be calculated from the weight of the precipitate. Difficulties in this technique are caused by deviations of the potassium chloroplatinate from its ideal formula and by the interference of rubidium and cesium, if present, whose chloroplatinates also are insoluble in ethanol.

The *perchlorate method*, also widely used, involves converting the alkali chlorides to perchlorates with perchloric acid. Sodium and lithium are removed by extraction with a mixture of butyl alcohol and ethyl acetate. The potassium perchlorate is then dried and weighed and the amount of potassium in the sample is calculated. As in the chloroplatinate method, rubidium and cesium perchlorates cannot be separated from the potassium perchlorate.

In the *tetraphenylboron method* (TPB), the potassium is converted to potassium tetraphenylboron, an insoluble salt. The sodium and lithium tetraphenylborons are removed in solution. The precipitate is filtered, dried, and weighed. As in the other methods, rubidium and cesium are precipitated with potassium. Another disadvantage of the method is that the sodium tetraphenylboron reagent is relatively unstable and will decompose and cause interference effects if the experimental conditions are not ideal (Cluley, 1955).

In the *cobaltinitrite method*, the potassium is precipitated by adding silvercobaltinitrite to an acidic solution of the alkali chlorides. This technique is difficult to do well, and because the composition of the precipitate may be uncertain the method is not widely used.

In all of these gravimetric methods, rubidium and cesium are precipitated and weighed with potassium. In the minerals commonly used for potassium-argon dating, the amount of cesium is negligible. Rubidium can be measured in the weighed potassium salt by flame photometry or X-ray fluorescence, and an appropriate correction can be applied to obtain the correct potassium value. The main disadvantage of the gravimetric methods is that the initial mineral or rock decompositions and alkali separations are difficult to make and, consequently, are very slow. The most widely used separation, the J. Lawrence Smith method, is extremely difficult, requiring the skill of an analytical chemist. For this reason, these techniques are seldom used for potassium-argon dating. The chief usefulness of the J. Lawrence Smith method and the accompanying gravimetric techniques is in the preparation of rock and mineral standards for calibrating the faster and easier methods that are necessary to produce results in volume.

For additional details and references, consult Müller (1966) or books on analytical chemistry, such as Hillebrand and others (1953).

INSTRUMENTAL METHODS

At the present time, most of the potassium measurements used in potassium-argon dating are made by means of the instrumental techniques. A few laboratories use the recently developed technique of atomic-absorption spectroscopy, but most do their potassium measurements by flame photometry.

Flame Photometry

The flame photometer operates on the principle that all elements emit a characteristic radiation when excited. Extremely high temperatures are required to excite most elements, but the alkali metals, either in their elemental state or in compounds, will emit radiation when burned in a gas-air flame. The emission occurs when electrons go from a high to a lower energy state. The wavelength emitted by any one element is characteristic of that element, and the intensity of the radiation is proportional to the amount of the element present. The flame photometer takes advantage of this property of elements and compares the intensity of the visible radiation from an unknown solution with the intensity of the visible radiation from known or standard solutions.

Two basically different flame photometric techniques have been used to measure potassium. One technique utilizes *direct measurement* of the intensity of the potassium radiation. In the other technique a *lithium internal standard* is added both to the unknown and the standard solutions, and the intensity of the potassium radiation is compared to that of the internal standard.

Direct-measurement techniques require that the alkalis be separated from both the directly and the indirectly interfering elements before the sample is measured with the flame photometer. Most of the techniques currently in use are based on the Berzelius method of dissolving the mineral or rock with hydrofluoric and sulfuric acids. Representative of these is the procedure described by Abbey and Maxwell (1960). After decomposition, silicon, fluorine, and excess acids are driven off by evaporation. Other unwanted elements are precipitated as insoluble sulfates and oxides and filtered out, leaving a final sulfate solution that contains the alkali metals and magnesium. This solution is then measured with a flame photometer, and the readings are compared with those from standard solutions. The direct-reading technique works well only if the interfering elements are properly removed from the final solution. Cooper (1963) made a systematic investigation of the interference effects in materials used for potassium-argon dating. He found that the presence of other elements, the type of burner and fuel used, and the potassium concentration all affected the potassium measurement. In addition to careful chemical preparation, the direct-reading technique requires a very good (and expensive) flame photometer to be accurate. For additional details about these techniques and the equipment required, see Ellestad and Horstman (1955) and Ingamells (1962).

For potassium-argon dating, the internal-standard technique is the one that is most commonly used. This technique has the advantages that the chemical procedures are simple and the instrument required is relatively inexpensive. A typical chemical procedure is described by Shapiro and Brannock (1962). The mineral or rock is dissolved in hydrofluoric, sulfuric, and nitric acids. Silicon is removed as SiF_4 by evaporation. The remaining solution is diluted with water, and a standard quantity of lithium (the internal standard) is added. The solution is then analyzed with a flame photometer equipped for a lithium internal standard. The use of the lithium internal standard minimizes indirect interferences from other elements (matrix effects).

Standard solutions for potassium flame photometry are made by dissolving a known amount of a potassium salt to get the desired concentration of potassium. A known amount of lithium, which is used as an internal standard, is added to both the standard and the unknown solutions. Lithium was

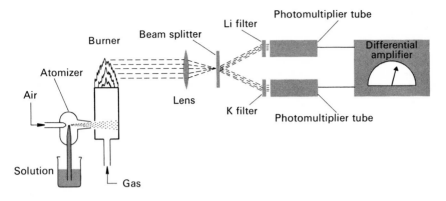

FIGURE 6-1
Schematic diagram of a flame photometer that utilizes a lithium internal standard.

chosen as the internal standard for alkali determinations because lithium is generally not very abundant in most rocks and minerals and because lithium emits only a single intense wavelength approximately midway in the spectrum between sodium and potassium. The only drawback to the use of lithium as an internal standard is that the presence of any appreciable quantity of lithium in the sample will decrease the potassium/lithium ratio in the photometer solution and lead to low results for potassium. Thus, for lithium minerals (for example, lepidolite), and for micas and feldspars from granitic pegmatites, it may be necessary to make a separate lithium measurement in order to correct the flame-photometer results.

The solution to be analyzed is atomized into a burner flame in the flame photometer (Fig. 6-1). The flame excites the potassium and the lithium in the solution, and each element emits its characteristic radiation, which is isolated using monochromators or filters. Most instruments employ a dual or split light path whose characteristic radiation is allowed to strike two photocells or photomultiplier tubes, one set to read only the intensity of the purple (wavelength = 7,700 Å) potassium radiation and the other set to read only the intensity of the red (wavelength = 6,708 Å) lithium radiation. The outputs of the potassium and lithium photomultipliers are applied to a differential amplifier that presents the difference on a meter or as a direct readout. This difference is proportional to the amount of potassium present in dilute solutions, and is compared with the differences produced by standard solutions of both higher and lower potassium contents. Because the potassium contents of the standard solutions are known, the potassium content of the unknown solution can be found from proportional parts using the data from the flame photometer. Once the concentration of potassium in the solution has been found, it is easy to calculate the percentage of K_2O

in the mineral from the concentration and the weight of the sample that was originally put into solution.

Suhr and Ingamells (1966) suggested a somewhat more rapid method of preparing samples for flame-photometer analysis that some laboratories use in place of the Shapiro-Brannock procedure. A mixture of the sample and lithium metaborate is fused and the melt is dissolved in nitric acid. An aliquant of the solution is analyzed on the flame photometer, the lithium from the lithium metaborate serving as the internal standard. This technique has the advantage of being quite rapid—a potassium measurement can be done in an hour or less. In contrast to the other flame-photometric techniques that utilize standard solutions, this method requires a set of analyzed mineral and rock standards for calibration. Nevertheless, the use of mineral and rock standards has the advantage that interferences from other elements can be minimized by using standards of the same bulk composition as the unknowns.

In addition to the effect of lithium in the sample on the potassium analysis,

TABLE 6-1

Comparison of potassium measurements of rocks and minerals by flame photometry and isotope dilution.

| | K_2O (wt percent) | |
Material	Flame photometry*	Isotope dilution
Hornblende	0.026	0.024
Hornblende	0.045	0.042
Hornblende	0.045	0.048
Hornblende	0.266	0.274
Pyroxene	0.054	0.052
Pyroxene	0.258	0.245
Plagioclase	0.302	0.301
Plagioclase	0.311	0.307
Plagioclase	0.600	0.599
Plagioclase	0.811	0.835
Biotite	9.17	9.15
Biotite	9.18	9.15
Diabase	0.656	0.652
Granite	5.54	5.60
Muscovite	10.40	10.35
Muscovite	10.20	10.39

* Lithium internal standard, sodium buffer (Cooper, 1963); lithium internal standard (Lanphere and others, 1968; Lanphere and Dalrymple, 1967).

rubidium also may interfere with the potassium determination because it is difficult to resolve the rubidium and potassium emission lines in most flame photometers. Cooper and others (1966) found that rubidium enhanced the potassium value by an amount equivalent to 0.5 part of potassium for each part of rubidium. Thus, for rubidium-rich minerals, it is necessary to determine rubidium by some other method, such as isotope dilution, and to apply a correction to the flame-photometric potassium value. As an alternative, interference filters can be used to minimize rubidium interference.

A precision of better than 1 percent is easily obtained for flame-photometric analyses of samples containing more than about 0.5 percent K_2O. Cooper (1963) reports that the standard deviation of a series of photometer readings on a sample solution is generally less than 0.5 percent. The precision is not as good for samples containing lower concentrations of potassium, because the radiation emitted is weaker and often is less stable. With careful work, however, good precision can be obtained on samples containing less than 0.1 percent K_2O. The accuracy of flame-photometric results is comparable to that of other methods and is a function of the accuracy of the standard solutions used. Table 6-1 gives a comparison of some determinations by flame photometry and isotope dilution. Isotope dilution is not influenced by any of the interference effects that have been discussed and thus provides a good basis for comparison.

Atomic-absorption Spectroscopy

Atomic-absorption spectroscopy is an analytical method for determining the concentration of an element in a sample on the basis of conversion of elements to individual atoms and the measurement of absorption of radiant energy by the atoms. The radiant energy absorbed produces narrow absorption lines, generally in the visible or ultraviolet parts of the spectrum, at wavelengths that are characteristic of the particular element being determined.

Atomic absorption and emission spectroscopy are related in a rather simple fashion. The basis for emission spectroscopy (the principle of flame photometry) is the emission of a photon when an atom goes from an excited state to the ground state; the basis for atomic-absorption spectroscopy is the formation of an excited atom from one in the ground state when it absorbs a photon. The intensity of an emission line is proportional to the number of excited atoms, which in turn is a function of temperature and the frequency of the emission line. In contrast, the only significant variable that affects the intensity of an absorption line is the number of atoms available to absorb photons. The chemical preparation of samples for atomic absorption is similar to that for flame photometry. The technique has the important advantage that rubidium does not give direct-line interference with potassium. But indirect interference from other elements (matrix effects) is just as serious

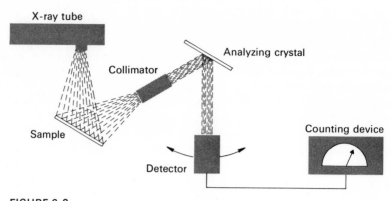

FIGURE 6-2
Schematic diagram of an X-ray fluorescence spectrometer.

as it is for flame photometry, and, unlike the instruments used for flame photometry, most instruments available for atomic-absorption spectroscopy do not allow the use of an internal standard to minimize these effects. Atomic absorption is not widely used in potassium-argon dating, and although the precision of the method is difficult to evaluate, it does appear to be slightly inferior to flame photometry.

PHYSICAL METHODS

X-Ray Fluorescence

X-ray fluorescence analysis, like flame photometry, is a type of emission spectroscopy. In X-ray fluorescence analysis, the material to be analyzed is bombarded with a beam of X-rays. Upon striking an atom, these X-rays eject an electron from one of the inner shells of the atom. The place of this electron is soon taken by an electron from one of the outer shells, whose place is then taken by an electron still farther out, and so forth. The atom thus returns to its normal state in a series of steps, in each of which a photon having a wavelength in the X-ray region is emitted. The wavelengths of the photons emitted from any given element are characteristic of that element and constitute its X-ray spectrum.

When a specimen is excited by irradiation with X-rays, the emitted radiation leaves the specimen in all directions (Fig. 6-2). Part of the emitted radiation is collimated into a beam that is directed onto an analyzing crystal, which in turn diffracts the X-ray spectrum according to Bragg's law. The intensity of the components of the dispersed X-ray spectrum are then measured with a detector, such as a Geiger counter, a scintillation counter, or a proportional counter. The intensity of the radiation is a function of the concentration of the emitting element. Thus the situation is similar to that in flame photometry; but instead of a flame, X-rays are used to excite the potassium atoms; instead of visible light, X-rays are emitted; and instead of a photomultiplier, an X-ray spectrometer is used to measure the intensity of the radiation. Because quantitative chemical data cannot be determined directly from the X-ray intensities, the measured intensities require calibration with analyzed standards.

X-ray fluorescence is normally subject to large errors because of interferences from other elements (matrix effects). To minimize these interferences, standards of the same composition as the sample are used, and this requires a large number of standards. Fortunately, the elements most likely to interfere with potassium are not common in rocks; consequently, interference is not a serious factor in the measurement of potassium. A single set of standards is usually sufficient for the purpose.

Sample preparation for X-ray fluorescence analysis is extremely important, because most of the incident X-rays penetrate only about 0.05 millimeters below the surface of the sample. For this reason, the surface must be representative of the entire sample, as inhomogeneities can cause significant errors but can be eliminated by fusing the sample into a uniform glass using a suitable flux.

The precision and accuracy of X-ray fluorescence is comparable to flame photometry or gravimetric methods, provided accurate standards are available. These standards must, of course, be analyzed by some other technique. Rose and others (1963) made replicate measurements on ten pairs of samples that contained between 0.5 and 8 percent K_2O. They report a coefficient of variation of 0.84 percent. The main advantage of X-ray fluorescence is that it is fast. Its disadvantages are that the necessary equipment is very expensive and that a carefully analyzed set of standards is required. Because of this latter point, the method is a secondary rather than a primary method of measurement. Comparisons of X-ray and chemical measurements of some rocks and minerals are given in Table 6-2. Figure 7-7 is a comparison of potassium values determined by both X-ray fluorescence and flame photometry.

Neutron Activation

The standard neutron-activation procedure for potassium is based on measuring the γ-activity of K^{42} as it decays to Ca^{42}. The half-life of K^{42} is 12.4 hours. The production of K^{42} is accomplished by neutron irradiation of K^{41}. Neutron activation is an extremely sensitive technique that has been used to measure very low potassium concentrations in silicate rocks

TABLE 6-2

Comparison of potassium measurements of rocks and minerals by X-ray fluorescence and chemical methods.

Material	K_2O (wt percent)	
	X-ray	Chemical
Tektite	1.60	1.6
Tektite	1.88	1.93
Tektite	2.38	2.43
Tektite	2.80	2.7
Shale	5.70	5.67
Rhyolite	6.25	6.34
Siderophyllite	7.60	7.60

Source: Data from Rose and others (1963).

(Morgan and Goode, 1966), but it has rarely been used to measure potassium for the purpose of age determination.

The powdered sample is irradiated in a thermal neutron flux together with either a flux monitor, which is used to measure the total neutron flux to which the sample was exposed, or a standard sample. Use of a standard eliminates the necessity of knowing the total neutron flux, because the activity of the sample is compared to the activity of the standard. After irradiation, the radionuclide K^{42} is chemically separated, and its activity is measured using counting equipment.

In Chapter 5 we described a method of determining potassium by measuring Ar^{39} produced by neutron interaction with K^{39}. This method, however, involves the measurement of radiogenic argon at the same time, and the technique has no particular advantage as a method for measuring only potassium.

Isotope Dilution

This method is particularly well suited for accurate analyses of minerals or rocks with low potassium contents. Potassium concentrations as low as a few tens of ppm can be determined accurately; the limiting factor at low concentrations is contamination from reagents. The basic principles of isotope dilution are outlined in Chapter 5, and the use of the method for potassium measurement differs only in chemical details from its use in argon analysis.

The chemical preparation of the sample is essentially the same as that for flame photometry. The rock or mineral is dissolved in a mixture of hydrofluoric and sulfuric acids. The isotope dilution tracer, or "spike," may be added at the same time as the acids (this is known as total spiking) or later if only a part of the sample solution is to be spiked. In the latter procedure the sample is first dissolved, and the solution is diluted to a predetermined volume. Then an aliquant is pipetted out, a known amount of potassium tracer solution is added to the aliquant, and the mixture is evaporated to dryness, leaving a residue. In total spiking, the evaporation is done immediately after the sample is dissolved. Any insoluble sulfates are separated by filtering or centrifuging before the solution is evaporated. Sometimes the potassium from samples with low concentrations of the element is concentrated by ion-exchange chromatography or by precipitation as potassium tetraphenylboron. A portion of the residue is loaded on a filament made of rhenium or tantalum ribbon. The filament is placed in a solid-source mass spectrometer, the filament is heated to ionize the potassium, and the isotope ratios of the spike-sample mixture are measured.

Natural potassium has the isotopic abundances $K^{39} = 0.9308$, $K^{40} = 0.0001$, $K^{41} = 0.0691$ (Table 3-1). Thus natural potassium consists largely of K^{39}, but includes a small fraction of K^{41}, and a much smaller fraction of K^{40}. A tracer highly enriched in K^{41} is used in many laboratories because if such a tracer is mixed with a sample the mixture will have a K^{39}/K^{41} ratio close to unity, which is ideal for potassium isotope dilution analysis. The use of a K^{40}-K^{41} "double spike," however, makes greater analytical precision possible. Solid-source mass spectrometry differs from gas-source spectrometry, the method used for argon analysis, in that discrimination or instrumental fractionation varies markedly from experiment to experiment. The variation in the measured isotope ratios of replicate measurements of a sample may be several percent in the potassium mass range. The extra isotope in the double-spike procedure allows the discrimination of the mass spectrometer to be calculated directly for each analysis. If a K^{41} spike is used the discrimination cannot be calculated directly, but is assumed to be a constant that is determined by periodic measurements of normal potassium.

COMPARISON OF METHODS

Potassium measurements of suitable precision can be obtained using several of the methods described in this chapter. Speed and simplicity are obviously important, but precision and accuracy cannot be sacrificed. Flame photometry using a lithium internal standard is the method that probably best fits these criteria. It is relatively inexpensive, easy to do, and utilizes standard solutions rather than mineral or rock standards. Data for 11 mineral or rock samples containing more than 1 percent K_2O (Table 7-2) indicate that the standard deviation of flame-photometer analyses is less than 1 percent for material containing from 1 to 19 percent K_2O. For material containing less than 1 percent K_2O the precision is in general not as good (Fig. 7-5), but for some of the examples given this may be caused by inhomogeneity of the sample material. A standard deviation of approximately 3 percent or less is possible, however, for samples containing between 0.2 and 1.0 percent K_2O. Reasonably precise potassium concentrations can be measured, with care, by flame photometry on material containing less than 0.5 percent K_2O. For material that contains less than about 0.2 percent K_2O, isotope dilution is preferable to flame photometry because good precision is possible at low potassium concentrations. The disadvantage of isotope dilution is that it requires a solid-source mass spectrometer and is therefore one of the most expensive techniques.

The precision and accuracy of atomic absorption may be comparable to flame photometry, but it is still subject to errors due to matrix effects. Although the equipment required for atomic absorption is somewhat more expensive than a flame photometer, it is not prohibitively so. The gravimetric methods suffer from the disadvantages of being difficult and slow. They are primarily useful as a source of analyzed mineral and rock standards for some of the other techniques. X-ray fluorescence is capable of precision nearly as good as flame photometry, but the equipment is expensive, and many carefully analyzed standards are required. Its main advantage is that it is extremely rapid; under favorable conditions 50 or more samples can be measured in a day.

The accuracy of potassium measurements is directly related to the error in calibrating the reference standards (flame-photometer standard solutions, X-ray fluorescence standards, isotope-dilution spike, and so forth). The calibration error generally is less than 1 percent if the calibration is carefully done. A good test of accuracy is provided by the results of samples measured by different methods in different laboratories. Data are given in Tables 7-3 and 7-5 for two mineral standards measured by a variety of methods in different laboratories. As we point out in Chapter 7, there seem to be no systematic variations that can be related to the analytical method used, and the agreement between methods and laboratories is remarkably good. The precision and accuracy of potassium measurements is discussed further in the next chapter.

7

ACCURACY AND PRECISION

The usefulness of an age determination is increased considerably if it is accompanied by some estimate of its reliability. In its simplest (and least useful) form this estimate may be only a statement to the effect that, "this age is (or is not) considered reliable." Usually, however, the reliability is expressed as a plus-or-minus figure appended to the age—for example, 100 million years ± 5 million years. What are these plus-or-minus figures? How are they derived? How can they be used? What factors contribute to errors in potassium-argon ages? Some of the answers to these questions form the content of this chapter.

For purposes of discussion, analytical errors will be divided into two categories—errors related to accuracy and errors related to precision. The term *accuracy* will be used to mean the degree to which the determinations represent the true K^{40} and Ar^{40} contents of the rock or mineral. *Precision* will be considered as the measure of reproducibility. When these terms are defined in this way, it is quite possible for the analytical data (or apparent age) to be very precise and at the same time be inaccurate. Thus, precision is a necessary condition but not necessarily an acceptable test for accuracy, for many of the factors that contribute to accuracy introduce systematic errors in the calculated age whereas errors due to precision tend to be more random.

In addition to analytical accuracy and precision, a third consideration is the overall validity or *geological accuracy* of an age determination. This is the degree to which a calculated age represents the true age of a geologic event, such as intrusion, metamorphism, or uplift. Geological accuracy is strongly dependent on the degree to which the basic assumptions obtain in nature. Especially important are the problems of argon loss, due either to nonretentive minerals or to heating events, and of extraneous Ar^{40}. No satisfactory general statement can be made about argon loss or extraneous Ar^{40} because they depend on both the history and the composition of the dated rock and will vary considerably from sample to sample. Therefore, it is necessary to consider the possibilities of argon loss and extraneous Ar^{40} for each age determination. These subjects are so important that they are discussed separately and in detail in Chapters 8 and 9. The remainder of this chapter will deal mostly with analytical accuracy and precision, for it is never possible to be sure how old a rock actually is.

It is assumed that the reader has a general knowledge of basic statistics. No attempt will be made here to review such things as the mean, standard deviation, standard error of the mean, variance, or normal distribution. The meaning and calculation of these parameters are covered in any beginning book on statistics.

THE MYSTERIOUS ±

The statistical parameters used to indicate the "error" in an age determination are by no means standardized. Most workers use either the standard deviation (68-percent confidence level) or the 95-percent confidence level. Others use the probable error, which is the 50-percent confidence level. Another parameter that is sometimes used is the coefficient of variation, which is the ratio of the standard deviation to the mean expressed as a percentage; it is sometimes called the percent standard deviation. If the meaning of the ± figures is not specified, it is probably safest to assume that they are standard deviations. It should be mentioned that all of these dispersion parameters are based on the assumption that the errors are normally distributed about the mean. For radiometric age determinations this may not be exactly true. For example, an error in the calibration of tracers would introduce a systematic, not random, error into the calculated age. An error in technique, such as inadvertently pumping away part of the argon during extraction or mass analysis of the sample could lead to a very large error that could not be treated statistically. There is very little information available concerning these types of errors, however, and at present there is no satisfactory alternative to the normal distribution hypothesis.

The ± figure that accompanies an age is usually only an estimate of precision for that particular determination. This is because the errors are highly variable, and there is no completely satisfactory way to calculate the uncertainty in a calculated age. Unless otherwise stated, these ± figures are most often estimates of what the standard deviation (or some other dispersion parameter) *would be* if a large number of measurements were made on that same sample. These estimates are based on the quality of the data, a knowledge of previous replication experiments, and an understanding of the way in which various factors affect the uncertainty in the calculated age. To estimate these errors is not necessarily bad practice, for there are more or less systematic ways of doing so. The main thing to remember is that a dispersion parameter, such as the standard deviation of analytical precision, means only that the geochronologist estimates that if he were to repeat the analysis on that particular rock or mineral the odds are about two out of three that the result would fall within the stated limits. Typically, standard deviations of analytical precision for a calculated age are in the range of 1 to 5 percent when the data are of good quality, but may be as high as 100 percent or more for some determinations.

Plus-or-minus figures may be related entirely to precision and be strictly a measure of reproducibility or they may be partly related to analytical accuracy and include some allowance for such things as the accuracy of analytical standards. Generally the ± figures quoted with a potassium-argon age do not take into account the uncertainties in the decay constants of K^{40} or in the isotopic abundances of potassium and atmospheric argon. The factors considered in estimating ± figures vary from worker to worker; these factors should be, but often are not, described. Whatever the case, it is the responsibility of the geochronologist to give a full explanation of what his ± figures represent and how they were determined. The user of potassium-argon ages has every right to expect this information.

Sample inhomogeneity may be a large source of analytical error in a potassium-argon measurement. Significant errors can easily be introduced by the use of inhomogeneous samples and poor splitting techniques,* but this is commonly overlooked when the ± figure is appended to the measured age. Both the potassium and the argon measurements are made on separate aliquants of a mineral concentrate or on separate fragments of rock samples. In other dating techniques, such as the rubidium-strontium and uranium-

---

*A sample is *split* when it is divided into aliquants or aliquots. Splitting may be done either by hand or with the aid of some mechanical device.

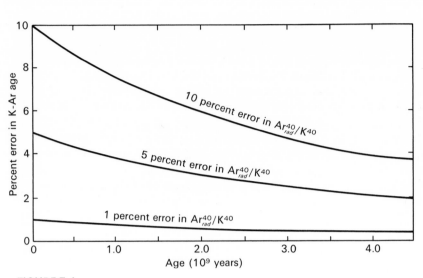

FIGURE 7-1
Percent error in potassium-argon age versus age for various errors in the ratio Ar^{40}_{rad}/K^{40}.

lead methods, all analyses are usually done on the same initial material, and hence many of the problems of sample inhomogeneity are avoided. This is not true for the potassium-argon method, and it is essential that the material analyzed for potassium or argon be a representative portion of the total sample.

FACTORS THAT AFFECT ACCURACY

The analytical accuracy of a potassium-argon age naturally depends on the accuracy of the potassium and argon measurements. It is important to realize, however, that the effect on the calculated age of errors in these quantities is not linear. The reason is that the age is a logarithmic function of the ratio Ar^{40}_{rad}/K^{40} (see equation 4-2). This means that the error in the calculated age for a given error in Ar^{40}_{rad}/K^{40} is time dependent. As shown in Figure 7-1, the error in the calculated age is about equal to the error in Ar^{40}_{rad}/K^{40} for young rocks and decreases as the ages become greater. Thus analytical errors do not introduce as large an uncertainty in the calculated ages of old rocks as they do for young rocks.

The analytical accuracy of an argon or potassium measurement depends ultimately on the absolute calibration of the Ar^{38} tracer and of the various potassium standards. The uncertainty in calibrating standards contributes a constant error to the analyses, and if the calibrations are done carefully, this error is generally less than 1 percent for each of the elements.

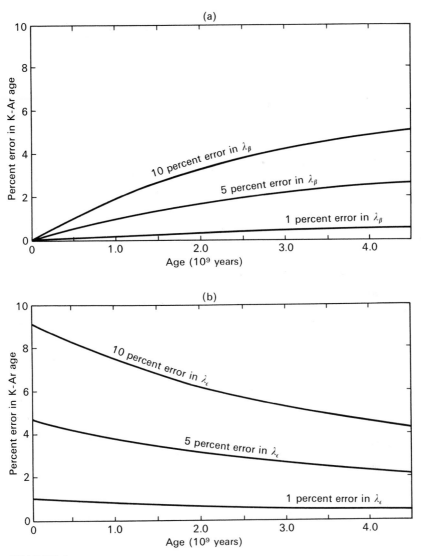

FIGURE 7-2
Percent error in potassium-argon age for various errors in (a) λ_β, and (b) λ_ϵ.

The uncertainties in the decay constants of K^{40} also produce a time-dependent error in the age. As shown in Figure 7-2, a, errors in λ_β have very little effect on the potassium-argon ages of rocks of Paleozoic age and younger. Even as much as a 10-percent error in λ_β would produce only a 1-percent error in the potassium-argon age of rocks as much as 500 million years old. As was discussed in Chapter 3, however, the uncertainty in λ_β

probably is small, and, because it is time-dependent, contributes a very small or negligible error to potassium-argon ages. In contrast, uncertainties in λ_ϵ, though also time-dependent, are not negligible for rocks of any age (Fig. 7-2, b). A 10-percent error in λ_ϵ produces slightly more than a 9-percent error in the calculated age for very young rocks, but this error exceeds 4 percent even at 4.5 billion years. Hence the error in λ_ϵ is important for rocks of all ages. The uncertainty in λ_ϵ probably is close to 3 percent or less, as was discussed in Chapter 3.

If more accurate determinations of λ_ϵ and λ_β become available, published ages can be recalculated from the analytical data. However, the most useful geologic information comes from comparing potassium-argon ages with each other, so a systematic change of a few percent in all of the potassium-argon ages probably would have little or no effect on the conclusions drawn from those ages. There are exceptions to this, of course, such as comparisons between potassium-argon ages and a previously established time scale.

Other factors that can affect the accuracy of the argon and potassium determinations, and hence the calculated age, are uncertainties in the isotopic compositions of tracers, of natural potassium, and of atmospheric argon. These uncertainties are usually very small, however, and generally contribute a negligible error to the calculated age.

FACTORS THAT AFFECT PRECISION

Because of the time and expense involved in making even a single measurement, multiple measurements are seldom made, and potassium-argon ages are usually the result of only one or two measurements. The choice that faces the experimenter is simply whether to make ten replicate measurements on a single sample and have a reasonably reliable estimate of precision for that sample, or to make one measurement on each of ten separate samples and to estimate the uncertainties for each sample. Usually (but not always) more can be learned by making one measurement on each of ten rocks than from ten measurements on one rock, and the geochronologist most often chooses to sacrifice a more exact knowledge of precision for a bulk increase in information. This makes it necessary to have some systematic way to estimate the precision of a single age determination. One of the ways of doing this is described in the next two paragraphs.

The largest error in precision is often related to the atmospheric argon correction, because of the effect produced when one large number is subtracted from another. Recall that the Ar^{40} from a sample consists primarily of two components, atomspheric Ar^{40} and radiogenic Ar^{40}. The atmospheric Ar^{40} must be subtracted from the total Ar^{40} in order to find the radiogenic

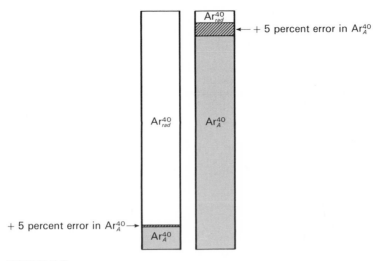

FIGURE 7-3

An error in the atmospheric argon correction is much more serious when the radiogenic argon percentage is small than when it is large.

Ar^{40} (the Ar^{40} in the tracer is usually very small and can be neglected for the purpose of this discussion).

$$Ar_{rad}^{40} = Ar_{total}^{40} - Ar_A^{40}. \tag{4-5}$$

If Ar_A^{40} is small, then the uncertainty in Ar_{rad}^{40} will be smaller than the uncertainty in Ar_A^{40}. But if Ar_A^{40} is large, then the uncertainty in Ar_{rad}^{40} will be quite large (Fig. 7-3). For example, if Ar_A^{40} makes up 90 percent of Ar_{total}^{40}, then a 1-percent error in Ar_A^{40} will produce approximately a 10-percent error in the quantity of Ar_{rad}^{40}. This effect is sometimes partially offset by the fact that as the amount of atmospheric argon increases, so does the signal-to-noise ratio of the Ar^{36} mass peak.

A formula for estimating the standard deviation of analytical precision, σ, in a potassium-argon age determination has been derived by Cox and Dalrymple (1967):

$$\sigma \cong \left[(\sigma_k)^2 + (\sigma_x)^2 + (\sigma_{38}^{40})^2 \left(\frac{1}{r}\right)^2 + (\sigma_{38}^{36})^2 \left(\frac{1-r}{r}\right)^2 \right]^{1/2}, \tag{7-1}$$

where

σ_k = standard deviation of the potassium analysis,

σ_x = standard deviation of the tracer calibration,

σ_{38}^{40} = standard deviation of the ratio Ar^{40}/Ar^{38},

σ_{38}^{36} = standard deviation of the ratio Ar^{36}/Ar^{38},

r = fraction of Ar^{40} that is radiogenic.

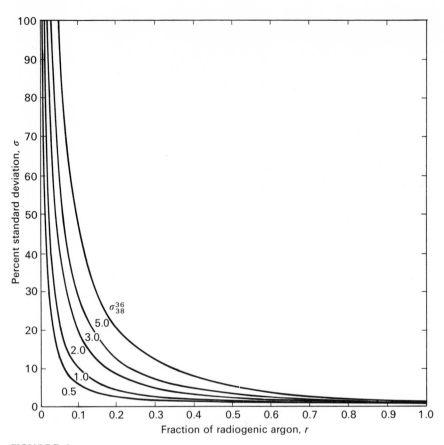

FIGURE 7-4

Percentage standard deviation, σ, in a potassium-argon age as a function of the fraction of radiogenic argon, r, for various values of σ_{38}^{36}. The curves were calculated from equation (7-1) using $\sigma_k = 0.5$ percent, $\sigma_x = 0.3$ percent, and $\sigma_{38}^{40} = 0.2$ percent. [After A. Cox and G. B. Dalrymple, Jour. Geophys. Res., v. 72, p. 2603-2614, 1967.]

On the basis of replication experiments, Cox and Dalrymple estimated σ_k to be about 0.5 percent. Their estimate of 0.3 percent for σ_x was based on repeated measurements of an intralaboratory standard biotite (Lanphere and Dalrymple, 1966) that gave a standard deviation of 0.6 percent; Cox and Dalrymple assumed that no more than one-half of this error was due to tracer variability. They estimated σ_{38}^{40} to be about 0.2 percent from mass spectrometric analyses of atmospheric argon in which the Ar[36] peak was sufficiently large to be comparable in signal-to-noise ratio to an average Ar[40] or Ar[38] peak. Using these values, they presented a set of curves for σ

TABLE 7-1

Comparison of precision determined from some replication experiments with estimates from Figure 7-4.

Description	K-Ar age (10^6 years)	Average r	σ (percent) calculated from repeated age determinations	σ (percent) estimated from Figure 7-4
12 whole-rock basalt specimens from same hand sample (Dalrymple and Hirooka, 1965)	3.4	0.72	1.90	1.5
7 whole-rock basalt samples from same flow (Dalrymple and Hirooka, 1965)	3.3	0.66	2.11	2.0
12 Ar and 10 K_2O measurements on muscovite (Lanphere and Dalrymple, 1965)	81.0	0.90	1.12	1.0
14 Ar and 3 K_2O measurements on biotite (Lanphere and Dalrymple, 1966)	159	0.92	0.77	1.0
Multiple Ar and K_2O measurements on 13 sanidine and obsidian samples (Doell and others, 1968)	0.4–1.0	0.56	3.98	4.0

Source: From A. Cox and G. B. Dalrymple, Jour. Geophys. Res., v. 72, p. 2603-2614, 1967.

versus r for several values of σ_{38}^{36}. These curves are reproduced here as Figure 7-4. Usually σ_{38}^{36} is about 1 to 2 percent but may decrease to 0.5 percent for small values of r because of an accompanying increase in signal-to-noise for the Ar^{36} peak. These error curves can never give a rigorous estimate of precision because all of the quantities may vary somewhat from experiment to experiment. Note also that the curves of Figure 7-4 do not take into consideration the time dependency of errors in Ar_{rad}^{40}/K^{40} shown in Figure 7-1. Nevertheless, the curves at least provide one reasonable way of obtaining an estimate of the precision of a single age determination. Some data that provide a partial check on the validity of these curves are given in Table 7-1. These results show that estimates obtained from Figure 7-4 are in general agreement with values actually calculated from replication experiments.

TABLE 7-2
Some data on the precision of potassium analyses.

Material	No. of analyses	Mean K_2O (wt percent)	Coefficient of variation
Plagioclase	12	0.178	3.5
Plagioclase	5	0.396	0.9
Plagioclase	25	0.933	1.2
Hornblende	53	0.294	3.0
Hornblende	29	0.492	1.6
Basalt	7	0.374	2.9
Basalt	8	0.674	0.6
Basalt	8	1.05	0.4
Basalt	46	1.31	1.1
Basalt	9	1.35	0.4
Basalt	10	2.58	0.4
Plastic clay	5	3.21	0.2
Biotite	31	7.69	1.1
Biotite	5	8.34	0.4
Biotite	45	8.40	0.7
Muscovite	8	10.2	0.1
Sanidine	21	10.4	0.9
Leucite	9	19.0	0.1

Source: Data from Evernden and Curtis (1965a), Dalrymple and Hirooka (1965), and unpublished U. S. Geological Survey sources. All measurements were made by flame photometry using a lithium internal standard, and all of the measurements on each sample were made by only one laboratory.

EMPIRICAL DATA ON ACCURACY AND PRECISION

The best way to evaluate precision is to make replicate measurements. From these, statistics can be calculated provided there are enough data. A few examples of precision data based on replication have already been given (Table 7-1).

Accuracy, too, can be partly evaluated empirically, but this generally involves more work and is slightly more complicated. Measurements on different minerals from the same rock, by different techniques and different laboratories on the same mineral, and on closely related rocks will give semiquantitative information about analytical accuracy as well as about precision. These measurements also provide some feeling about geological accuracy. In this section we present a few examples of such empirical data.

Potassium Measurements

Table 7-2 presents some data on the precision of flame photometric K_2O measurements. These data, from the U.S. Geological Survey Menlo Park laboratory and the Department of Geology and Geophysics of the University of California at Berkeley, are on a variety of intralaboratory standard materials. The data show that the standard deviation of precision is generally less than 1 percent for minerals and rocks with more than 1 percent of K_2O. As the K_2O content decreases to less than 1 percent, the standard deviation of precision may rise to several percent or more (Fig. 7-5). This

FIGURE 7-5

Comparison of precision versus K_2O content for data of Table 7-2.

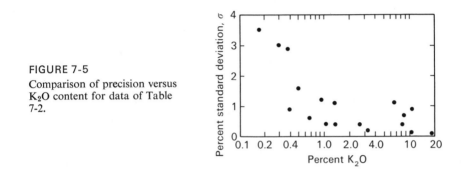

is because small K_2O concentrations are more difficult to measure than large concentrations (Chapter 6). Because each material listed in Table 7-2 was measured by the same technique and only in one laboratory, the data contain little, if any, information about accuracy.

FIGURE 7-6

Comparison of flame-photometric and isotope dilution measurements of K_2O on the same mineral. The symbols indicate the range of values for both the abscissa and the ordinate. Data from Table 6-1. The outer limits of the shaded band are ± 10 percent from perfect agreement (solid line).

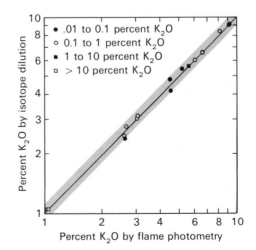

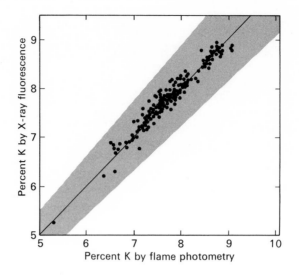

FIGURE 7-7

Comparison of flame-photometric and X-ray fluorescence
measurement of potassium (K) on the same mineral.
The outer limits of the shaded band are ±10 percent
from perfect agreement (solid line). [After Wanless and
others (1965).]

Comparison of potassium contents measured on the same mineral by
different techniques indicates that discrepancies are rarely greater than 5
percent (Tables 6-1 and 6-2, and Figs. 7-6 and 7-7). This also is good evidence
that the measurements are probably accurate to within a few percent,
especially when the techniques are based upon quite different physical
principles.

Interlaboratory Standards

Interlaboratory standard minerals are a source of valuable information about
the precision to be expected when comparing potassium-argon ages determined in different laboratories. Two such international potassium-argon
standards have been widely circulated and analyzed—M.I.T. standard biotite B3203 and U.S. Geological Survey standard muscovite P-207.

The reproducibility of both potassium and argon values for biotite B3203
(Tables 7-3 and 7-4) is remarkable, especially in view of the fact that many of
the measurements were made before 1960, when techniques were still being
refined. In spite of this, and the additional condition that a variety of ana-

TABLE 7-3

Potassium determinations of the M.I.T. standard biotite B3203.

Laboratory	Method	K_2O (wt percent)
M.I.T.	G	8.92
	FP	9.13
	NA	9.40
U. of Chicago	FP	9.07
U.S.G.S., Washington	FP	8.92
U. of Minnesota	G	8.94
Brookhaven	FP	9.17
	G	9.25
Shell Development	G	9.28
Lamont	ID	9.15
Geological Survey, Canada	FP	9.16
U. of California, Berkeley	FP	9.17
U. of Arizona	FP	8.92
Carnegie Institution	G	9.09
U.S.G.S., Menlo Park	FP	8.95
Australian National Univ.	FP	9.17
	ID	9.15

Mean = 9.11

Coefficient of variation = $\pm 1.5\%$

G = gravimetric
NA = neutron activation
ID = isotope dilution
FP = flame photometry

Source: Data from Hurley (1962), Lanphere and Dalrymple (1965), Cooper (1963), Evernden and Curtis (1965a).

lytical methods were used, the total spread of the argon and potassium measurements is only ± 3.5 percent and ± 2.6 percent, respectively, and the standard deviations only ± 1.8 percent and ± 1.5 percent.

Probably the most widely analyzed potassium-argon standard for which data are available is muscovite P-207. A recent compilation of results available from January 1964 through January 1967 is presented in Table 7-5. From these data it can be seen that the standard deviation of precision of laboratory means is less than 2 percent for both potassium and argon

TABLE 7-4

Argon determinations of the M.I.T. standard biotite B3203.

Laboratory	No. of Measurements	Ar_{rad}^{40} (10^{-8}mole/gram)
Lamont	8	1.72
University of Kyoto	—	1.74
U.S. Geological Survey, Washington	2	1.74
Carnegie Institution	1	1.72
Fermi Institute	2	1.73
Massachusetts Inst. of Technology	6	1.74
University of Arizona	1	1.76
Shell Development	3	1.70
University of Minnesota	—	1.79
U.S. Geological Survey, Menlo Park	4	1.73
California Institute of Technology	4	1.67
		Mean = 1.73
	Coefficient of variation = 1.8%	

Source: Data from Hurley (1962), Hanson and Himmelberg (1967), Lanphere and Dalrymple (1965), Bogard and others (1968).

determinations. As is expectable, the precision within the average single laboratory is slightly better than the precision between different laboratories. When ages are calculated from the potassium and argon values, the resulting standard deviation is still only 2.6 percent. Moreover, it is important to note that there does not appear to be any systematic variation in analytical results with technique.

Additional Data

One way to obtain a feeling for the validity, or geological accuracy, of potassium-argon ages is to compare the results when the technique is applied to two minerals from the same rock.

Different minerals usually have quite different potassium contents and argon diffusion parameters. This makes concordance of potassium-argon ages highly unlikely unless all of the basic assumptions of the method are fulfilled.

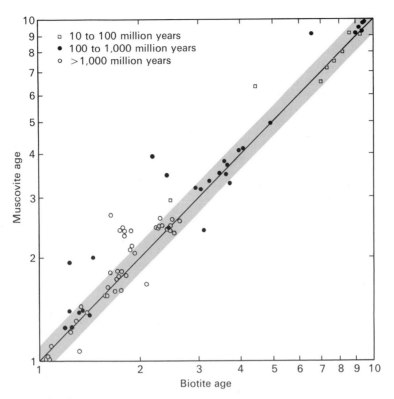

FIGURE 7-8

Potassium-argon ages determined from biotite and muscovite samples from the same rock. The symbols indicate the range of values for both the abscissa and the ordinate. The outer limits of the shaded band are ±10 percent from perfect agreement (solid line). [Data from Wanless and Lowdon (1961, 1963a, 1963b) and Wetherill and others (1965).]

Figure 7-8 is a comparison of potassium-argon ages on biotite and muscovite from the same rock. Note that in most cases the ages agree relatively well, indicating that the potassium-argon ages are probably reasonable estimates of the time of formation of the rock. The data are from both igneous and metamorphic rocks, and no attempt was made to distinguish those rocks that might have undergone later heating events. Consequently, about one-quarter of the data are discordant. With only a few exceptions, the discordance can be attributed to post-formation heating.

Comparing ages determined by two techniques on the same mineral is another test of the validity of potassium-argon ages. This is a slightly more powerful test than that provided by two minerals from the same rock, because each technique uses independently determined decay constants;

TABLE 7-5

Potassium and argon measurements on P-207, the U.S.G.S. interlaboratory standard muscovite.

Laboratory	Method*	Potassium measurements			Argon analyses		
		Number of analyses		Mean K_2O† (wt percent)	Number of analyses	Mean Ar_{rad}^{40}† (10^{-9} mole/gram)	Calculated age‡ (10^6 years)
Australian National Univ.	FP	2		10.38 ± 0.01	5	1.246 ± 0.018	79.5
Bundesanstalt für Bodenforschung (W. Germany)	FP	6		10.38 ± 0.04			
Geochron Labs	FP	4		10.04 ± 0.17	3	1.251 ± 0.005	82.5
Geol. Survey of Canada	X	1	10.43	10.36 ± 0.14	1	1.283	82.0
	ID	5	10.35 ± 0.15				
Geol. Survey of Japan	KTPB	3	10.48 ± 0.10	10.37 ± 0.17	3	1.258 ± 0.005	80.4
	FP	2	10.22 ± 0.09				
Isotopes, Inc.	ID	4		10.23 ± 0.17	2	1.244 ± 0.006	80.6
Lamont Geol. Obs.	ID	5		10.38 ± 0.08	4	1.257 ± 0.022	80.2
Max Planck Inst.	FP	6	10.40 ± 0.04	10.39 ± 0.05	3	1.258 ± 0.008	80.2
	ID	2	10.35 ± 0.07				
Min. Inst., Bern	FP	2		10.36 ± 0.04			
Oxford	FP	12		10.44 ± 0.21	4	1.264 ± 0.009	80.2
Socony Mobil	KTPB	4		10.42 ± 0.02	3	1.245 ± 0.006	79.2
Shell Development					3	1.245 ± 0.013	
Tohoku Univ.	FP	3		10.14 ± 0.02	3	1.341 ± 0.014	87.5

Univ. Alberta	FP	2	10.34 ± 0.02	10.34 ± 0.09	3	1.263 ± 0.003	80.9
	KTPB	5	10.34 ± 0.11				
Univ. Amsterdam	FP	6		10.24 ± 0.16			
Univ. Arizona	FP	5		10.43 ± 0.09	3	1.270 ± 0.007	80.7
Univ. California, Berkeley	FP	8		10.29 ± 0.02	1	1.265	81.4
Univ. California, La Jolla	AA	1		10.16	4	1.245 ± 0.009	81.2
Univ. Hawaii	FP	7		9.92 ± 0.16	(5)	(1.254 ± 0.025)	(83.7)
Univ. Tokyo	KTPB	3		10.40 ± 0.04	2	1.223 ± 0.014	78.0
Univ. Toronto					5	1.273 ± 0.007	
Penn. State	JLS	1		10.22			
Cambridge Univ.	FP	6		10.31 ± 0.07			
U.S. Geol. Survey	FP	12	10.20 ± 0.09	10.21 ± 0.10	12	1.253 ± 0.008	81.3
	ID	1	10.39				
Number of analyses, N		118			64		
Mean, $\bar{x}$, of lab. means				10.29		1.260	81.0
Median, $\tilde{m}$, of lab. means				10.35		1.258	80.6
Std. dev., s, of lab. means (= interlab. std. dev.)				0.13 or 1.26% of $\bar{x}$		0.024 or 1.90% of $\bar{x}$	2.1 or 2.59% of $\bar{x}$
Std. error, $s_{\bar{x}}$, of lab. means				0.03 or 0.29% of $\bar{x}$		0.006 or 0.48% of $\bar{x}$	0.5 or 0.61% of $\bar{x}$
Intralab. std. dev., s_0				1.18% of value		1.01% of value	1.55% of value
Is interlab. std. dev. different from the intralab. std. dev. at 5% significance level?				No		Yes	Yes

Source: From M. A. Lanphere and G. B. Dalrymple, Geochim. Cosmochim. Acta, v. 31, no. 6, p. 1091-1094, 1967.

* FP = flame photometry, ID = isotope dilution, KTPB = potassium tetraphenylboron precipitation, X = X-ray fluorescence, JLS = J. Lawrence Smith method, AA = atomic absorption. Data in parentheses were not included in interlaboratory statistics because P-207 was used for tracer calibration.

† The ± figures are calculated standard deviations.

‡ $\lambda_\epsilon = 0.585 \times 10^{-10}/\text{yr}$, $\lambda_\beta = 4.72 \times 10^{-10}/\text{yr}$, $K^{40}/K_{total} = 1.19 \times 10^{-4}$ mole/mole.

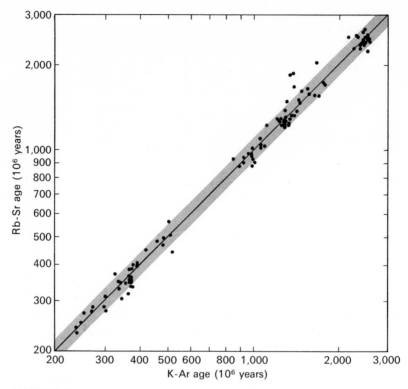

FIGURE 7-9

Potassium-argon versus rubidium-strontium ages for biotite from igneous rocks and for muscovite from pegmatite, granite, and gneiss. The outer limits of the shaded band are ±10 percent from perfect agreement (solid line). [Data from Kulp and Engels (1963).]

therefore, there is not as much possibility of systematic errors. Kulp and Engels (1963) compiled data of this kind. They compared potassium-argon and rubidium-strontium ages on biotite available through 1963; their data are presented in Figure 7-9. The figure includes only those data that probably were not affected by later heating. Consequently, there are fewer large discordances than in Figure 7-8. Few of the data differ by more than 10 percent, indicating again that potassium-argon ages can provide reasonable estimates of age if the geologic conditions are favorable.

Within the past few years, whole-rock basalts have been used increasingly as dating material, especially in areas of Cenozoic volcanism. Young volcanic flows offer a good test of precision and accuracy because, unlike many metamorphic and plutonic igneous rocks, they are relatively simple systems; they cool quickly and are seldom reheated or metamorphosed.

TABLE 7-6

Comparison of multiple potassium-argon age measurements on specimens from the same hand sample and from the same flow.

Sample no.	Percent K_2O	Calculated age (10^6 years)
Within same hand sample		
509-62-5	2.58	3.39
	2.59	3.38
	2.58	3.43
	2.56	3.42
	2.59	3.51
	2.56	3.46
	2.54	3.41
	2.58	3.44
	2.58	3.54
	2.58	3.37
	2.60	3.28
	2.58	3.39
		Mean = 3.42
	Coefficient of variation = 1.90%	
Within same flow		
509-62-2	2.18	3.31
509-62-3	2.63	3.38
509-62-4	2.74	3.24
509-62-5	2.58	3.39
3V121-0	2.39	3.30
3V124-0	2.46	3.20
3V128-0	2.44	3.41
		Mean = 3.32
	Coefficient of variation = 2.11%	

Source: Data from Dalrymple and Hirooka (1965).

Table 7-6 shows the variability that can be expected within a single basalt hand specimen and within a single basalt flow. The seven samples from within the same flow were collected from a lateral span of about 3 kilometers. The standard deviations of the calculated ages in both groups of samples are about 2 percent. Note that this is true even though the K_2O percentage of the within-flow samples varies by more than 22 percent.

TABLE 7-7
Potassium-argon ages of whole-rock basalts from Steens Mountain, Oregon.
The six lava flows are listed in stratigraphic order.

Lava no.	Core no.	Percent K	Percent Ar_{atm}^{40}	Calculated age (10^6 years)
11 (youngest)	3	1.53	19	15.3
			24	15.1
	4	1.51	40	15.2
			32	14.9
	7	1.50	16	15.1
17	4(i)	0.84	48	15.0
			44	15.1
	4(ii)	0.83	42	14.9
	6	0.84	47	14.8
51	1	1.31	61	14.8
	2	1.34	64	15.4
	5	1.27	57	15.4
			35	15.2
	6	1.27	93	14.9
			18	14.8
61	1	0.98	95	15.0
			94	14.9
	6	0.87	68	15.5
			54	14.9
	7	0.88	49	15.0
			67	15.0
68	1	0.89	76	15.0
			93	15.0
	4	1.00	91	15.2
	5	0.92	94	15.3
	6	1.00	71	15.5
70 (oldest)	3	0.95	74	14.7
	5	0.83	66	15.0

Mean = 15.1

Coefficient of variation = $\pm 1.4\%$

Source: Data from Baksi and others (1967).

An example of replicate potassium-argon ages on six basalt flows in stratigraphic succession is given in Table 7-7. In this example the potassium contents of the flows vary by nearly a factor of two, and yet the standard

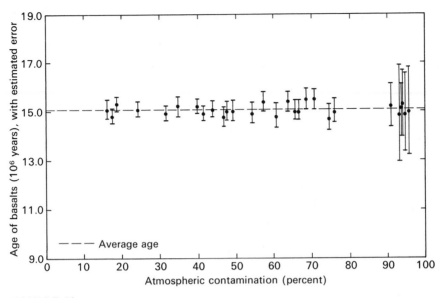

FIGURE 7-10

Potassium-argon age versus atmospheric argon contamination for the basalts from
Steens Mountain, Oregon (Table 7-7). Note that the calculated ages do not vary with
the size of the atmospheric argon correction. [After A. K. Baksi, D. York, and
N. D. Watkins, Jour. Geophys. Res., v. 72, p. 6299-6308, 1967.]

deviation of precision for the calculated ages is still less than 2 percent.
Note also that the ages do not vary systematically with the size of the atmospheric argon correction (Fig. 7-10). This indicates that there are no large
errors in the way that this correction is made.

The foregoing examples show that the analytical precision of potassium-
argon ages can be approximately 2 percent and, in some cases, even less.
Remember, however, that these replication experiments were all done on
carefully selected material and that the atmospheric corrections in most of
the ages were small. Thus they probably more nearly represent the best
that can be done rather than the precision of the average potassium-argon
age. It is reasonable to expect a standard deviation of precision of 2 to 5
percent for samples with 30 percent or more radiogenic argon. Geological
accuracy is much more difficult to evaluate, but comparisons of potassium-
argon ages on two minerals from the same rock and of potassium-argon ages
with rubidium-strontium ages on the same mineral suggest that potassium-
argon ages probably provide reasonable estimates (within 10 percent or
better) of the actual ages (of crystallization, cooling, metamorphism, and so
forth) where the rocks have not been disturbed by later thermal or chemical
events.

DECISION MAKING

One of the principle reasons for obtaining estimates of precision is to provide an objective and quantitative basis for making decisions concerning the probable reality of apparent age differences. Suppose that age measurements have been made on two related rocks and the calculated ages are somewhat different. Is there any *real* difference in the ages of the rocks? What is the actual difference likely to be? What are the odds that these two rocks are the same age? These are the kinds of questions that statistics can help to answer.

A detailed discussion of the criteria for decision making is beyond the scope of this book; for this the reader is referred to texts on statistics. An article by McIntyre (1963) on the application of statistics to geochronology also may be of interest to the reader. A few examples will be given, however, to illustrate the problem and the general approach.

In order to claim, at 95-percent confidence, that there is a real difference between the calculated ages of two rocks, the apparent difference, $|\bar{x}_1 - \bar{x}_2|$, must exceed the Critical Value,

$$\text{C.V.} = 1.960 \left(\frac{\sigma_1^2}{n_1} + \frac{\sigma_2^2}{n_2} \right)^{1/2}, \tag{7-3}$$

where σ_1 and σ_2 are the standard deviations of the ages and n_1 and n_2 are the number of measurements made on each rock. Suppose that single potassium-argon ages have been determined for two rocks and that $\sigma_1 = \sigma_2 = 3$ percent. Then

$$\text{C.V.} = 1.960 \left(\frac{3^2}{1} + \frac{3^2}{1} \right)^{1/2} = 8.3 \text{ percent.}$$

For rocks 100 million years old, this means that the apparent age difference must be greater than 8.3 million years before it is possible to state, with 95-percent confidence, that any real difference has been detected. If two determinations have been made on each rock, then C.V. is reduced to 5.9 percent. Note that when the apparent age difference exceeds C.V., it means only that a difference has been detected; the apparent difference is not necessarily the real difference.

If $|\bar{x}_1 - \bar{x}_2|$ does not exceed C.V., it does not follow that the two rocks are the same age. It is virtually impossible to prove that two rocks are the same age. About the most that can be said when $|\bar{x}_1 - \bar{x}_2| < \text{C.V.}$ is that the age difference, if any, is too small to be detected, and therefore the age measurements are consistent with the hypothesis that the two rocks are the same age.

8

EXTRANEOUS ARGON

One of the fundamental assumptions in potassium-argon dating is that the material analyzed contains no radiogenic Ar^{40} in addition to that which has been produced by the decay of K^{40} since the time of formation of the rock or mineral. In other words, D_o in equation (2-12) can be neglected. The large number of concordant ages reported in the literature suggests that this assumption is valid for most rock systems to which the potassium-argon method normally is applied. Nevertheless, several workers have reported anomalously old ages which they have attributed to extraneous argon.

There are several ways in which extraneous argon can originate, and a consistent terminology that reflects the origin is both desirable and necessary. Basically, we will use the terminology of Damon (1968), slightly modified to make it more specific. Ar^{40} that somehow is incorporated into rocks and minerals by processes (for example, diffusion) other than *in situ* radioactive decay of K^{40} is called *excess* Ar^{40}. Any Ar^{40} that is produced within mineral grains by the decay of K^{40} before the event being dated is called *inherited* Ar^{40}. Inherited Ar^{40} may be further subdivided into *inherited* (*metamorphic*) Ar^{40}, which is Ar^{40} that was generated during the premetamorphic history of the rock and that has survived the metamorphic event, and *inherited* (*contamination*) Ar^{40}, which is due to incorporation of older contaminating mineral grains into the dated sample. Inherited (contamination) Ar^{40} may be caused by xenoliths or xenocrysts from the natural environment or may be inadvertently introduced in the laboratory. Both inherited Ar^{40} and excess Ar^{40} are collectively called *extraneous* Ar^{40}. Obviously, it is not always possible to tell excess Ar^{40} from inherited Ar^{40}.

Inherited (metamorphic) Ar^{40} is caused by incomplete resetting of the potassium-argon clock, as was discussed in Chapter 4. The remainder of this chapter will be devoted to the origins and effects of excess Ar^{40} and inherited (contamination) Ar^{40}.

OCCURRENCE OF EXCESS ARGON

Excess inert gas in minerals was first reported in 1908 by Lord Rayleigh (Strutt, 1908), who found that beryl, sylvite, halite, and carnallite contained helium in excess of the amount that could be produced by the radioactive decay of uranium and thorium in these minerals. These observations have since been confirmed by numerous workers, and the occurrences of excess helium have been reviewed by Damon and Kulp (1958). Excess Ar^{40} in minerals was first reported by Aldrich and Nier (1948b). To date, more than fifty apparently anomalous ages have been attributed to excess Ar^{40}. The occurrence of excess Ar^{40} has been reported in beryl, cordierite, tourmaline, hornblende, feldspar, phlogopite, biotite, pyroxene, sodalite, basalt, and fluid inclusions in quartz and fluorite. Table 8-1 is a summary of most of the published data for which excess Ar^{40} has been claimed.

In order to test for excess Ar^{40}, it is necessary to establish the age of the rock or mineral by some independent means. This is not always easy, and many claims of excess Ar^{40} are based on comparisons with radiometric ages on coexisting minerals; the possibility that the comparison age is too low also must be considered. Once the existence of extraneous Ar^{40} has been established, it is then necessary to preclude the possibility that the extraneous Ar^{40} is inherited Ar^{40} rather than excess Ar^{40}. In some of the materials listed in Table 8-1, the existence of excess Ar^{40} is questionable. In order to make a realistic evaluation of the importance of excess Ar^{40} to potassium-argon dating, it is necessary to examine each material and determine whether there is sufficient evidence to claim the existence of excess Ar^{40}. For this reason, the evidence is reviewed briefly below for various geologic materials.

TABLE 8-1
Summary of data on excess Ar^{40} in geological materials.

Material	Occurrence	No. reported	Excess Ar^{40}		References
			10^{-11} mole/gram	Percent of total radiogenic Ar^{40}	
Beryl	Pegmatites	14	201–143,000	82–>99.9	Aldrich and Nier (1948b); Damon and Kulp (1958)
Cordierite	Metabasite, schist	5	607–3,570	44–>99.3	Damon and Kulp (1958)
Phlogopite	Altered eclogite, breccia pipe filling, peridotite, kimberlite	5	42.8–580	14–70	Lovering and Richards (1964); Zartman and others (1967)
Plagioclase	Quartz monzonite, gneiss, pegmatite, basalt	7	0.01–12.1	11–100	Livingston and others (1967); Damon and others (1967); Dalrymple (1969)
Orthoclase	Quartz monzonite	1	27.1	20	Livingston and others (1967)
Pyroxene	Gneiss, amphibolite, eclogite, mafic dike	11	1.5–50.6	~25–98	Hart and Dodd (1962); McDougall and Green (1964); Lovering and Richards (1964); Allsopp (1965)
Sodalite	—	—	17.4–66.9	—	York and others (1965)
Fluid inclusions	Vein and pegmatitic quartz and fluorite	7	0.16–53.5	~50–100	Rama and others (1965); Lippolt and Gentner (1963)
Tourmaline	Pegmatite	2	80–520	60–95	Damon and Kulp (1958)
Amphibole	Hornblendite, camptonite	2	0.45–86	~30–60	Pearson and others (1966); Damon and others (1967)
Basalt	Lava flows, dikes	3	0.025–1.02	60–100	Dalrymple (1969); Damon and others (1967)
Olivine	Basalt	1	0.34	100	Damon and others (1967)

There is no question that excess Ar^{40} exists in some rocks and minerals, especially those that form in environments where a high gas pressure might be expected. The occurrence of excess Ar^{40}, however, probably is rare and poses no serious threat to the routine use of potassium-argon dating. This is especially true when potassium-argon age determinations are numerous and have not been made independent of other direct geological evidence, but are part of a large and integrated geochronological study. From the evidence available at present, we conclude that the occurrence of excess Ar^{40} is too rare to provide a satisfactory explanation for very many potassium-argon ages that may appear anomalous.

Cyclosilicates

In their study of five essentially potassium-free Paleozoic and Precambrian beryls, Aldrich and Nier (1948b) found that three contained radiogenic Ar^{40} that could not be attributed to the potassium contents of these minerals.

Damon and Kulp (1958) determined the amount of radiogenic helium and argon in pegmatitic beryl, cordierite, and tourmaline and found abundant evidence of excess inert gas in all of these minerals. By comparing the apparent potassium-argon ages with the known geologic ages of the minerals, they showed that some beryl contained as much as 1.4×10^{-6} mole of excess Ar^{40} per gram. In addition, they noticed an increase in the helium and argon contents of beryl and cordierite with age (Fig. 8-1), which they attributed to a more extensive degassing of the mantle and crust during earlier times as a result of the greater heat production that then prevailed. According to

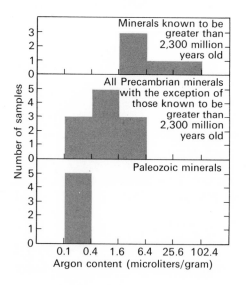

FIGURE 8-1

Argon content of beryl and cordierite of different ages for class intervals arranged according to a geometric progression. [After Damon and Kulp (1958).]

their interpretation, this excess gas represented a sample of the magmatic gases in the environment during crystallization and was occluded by the minerals as they formed. Damon and Kulp point out that any mineral whose lattice has "voids" large enough to accommodate argon (radius = 1.91 Å) should be considered as a possible source of excess inert gas, including the amphiboles in which the alkali cation position is seldom completely filled. This reasoning can no doubt be extended to all minerals, for even though the ideal lattice may not have large voids, virtually all crystals are imperfect and therefore are capable of containing the argon atom.

Pyroxene

Because of the lack of structural vacancies in the pyroxene structure, this group of minerals would seem to be an unlikely host for excess Ar^{40}. Nevertheless, good evidence for excess Ar^{40} in eight samples of enstatite, diopside, and omphacite from metamorphic rocks has been presented by Hart and Dodd (1962) and McDougall and Green (1964) (Table 8-2). Particularly convincing are the five samples that give apparent ages greater than the probable age of the earth (about 4,500 to 4,600 million years), for this effect obviously could not be produced by inherited Ar^{40}. Hart and Dodd (1962) have suggested that the excess Ar^{40} in pyroxene is held in crystal imperfections.

Ages between 721 and 1,407 million years on clinopyroxene from eclogite xenoliths have been interpreted by Lovering and Richards (1964) as probably due to excess Ar^{40}. Their interpretation is less convincing, however, than the interpretations given by Hart and Dodd (1962) and McDougall and Green (1964) because these xenoliths commonly are interpreted as accidental inclusions of ancient material, and the ages found by Lovering and Richards are consistent with this alternate interpretation. Thus their calculated ages might represent true minimum ages for the inclusions.

Igneous clinopyroxenes typically do not show effects of excess Ar^{40} (Hart, 1961; McDougall, 1961, 1963), but an age of 3,500 million years on an orthopyroxene from the Great Dyke of Southern Rhodesia has been interpreted by Allsopp (1965) as due to excess Ar^{40} (Table 8-2). Biotite from the dike gives concordant potassium-argon and rubidium-strontium ages of about 2,530 million years. Another possible exception is pyroxene from a 110- to 122-million-year-old tinguaite dike from Mont Royal, Quebec. An apparent age of 163 million years on the pyroxene is attributed by Hart (1961) to either excess Ar^{40} or sample contamination.

Olivine

Damon and others (1967) have measured a potassium-argon age of 114 million years on olivine from a basalt of unquestionably Recent age. Although

TABLE 8-2

Occurrence of excess Ar40 in pyroxene, amphibole, feldspar, mica, and basalt. Included are data from samples in which the excess Ar40 was 20 percent or more of the total radiogenic Ar40.

Mineral	Rock	Calculated age (10^6 years)	Geologic age	Excess Ar^{40} (10^{-11} mole/gram)	Excess Ar^{40} (%)	Reference
Enstatite with some augite	Pyroxene gneiss	1,500	1,050-1,150 million years, concordant U-Pb ages on zircons; 900-1,000 million years, K-Ar on horn-blendes	14.69	35.1	Hart and Dodd (1962)
Diopside	Skarn in amphibolite	10,400		40.93	94.7	
Diopside	Eclogite pegmatite lens in gneiss	4,760	1,750 million years, K-Ar on coexisting amphibole	18.47	85.5	McDougall and Green (1964)
Diopside		5,050		14.98	87.7	
Enstatite		3,800		5.12	74.4	
Omphacite		4,470		12.38	82.8	
Diopside	Eclogite lens in peridotite	8,100	1,850 million years, K-Ar on coexisting amphibole	44.28	96.5	
Diopside		7,350		50.63	97.7	
Albite	Pegmatite	396	324 million years, K-Ar on coexisting muscovite	6.15	20	Damon and Kulp (1957)

Albite	Quartz monzonite	298	58 million years, K-Ar on coexisting biotite	12.1	82	Livingston and others (1967)
Plagioclase-quartz	Quartz monzonite	69.4	47.4-54.2 million years, K-Ar on coexisting biotite and muscovite	1.5	30	
Albite	Pegmatite	1,180	50.7 million years, K-Ar on coexisting muscovite	2.1	95	
Albite	Pegmatite	384	254 million years, K-Ar on coexisting muscovite	3.5	33	
Orthoclase	Plutonic quartz monzonite	73	58 million years, K-Ar on coexisting biotite	27.1	20	
Orthopyroxene	Mafic dike	3,500	2,530 million years, K-Ar and Rb-Sr on coexisting biotite	8.93	47.3	Allsopp (1965)
Clinopyroxene	Eclogite xenolith in tuff	1,407	<2 million years, K-Ar on related lavas	8.48	99.2	
Clinopyroxene	Eclogite xenolith in breccia pipe	721-911	~170 million years, K-Ar on coexisting hornblende	1.45	79.4	Lovering and Richards (1964)
Phlogopite	Altered eclogite in kimberlite	142	68 million years, K-Ar on coexisting pyroxene; Cretaceous on geologic evidence	121	53.3	
Hornblende	Hornblendite intruding gneiss	2,020	1,240 million years, K-Ar on coexisting phlogopite and K-Ar and Rb-Sr ages of about 1,200-1,400 million years on related rocks	86	~60	Pearson and others (1966)
Basalt	Basalt flow from Hualalei, Hawaii	1.1	Historic flow, erupted in 1801	0.15	100	Dalrymple (1969)
Basalt	Basalt flow from Sunset Crater, Arizona	0.225	1,065 A.D. from tree-ring analysis	0.026	100	Dalrymple (1969)

(continued)

TABLE 8-2 (continued)

Mineral	Rock	Calculated age (10^6 years)	Geologic age	Excess Ar^{40} (10^{-11} mole/gram)	(%)	Reference
Biotite	Kimberlitic diatreme	368-408	Cretaceous(?), intrudes Upper Pennsylvanian	370-440	~65	Zartman and others (1967)
Biotite	Kimberlitic dike	420-493	136 million years, Rb-Sr on same mineral; 145 million years, K-Ar on coexisting, fine-grained biotite	450-600	~70	
Biotite	Peridotite dike	255-371	118 million years and 146 million years, Rb-Sr on same mineral; 150 million years, K-Ar on coexisting, fine-grained biotite	160-320	~55	
Plagioclase	Basalt flow	9.3	Late Pliocene on geologic evidence; 2.4 million years, K-Ar on whole rock; younger than flow with K-Ar age of 6.2 million years	0.16-0.25	67-75	Damon and others (1967)
Plagioclase	Basalt flow	0.13	Historic flow, erupted in 1915	0.01	100	Dalrymple (1969)
Kaersutite	Camptonite dike	5.2	3.7 million years, K-Ar on whole rock from dike interior	0.45	30	Damon and others (1967)
Camptonite (chilled border)	Camptonite dike	9.3	3.7 million years, K-Ar on whole rock from dike interior	1.02	60	Damon and others (1967)

the calculated age of the olivine is quite high, the actual amount of excess Ar^{40} is rather small; the low potassium content enhances the effect of the excess Ar^{40}.

Olivine nodules from lava flows frequently give anomalously old ages, and it is likely that the number of reported cases of excess Ar^{40} in olivine will increase as more of these nodules are studied. It is debatable, however, whether the extraneous Ar^{40} in these nodules should be called excess Ar^{40} or inherited Ar^{40}.

Feldspar

Damon and his co-workers at the Geochronology Laboratories of the University of Arizona recently have reported data that suggest that some pegmatitic and plutonic plagioclase may contain excess Ar^{40} (Livingston and others, 1967). Particularly striking are the 298-million-year age of plagioclase from an early Tertiary pluton and ages of 1,180 and 1,160 million years on plagioclase from the Tertiary Canoa Ranch pegmatite in Arizona (Table 8-2). The rocks studied by Damon and his colleagues are from an area that is underlain largely by Precambrian rocks, and the possibility that the anomalies are caused by inherited Ar^{40} cannot be precluded. Nevertheless, inherited Ar^{40} seems unlikely in view of the extended cooling times at high temperatures of most pegmatites and plutons.

Damon and others (1967) have reported concentrations of excess Ar^{40} ranging from 1.6 to 2.5×10^{-12} mole per gram from plagioclase phenocrysts from a late Pliocene basalt. It is their view that the problem of excess Ar^{40} in volcanic rocks can be minimized by avoiding the use of large phenocrysts as sample material.

Measurements by Dalrymple (1969) of the ratio of Ar^{40}/Ar^{36} in plagioclase from two historic lava flows gave mixed results. A single large crystal, about 1 cm in diameter, from the 1964 eruption of Surtsey, Iceland, gave an Ar^{40}/Ar^{36} ratio indistinguishable from atmospheric argon. The calculated upper limit (95-percent confidence) for excess Ar^{40} in this sample is 2.4×10^{-13} mole/gram. In contrast, plagioclase from the 1915 dacite flow of Mt. Lassen, California, gave an Ar^{40}/Ar^{36} ratio of 309.1, indicating about 1.1×10^{-13} mole/gram of excess Ar^{40} and an apparent age of about 125,000 years.

The single case of excess Ar^{40} that has been reported for potassium feldspar (Livingston and others, 1967) is not convincing, because the age of 73 million years is consistent with the geologic age. The comparison age of 58 million years on biotite could be too low because of argon loss, as the authors readily admit.

Evernden and Curtis (1965a) report that feldspar from three historic lavas from Italy, Alaska, and New Guinea have yielded "zero" ages. But

TABLE 8-3

Maximum excess (or inherited) Ar^{40} in sanidine from the Mono Craters, California. The figures are only upper limits. There is no evidence that the samples actually do contain excess Ar^{40}.

Sample no.	Maximum excess or inherited $Ar^{40}(10^{-13}$ mole/gram)
5G201 and 6G005	0.89
5G202	0.68
5G203	0.74
5G204	0.71
6G006	1.29
6G016	1.13
6G017	1.05

Source: Data from Dalrymple (1968).

since their report does not include the data on these analyses, it is not possible to establish the upper limits for the amounts of excess Ar^{40} in these minerals.

Dalrymple (1968) has calculated upper limits for excess Ar^{40} in sanidine from the Mono Craters of California (Table 8-3). This was done by assuming that the apparent potassium-argon ages of the samples (between 6,000 and 12,000 years) was due primarily to excess Ar^{40} and not to radiogenic Ar^{40}. The amounts are quite small and, if present, would pose no serious problem for routine potassium-argon measurements of older rocks. It must be emphasized that there is no evidence that these samples do contain excess Ar^{40}, but if they do the amounts must be less than given in Table 8-3.

Feldspathoids

The occurrence of excess Ar^{40} in sodalite has been noted by York and others (1965), and Macintyre (Univ. Toronto Ph.D. Thesis, 1966) has reported several occurrences of excess Ar^{40} in sodalite and cancrinite. However, the details of these studies have not been published.

Mica

Excess Ar^{40} has been reported in three biotites and one phlogopite (Table 8-2). The phlogopite reported by Lovering and Richards (1964) occurs in eclogitic inclusions from a kimberlite pipe. Although this phlogopite age is distinctly greater than that of the kimberlite, it is quite possible that it represents incomplete degassing of an older inclusion; that is, it is a "relict" age and is due to inherited Ar^{40}.

The excess Ar^{40} in the three biotites reported by Zartman and others (1967) is well documented. Both geologic and independent isotopic age evidence show conclusively that the crystals contain far more radiogenic Ar^{40} than can be accounted for by the decay of K^{40}. In addition, these workers found that the quantity of excess Ar^{40} varied by as much as 9 percent between repeat measurements on the same mineral concentrate, even though the K_2O content varied by less than 1 percent. Apparently the excess Ar^{40} is not uniformly distributed among grains of this coarse-grained mica.

Excess Ar^{40} may also be the explanation for the potassium-argon ages of 665 million years determined on phlogopite from the Mesozoic kimberlite breccia pipes of Siberia (Davidson, 1964). These were interpreted by Davidson to indicate a two-stage process of formation, the initial emplacement occurring 665 million years ago. Again, inherited Ar^{40} is a distinct possibility.

Excess Ar^{40} in mica has been reported in the Russian literature, but the details are not summarized here. The references to these works can be found in Zartman and others (1967).

On the more positive side are the results of Damon and Kulp (1957), who analyzed two samples of the calcium mica margarite and detected no excess Ar^{40}. Damon (1965) established an upper limit of 0.2×10^{-11} mole/gram for the excess Ar^{40} content of these minerals. Margarite has a very low potassium content—about two orders of magnitude less than biotite or muscovite—and thus should be a sensitive indicator of excess Ar^{40}. Hart (1966) has made similar tests on samples of margarite and chlorite and found no evidence of excess Ar^{40}. Hart's upper limits for excess Ar^{40} in these two minerals were less than 2.2×10^{-12} mole/gram for margarite and less than 9×10^{-13} mole/gram for chlorite.

Amphibole

Excess Ar^{40} has been reported for two amphiboles. Concordant potassium-argon and rubidium-strontium ages of 1,200 to 1,400 million years make the hornblende age of 2,020 million years reported by Pearson and others (1966) look anomalous indeed. Only a single analysis was made, however, and the possibility of an analytical error or of laboratory contamination cannot be precluded. Moreover, the authors themselves do not completely reject the hypothesis that the hornblende age represents the minimum age of the hornblendite and that the comparison ages are low. The claim by Damon and others (1967) of excess Ar^{40} in kaersutite (a titanium-rich amphibole similar to oxyhornblende) is even less convincing because the true age of the dike is uncertain. These workers readily admit that their interpretation is equivocal.

TABLE 8-4

Analyzed historic lava flows in which no excess Ar^{40} was detected. See also Figure 8-2.

Location	Year of Eruption
Mt. Mihara, Japan	1951
Sakurajima, Japan	1946
Kilauea, Hawaii	1750
Kilauea, Hawaii	1955
Mauna Loa, Hawaii	1907
Mt. Etna, Sicily	252
Mt. Etna, Sicily	1329
Mt. Etna, Sicily	1444
Mt. Etna, Sicily	1536
Mt. Etna, Sicily	1669
Mt. Etna, Sicily	1886
Mt. Vesuvius, Italy	1944
Askja, Iceland	1875
Laxa Canyon, Iceland	~1500 B.C.
Lakagigar, Iceland	1783
Ngauruhoe, New Zealand	1954
Paracutin, Mexico	1944
Augustine, Alaska	1935
Cinder Cone, California	1851

Source: Data from Dalrymple (1969).

Basalt

An obvious and simple test for excess Ar^{40} in lava flows is to "date" flows that have erupted during historic times. If the hypothesis of no Ar$^{40}_{rad}$ at the time of eruption is valid, then radiogenic argon should not be detected, and the calculated potassium-argon "age" should be zero, or nearly so. This has been done for 22 historic basalts and andesites from Iceland, Italy, Sicily, Japan, New Zealand, Mexico, Alaska, Hawaii, and California (Table 8-4). In all but three of these flows no excess Ar^{40} was detected (Dalrymple, 1969). The upper limits for excess Ar^{40} in these 19 flows are plotted in Figure 8-2. These calculated "permissible maximums" vary because the sensitivity of the test varies inversely with the amount of atmospheric argon present. But if any excess Ar^{40} is present in these flows, it is in such small amounts as to pose no problem for potassium-argon dating.

Three of the flows gave ratios of Ar^{40}/Ar^{36} that were demonstrably greater than the atmospheric value of 295.5 (Table 8-5). In two of these

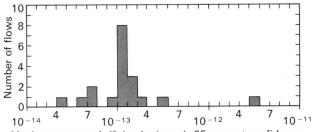

FIGURE 8-2

Upper limits for excess Ar^{40} in some historic lava flows. Excess Ar^{40} was *not* detected in these samples. The flows analyzed are listed in Table 8-4. [After Dalrymple (1969).]

TABLE 8-5
Historic lava flows in which excess Ar^{40} was found.

Lava flow	Year of eruption	Excess Ar^{40} $(10^{-12} \text{ mole/gram})$	Apparent age (10^6 years)
Hualalei, Hawaii	1801	1.5	1.1
Sunset Crater, Arizona	1065	0.26	0.22
Mt. Etna, Sicily	1792	0.35	0.15

Source: Data from Dalrymple (1969).

flows, Sunset Crater and Mt. Etna, the amounts of excess Ar^{40} were small, and the apparent ages were only on the order of 10^5 years. These amounts would not introduce serious errors except in the dating of rocks less than a few million years old. The 1801 flow from Hualalai, however, gave an apparent age of more than 1 million years. It is probably significant that all three of these flows contain ultramafic xenoliths—in fact, the Hualalai flow is well known for the abundance and variety of its inclusions. These xenoliths frequently give potassium-argon ages in excess of 1 billion years (J. G. Funkhouser, Univ. Hawaii Ph.D. thesis, 1966). In addition, the olivine crystals in these xenoliths contain fluid inclusions (or bubbles) that have been shown to contain large quantities of excess Ar^{40}. Although fluid inclusions are not apparent in the flows from Sunset Crater and Mt. Etna, it may be that the excess Ar^{40} in some way is connected with ultramafic xenoliths and xenocrysts. As will be discussed later in this chapter, inherited (contamination) Ar^{40} is much more of a problem in volcanic rocks than is excess Ar^{40}.

Damon and others (1967) have reported finding excess Ar^{40} in the chilled borders and in phenocrysts from a volcanic dike. As they admit, however, their data do not lead to an unequivocal interpretation, and their evidence for excess Ar^{40} in the dike is not strong.

Submarine Basalt

The recent and vigorous interest in the history and development of the world's ocean basins has prompted a number of laboratories to turn their attention to dating basalt flows from the ocean floor. The work on historic continental lava flows has demonstrated that the problem of excess Ar^{40} there is not severe. But what about lava that cools under the sea? What is the effect of rapid quenching, at near-zero temperatures, on lava erupted onto the sea floor? What is the effect of the hydrostatic pressures in the ocean depths?

To answer these questions and to test the possibility that excess Ar^{40} is present in submarine basalts, Dalrymple and Moore (1968) studied lavas dredged from the submarine part of the still-active east rift of Kilauea Volcano, Hawaii. All available evidence indicates that these lavas erupted during historic times or at most a few thousand years ago; they should give zero potassium-argon ages. On the contrary, ages as great as 43 million years were found!

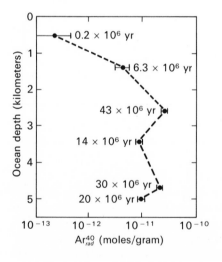

FIGURE 8-3

Excess Ar^{40} and apparent age as a function of ocean depth for Kilauea submarine basalts. Samples from the outer glassy crusts of pillows were analyzed. Horizontal bars are analytical uncertainty at 95-percent confidence. [Data from Dalrymple and Moore (1968).]

Fortunately, patterns could be seen in these anomalously old ages—there was a systematic increase in excess Ar^{40} with ocean depth (Fig. 8-3) and a decrease in excess Ar^{40} from the rim inward in a single pillow (Fig. 8-4). This was interpreted to mean that the excess Ar^{40} content was a function of both hydrostatic pressure and of cooling rate. These results have been confirmed by Noble and Naughton (1968), who also reported excess helium in the Kilauea submarine lavas.

Apparently, lava erupted under pressure contains excess Ar^{40} (and other gases as well) dissolved in the molten rock. Because the solution of gases in liquids is directly influenced by pressure, the amount of excess Ar^{40} decreases as the pressure lessens and the argon comes out of solution. Thus lava erupted at great ocean depths can be expected to contain large amounts of excess Ar^{40} whereas lava erupted in shallow water or in the atmosphere will not. If a lava that contains excess Ar^{40} is rapidly quenched, as are the rims of pillows, the excess Ar^{40} will be "frozen" into the rock. On the other hand, if the lava is allowed to cool more slowly, as do pillow interiors, the excess Ar^{40} is given another opportunity to escape; this is illustrated in Figure 8-4.

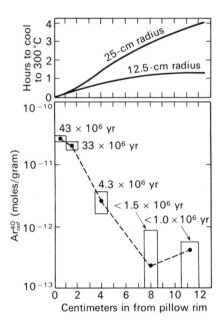

FIGURE 8-4

Excess Ar^{40} and apparent age within a single pillow from a depth of 2,590 meters (Kilauea Volcano, Hawaii). Width and height of boxes indicate width of sample and analytical uncertainty (95-percent confidence), respectively. Upper curves show cooling times for pillows. [After G. B. Dalrymple and J. G. Moore, Argon 40: Excess in submarine pillow basalts from Kilauea volcano, Hawaii, Science, v. 161, p. 1132-1135, September 1968. Copyright 1968 by the American Association for the Advancement of Science.]

At present, it is not known for sure if the pattern of excess Ar^{40} found in the Kilauea samples will also be found in other submarine basalts, but quite likely it will be. Does this mean that all submarine lava flows are not good potassium-argon clocks? Not at all. It does mean, however, that dating of submarine rocks will have to be done with a different set of rules than those used for continental lavas. At present, these new rules are inadequately known. The Kilauea results suggest that perhaps coarse-grained samples and samples from rocks erupted in shallow water eventually may prove reliable. Only additional experiments may solve this problem. In the meantime, potassium-argon ages on submarine rocks must be used with caution unless there is strong confirmatory evidence, such as concordant ages for two minerals from the same rock.

ORIGIN OF EXCESS ARGON

The evidence reviewed in the preceding section shows that excess Ar^{40} does occur in a wide variety of geological materials, but also that the proven occurrences are not numerous. From the data available, it is possible to draw two generalizations about its recognized occurrences. First, it has been found more often in minerals of low potassium content, especially pyroxene, than in minerals of high potassium content. This is because a small amount of excess Ar^{40} will produce the biggest effect on the apparent potassium-argon age of minerals with very low potassium contents. For example, 4×10^{-10} mole/gram of excess Ar^{40} in a pyroxene that contains 0.01 percent K_2O would produce an age greater than the age of the earth, whereas the same amount of excess Ar^{40} probably would not be noticed in a 500-million-year-old biotite. So it may be that excess Ar^{40} occurs in many minerals, but is noticeable primarily in those minerals with low potassium contents. Thus, pyroxene should not be regarded as having some special affinity for excess Ar^{40}. Second, large amounts of excess Ar^{40} are most often found in those geologic environments where a high gas pressure might be expected to have prevailed during emplacement—kimberlite pipes, high-grade metamorphic terranes, pegmatites, and so forth. Proven occurrences in plutonic, hypabyssal, or continental extrusive rocks are infrequent; where excess Ar^{40} does occur in these environments, the amounts are small and generally would cause problems only in potassium-argon dating of relatively young rocks. Thus it is probably the geologic environment rather than particular mineral species that should be blamed for excess Ar^{40}.

Where does excess Ar^{40} come from, and how does it find its way into rocks and minerals? Before the several hypotheses on the origin of excess Ar^{40} are discussed, it will be valuable to explore the idea that argon, enriched in mass 40, is present as a free gaseous phase or is dissolved in melts in the crust and mantle.

The Availability of Ar^{40}

A simple calculation, based on estimates of the abundance of potassium in the earth's crust and mantle, shows that the Ar^{40} in the atmosphere is only a fraction of what probably has been produced by radioactive decay of K^{40} since the earth formed. The rest, then, must still be locked within the rocks of the crust and mantle. The formation of igneous rocks is generally thought to involve complete or partial melting, and this process would release radiogenic Ar^{40}. Metamorphism, too, can be expected to result in complete or partial release of radiogenic argon because of the high temperatures and ionic mobility characteristic of the metamorphic process. What becomes of

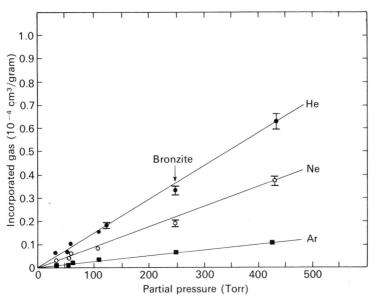

FIGURE 8-5

The amounts of inert gases incorporated in solidified enstatite melts at various partial pressures. $T = 1{,}500°C \pm 2$ percent. [After T. Kirsten, Jour. Geophys. Res., v. 73, p. 2807-2818, 1968.]

this gas? Does it rapidly escape into the atmosphere, or does it remain in the crust and mantle where it is available as a source of excess Ar^{40}?

Studies by Boato and others (1952), Zartman and others (1961), Wasserburg and others (1963), and Ferrara and others (1963) on natural gases that emanate from wells and fumaroles have shown that the argon in many of these gases is highly radiogenic. Ratios of Ar^{40}/Ar^{36} in excess of 30,000 have been reported (compared to the atmospheric value of 295.5). In addition, the He^4/Ar^{40} ratio in these gases is approximately equal to the production ratio from uranium, thorium, and potassium in average rock types. This indicates that these radiogenic gases are freed during outgassing of crustal and subcrustal material. It seems highly probable, therefore, that radiogenic Ar^{40} is available as a gaseous phase to minerals crystallizing under igneous and metamorphic conditions.

The anomalously high argon contents of the quenched Kilauea submarine basalts discussed on page 134 demonstrate conclusively that significant quantities of Ar^{40} can be dissolved in basalt melts even at low to moderate pressures. Because this is true for basaltic magma, it is also reasonable to suppose that it may be true for melts of other compositions.

Recent laboratory experiments by Kirsten (1968) have shown that enstatite melts, when cooled in the presence of an inert gas, will incorporate a portion of the gas. The amount incorporated into the melt was found to be proportional to the partial pressure and to the atomic mass (Fig. 8-5). Kirsten was able to show that much of the argon, helium, and xenon was actually in solution in the enstatite melt and not merely adsorbed onto surfaces.

Experiments by Fyfe and others (in press) show that up to 7×10^{-10} mole/gram of radiogenic Ar^{40} can be dissolved in a melt of granitic composition at pressures of only 2 kilobars.

In summary, the few relevant laboratory experiments and studies of natural systems demonstrate that radiogenic Ar^{40} is available as a gaseous phase in the crust and mantle and that it can be, and sometimes is, dissolved in silicate melts. The occurrence of excess Ar^{40} in minerals and rocks shows that some of this argon actually can be incorporated into crystals during or after crystallization. The mechanism whereby this takes place is not clear. The possibilities, however, are limited, and the more important theories and laboratory experiments concerning the origin of excess Ar^{40} will be reviewed briefly.

Incorporation of Excess Argon

There are three basic hypotheses that might explain excess Ar^{40} in minerals (Damon and Kulp, 1958):

1. The argon is created within the minerals either by an unknown source of radioactivity or by nuclear reactions.

2. The argon diffuses into the minerals after they form.

3. The argon is occluded by the minerals at the time of formation.

The first hypothesis can be dismissed on physical grounds. Neither nuclear reactions nor an unknown radioactive parent can account for the quantities of excess Ar^{40} found in minerals.

It is not possible, at present, to choose between the two remaining hypotheses. In fact, it is likely that both may be important mechanisms. The occlusion and diffusion hypotheses require further discussion.

Diffusion Hypothesis   The arguments against the diffusion hypothesis were expressed more than 10 years ago by Damon and Kulp (1958). First, they believed that the partial pressure of inert gas in the intergranular spaces of rocks would be much lower than in the minerals. Because gas diffuses from areas of high gas concentration to areas of low gas concentration, diffusion into minerals would, therefore, be improbable. Second, a 2,700-million-year-old beryl has, on the average, about 500 times more inert gas than a 100-million-year-old beryl, yet their ages differ only by a factor of 27. This would

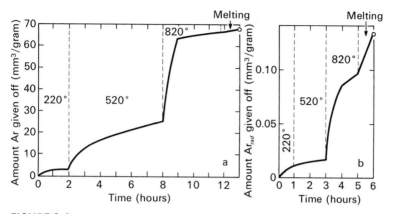

FIGURE 8-6

Argon-release curves for (a) muscovite into which argon was introduced at high temperatures and high argon pressures, (b) natural muscovite. The similarity of the two curves indicates that much of the injected argon had entered the mineral lattice. [After T. B. Karpinskaya, I. A. Ostrovskiy, and L. L. Shanin, Akad. Nauk SSSR, Izv. Acad. Sci., USSR, Geol. Ser., no. 8, p. 87-89, 1961. Transl. by American Geological Institute.]

not be true if the gas had been diffusing into the minerals for much of their history. Finally, diffusion could not explain the inhomogeneities found by Damon and Kulp (1958) within single crystals.

These objections, though valid, do not completely rule out the diffusion hypothesis. It could be that high argon partial pressures are maintained in a rock system for a considerable length of time after formation or that the argon pressure fluctuates irregularly. If this were the case, diffusion might lead to complex relationships that could not be dismissed easily. Another possibility is that argon might diffuse from a high-potassium mineral into an adjacent low-potassium mineral. The concentration gradient would be in the correct direction, and this might well happen if the grain boundary did not provide a path of escape for the diffusing argon.

Karpinskaya and others (1961) have subjected muscovite to argon pressures of 2,800 to 5,000 atmospheres in the temperature range of from 740° to 860°C, for periods of from 3 to $10\frac{1}{2}$ hours. The muscovite absorbed significant quantities of argon—from about 4×10^{-7} to 40×10^{-7} mole/gram. Apparently the argon diffused into the crystals. When these same crystals were then heated in vacuum, about 60 percent of this argon could be released only at temperatures above 520°C. In addition, the argon-release curve (Fig. 8-6, a) for this muscovite was similar to that of the natural muscovite (Fig. 8-6, b). This led Karpinskaya and her colleagues to conclude that the argon had actually entered into the mineral lattice and was not just adsorbed on crystal surfaces.

Occlusion Hypothesis   Although there is no evidence that precludes the diffusion hypothesis, occlusion seems to be the most likely explanation for most of the excess Ar^{40} occurrences. As is evident from Table 8-1, the amount of excess argon in minerals increases with the degree of "openness" of the mineral lattice. For example, the cyclosilicates, with their large tunnel-like structures, contain much more excess Ar^{40} than the very tightly structured pyroxenes. This suggests that the amount of excess Ar^{40} depends partly on the amount of space available for it—a condition seemingly at odds with diffusion models but not with occlusion.

A second observation in support of occlusion is that the helium-to-argon ratio in the cyclosilicates is similar to that which would be predicted for a normal pegmatitic environment (Damon and Kulp, 1958). In view of the very different diffusion rates of helium and argon—helium diffuses much more rapidly than argon because of its small diameter and low atomic weight—this observation is difficult to reconcile with a diffusion model.

Furthermore, occlusion would explain the different concentrations of inert gas in different parts of the same crystal. This could be interpreted as a result of continual variation in the partial pressure of the gas as crystallization progressed (Damon and Kulp, 1958).

Finally, the existence of excess Ar^{40} in fluid inclusions (Table 8-1) is strong evidence for occlusion. There is no reasonable way in which argon diffusing into a mineral would concentrate in pre-existing gas bubbles.

Karpinskaya (1967) has demonstrated that it is possible for muscovite to occlude argon during crystallization. In her experiment she synthesized muscovite from a colloidal gel at 640°C under an argon and water vapor pressure of 3,500 to 4,200 atmospheres. The muscovite occluded up to 0.5 percent by weight of argon! This experiment has not been done for other minerals, but it would be surprising if any mineral would not occlude argon, provided the argon partial pressure were high enough.

Thus occlusion appears to be a more plausible explanation for excess Ar^{40} than is diffusion, although the latter may be possible under certain conditions. Occlusion has been the explanation favored by most workers.

INHERITED (CONTAMINATION) ARGON

Inherited (contamination) Ar^{40}, as defined previously, is extraneous Ar^{40} that is caused by older contaminating material. The influence of this kind of contamination is obvious: if either older or younger material is inadvertently included in the dated sample, the potassium-argon age will be incorrect. Contamination can come primarily from two sources: from the laboratory during sample preparation, and from foreign material (xenoliths and xenocrysts) picked up by the rock during emplacement.

Sources of Contamination

Contamination in the laboratory, although an ever-present problem, is easy enough to prevent. All it takes is care. It is simply a matter of taking the time to clean thoroughly all of the equipment that is used to process samples and of being certain that the material is kept well covered at all times. It is usually wise to clean the entire sample-preparation laboratory before beginning work on a sample. This is especially advisable when working with very young rocks. Sieves must be inspected carefully to be sure that they are completely free of foreign grains. Often this requires hand-cleaning with a magnifying glass and needle—a tedious but necessary job. Besides keeping the equipment clean, the samples should be stored in sealed bottles or vials and never left uncovered where a gust of wind might add a few grains of unwanted material.

Contamination by natural processes poses a much more difficult problem. Plutonic or metamorphic rocks seldom contain xenolithic material, and any that is present has usually been thoroughly degassed. In these rocks excess Ar^{40} and inherited (metamorphic) Ar^{40} are probably more of a problem than inherited (contamination) Ar^{40}. In contrast, volcanic rocks commonly contain foreign inclusions. In fact, it is rare to find a volcanic rock that does not contain at least a few xenoliths, however small. Welded tuffs are especially notable in this respect. Because the processes that lead to their formation are especially violent, ash flow tuffs nearly always contain xenoliths and xenocrysts torn from the conduit walls or picked up as the gas-charged material rolled across the countryside. Thus inherited (contamination) Ar^{40} is more of a problem in volcanic rocks than is excess Ar^{40}. In sedimentary rocks contamination frequently comes from detrital material. For example, a glauconite sample may contain two components, one detrital and one authigenic. In addition, authigenic material may form by using an older grain as a nucleus upon which to grow. This kind of contamination is especially insidious and is very difficult to recognize.

Sometimes contaminating grains can be recognized and eliminated by hand-picking under a microscope, but this is a risky procedure because some grains may escape notice. Samples often have to be discarded as unsuitable for dating because contaminants cannot be removed.

A rather thorough discussion of the contamination processes in volcanic and sedimentary rocks is given by Curtis (1966), to whose work the reader is referred for additional information on this subject.

Effects of Inherited (Contamination) Argon

The effect of inherited (contamination) Ar^{40} depends on the radiogenic argon contents of the sample and the contaminant, as well as on the relative

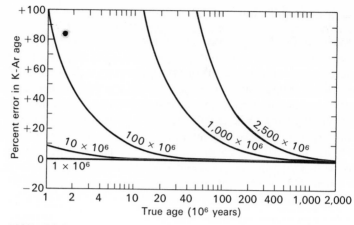

FIGURE 8-7

Percent error in potassium-argon age versus true age for samples contaminated with 1 percent of foreign material of the same potassium content. The different curves represent various ages for the contaminant.

proportion of contaminating grains. This effect can be estimated using the formula

$$t_1 = t_3 + f t_2 \frac{K_2}{K_1}, \tag{8-1}$$

where t_1 = apparent age of the sample, t_2 = apparent age of the contaminant, t_3 = true age of the sample, f = fraction of contaminant in the sample, K_2 = potassium content of the contaminant, and K_1 = potassium content of the uncontaminated sample. This formula is useful only for samples and contaminants of Mesozoic age or younger. It does not take into account the exponential decay of potassium and therefore cannot be used on older samples.

Figure 8-7 shows the percentage error introduced into a potassium-argon age determination by 1 percent of contamination of various ages. These curves were calculated using an exact expression rather than formula 8-1. As is evident from the figure, the problem of inherited (contamination) Ar[40] is much more severe for young rocks than for old ones. A young sample that contains only a small fraction of a percent of contaminating foreign material may give a highly inaccurate age. A second point that is obvious from these curves is that the error is quite small if the contamination is younger than the sample. Only rarely, however, is such contamination present in samples, and if it is present it must have been introduced in the laboratory or during field collection rather than during the formation of the rock.

TABLE 8-6
Potassium-argon ages determined for the Bishop Tuff, California.
The bulk samples were contaminated by older foreign material.

Sample no.	K-Ar age (10^6 years)	Reference
Measurements made on sanidine from bulk samples		
KA 210R	0.681, 0.783	Evernden and others (1957)
KA 210 R1	0.830, 0.955	
KA 277	0.9	
KA 278	1.2	
KA 305	0.96	Evernden and Curtis (1965b)
KA 320	0.96	
KA 321	0.91	
KA 328	0.91	
Measurements made on sanidine from pumice fragments		
4G 001	0.736, 0.754	
4G 002	0.730, 0.692	Dalrymple and others (1965)
4G 003	0.639, 0.717	

As has been explained by Curtis (1966), it was once thought that the high temperatures of emplacement of lava flows and welded tuffs would effectively degas any xenoliths or xenocrysts. On the contrary, the evidence now at hand indicates that this is not true. Apparently volcanic rocks cool much too quickly, leaving insufficient time for complete degassing to occur.

To test the extent to which xenoliths are degassed, Dalrymple (1964a) analyzed potassium feldspar from a granitic xenolith in a late Pleistocene basalt flow (ca. 60,000 years old) and obtained an apparent potassium-argon age of 2.0 million years. The xenolith came from a pluton with an age of about 90 million years and thus had retained slightly more than 2 percent of its radiogenic argon, in spite of the fact that the temperature of the flow when it erupted was probably about 1,100°C. Xenoliths in welded tuffs can be expected to retain even more of their radiogenic argon, because welded tuffs are erupted at temperatures several hundred degrees lower than basalt. Curtis (1966) reports that granitic xenoliths from the tuff at Katmai, Alaska, (1912 eruption) and the Bishop Tuff of California (0.7 million years old) gave potassium-argon ages of about 4 million years.

Determinations of the age of the Bishop Tuff serve as an example of the hazard of dating contaminated samples. The Bishop Tuff is important because it overlies glacial till and outwash from one of the early glaciations in the Sierra Nevada, California (Sharp, 1968). The tuff contains foreign material. Granitic and metamorphic xenoliths are common, and the tuff, no doubt, contains xenocrysts as well. The first attempts to determine the age of the Bishop Tuff were made by G. H. Curtis and J. F. Evernden of the University of California in 1957. In spite of the inherited (contamination) Ar^{40} problem that became apparent later, these early potassium-argon measurements were truly remarkable. Made when the technique was still in its early stages of development, their measurements forcefully demonstrated that potassium-argon dating could be applied profitably to rocks less than 1 million years old. The first group of age determinations were made on sanidine separated from bulk samples of the welded tuff. These ages were discordant by nearly a factor of two, and ranged from 0.68 to 1.2 million years (Table 8-6). Later measurements on sanidine separated from carefully picked and uncontaminated pumice fragments were not only concordant within the analytical uncertainty, but were younger.

Our final example is one briefly described by Curtis (1966). A tuff from the Eifel District, Germany, had an approximate age of 12,000 years based on C^{14} dating. Sanidine from this same tuff gave much older and discordant potassium-argon ages. Five measurements ranged from 200,000 years to 500,000 years! The marked discordance is probably due to uneven distribution of the contaminant in the sample and also may be coupled with the problems of obtaining representative sample aliquants.

9

ARGON LOSS

The loss of argon from potassium-bearing minerals has the effect of lowering their potassium-argon ages. If the loss is complete, then the potassium-argon clock is reset completely and will reflect the event that caused the loss. Argon loss is often incomplete, however, which makes the resulting "age" more difficult to interpret because it results from a complex history involving perhaps both accumulation and loss (see, for example, Fig. 4-2). In addition, the argon loss may be episodic or it may take place over a long period of time. These factors, when combined, can produce a nearly infinite variety of results.

There are seven geologic factors that can cause argon to be lost from minerals.

1. *The inability of a mineral lattice to retain argon.* Some minerals are not capable of retaining argon even at room temperature and pressure. The suitability of various mineral species for dating is discussed in the next chapter.

2. *Melting.* Formation of a new igneous rock by complete or partial melting nearly always resets the potassium-argon clock. The submarine pillow basalts discussed in Chapter 8 are apparent exceptions.

3. *Metamorphism.* The chemical and physical reconstitution resulting from metamorphism at elevated temperatures and pressures usually causes complete argon loss. But if the metamorphism is of short duration or of low grade, argon loss may be only partial, in which case inherited (metamorphic) Ar^{40} will be present in the rock. Fortunately, metamorphism of an igneous or sedimentary rock can usually be recognized and the accompanying argon loss anticipated.

4. *Weathering and alteration.* These processes can produce either complete or partial argon loss. Total degradation of a mineral will result in total loss of argon. Often, however, weathering does not result in complete breakdown of the mineral lattice, and weathered rocks may retain some of their argon. The effects of weathering and alteration usually can be recognized in hand specimen or thin section.

   Under some circumstances, alteration apparently can produce ages that are too old. Doell and others (1968) found such an effect in their study of volcanic rocks from the Valles Caldera, New Mexico. Some of the rhyolitic domes and flows that occur within the caldera show the effects of hydrothermal or other aqueous alteration. Sanidine (3 samples from 3 units), biotite (2 samples from one unit), and plagioclase (one sample) from the altered units gave potassium-argon ages significantly greater than ages on unaltered rocks that are older on the basis of field relations. Not only were the potassium-argon ages too old, they were also very discordant. Ages determined from coexisting biotite, sanidine, and plagioclase differed by more than a factor of two! The exact cause of these anomalous ages is unknown, but the phenomenon is limited to the altered zone of the caldera, and it is reasonable to assume that it is connected in some way with the alteration.

5. *Recrystallization.* Easily soluble minerals are subject to dissolution by ground water or other fluids and to subsequent recrystallization. Such recrystallization is seldom recognized easily and is one of the primary difficulties in dating potassium-bearing salts, such as sylvite.

6. *Reheating.* Prolonged reheating at temperatures of a few hundred degrees centigrade is sufficient to cause some loss of argon in most minerals. Such reheating can be caused by deep burial, the intrusion of a nearby dike or batholith, or very mild metamorphism. The effects of reheating are often difficult to recognize because there may be no obvious physical or chemical changes in the rock. Thus reheating is an important cause of incorrect potassium-argon ages.

7. *Physical damage.* It is possible that such things as radiation damage, high-velocity shock, or deformation could cause argon to be lost from minerals. For example, Brandt and others (1966) found that a 188-million-year-old sylvite lost about 18 percent of its radiogenic argon when subjected to a pressure of 10 tons/cm². Plastic flow in the sylvite began at 5 to 6 tons/cm², so the loss of argon is not surprising. Although there is very little evidence for or against the possible loss of argon because of physical damage, these mechanisms are probably not important in potassium-argon dating simply because physically damaged mineral and rock samples are not normally used.

In addition to these geologic factors, argon loss can occur during sample preparation or handling. Excessive heating in laboratory ovens or treatment with chemicals that attack the mineral lattice may cause loss of argon. Grinding, if carried to extremes, can also result in argon loss. Gentner and Kley (1957) have shown that feldspars lose argon readily during grinding as soon as the grain size is reduced to below 100 microns (Fig. 9-1). Mica, too, will lose argon when finely ground in a mortar or filed, as shown by the experiments of Gerling and others (1961) (Fig. 9-2). Using X-ray techniques, they were able to demonstrate that the mechanical grinding damaged the structure of the mica, and probably caused the argon loss.

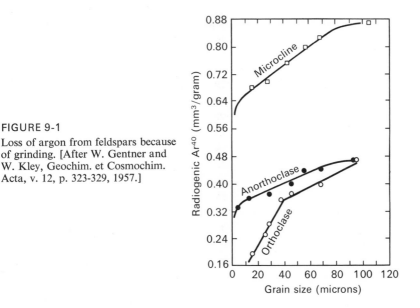

FIGURE 9-1

Loss of argon from feldspars because of grinding. [After W. Gentner and W. Kley, Geochim. et Cosmochim. Acta, v. 12, p. 323-329, 1957.]

Generally, argon is lost from minerals by diffusion. Because of its importance to potassium-argon dating, the diffusion of argon in geologic materials has been much studied, both theoretically and experimentally. There are two excellent reviews of argon diffusion work; one by H. Fechtig and S. Kalbitzer of the Max Planck Institute in Heidelberg (Fechtig and Kalbitzer, 1966), the other by Alan E. Mussett of the Chadwick Laboratory, University of Liverpool (Mussett, in press). Readers who are interested in pursuing argon diffusion in more detail than is presented in this chapter are encouraged to read these papers.

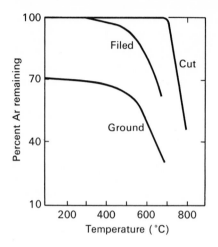

FIGURE 9-2

Percentage of argon retained in cut, filed, and ground muscovite after heating for two hours at the indicated temperatures. [After E. K. Gerling, I. M. Morozova, and V. V. Kurbatov, Ann. N. Y. Acad. Sci., v. 91, no. 2, p. 227-234, 1961. Copyright 1961 by New York Academy of Sciences.]

THE PROCESS OF DIFFUSION

Diffusion is a process whereby material is transferred from one place to another by random molecular motion. Because each atom or molecule moves independently of all others and in a purely random manner, the diffusing material gradually moves from areas of higher concentration to areas of lower concentration. Thus, diffusion tends to smooth out and eventually cancel differences in the concentration of the diffusing molecules.

Because the motion of each molecule is random, it is not possible to determine the direction of any single molecule at a particular moment. It is not difficult, however, to see why the net transfer of material must be toward the area of lower concentration and why the process is irreversible. Consider two small adjacent volumes, A and B, containing unequal gas concentrations C_A and C_B (Fig. 9-3). Because the molecules are moving randomly, the same fraction of molecules will move from A to B as from B to A. If this fraction is X, then the number of molecules moving from A to B will be XC_A, and the number moving from B to A will be XC_B. Because $C_B > C_A$, there must be more molecules moving from B to A than from A to B. Familiar examples of the phenomenon are the way in which sugar diffuses throughout an unstirred cup of coffee, and the way that smells permeate a room even if there is no air circulation.

The mathematics that describe diffusion are fundamentally the same as for heat conduction. This is very convenient because heat conduction studies have provided solutions to many of the difficult mathematical problems of diffusion and vice versa. Detailed discussions of the mathematics of diffusion and heat conduction are given by Crank (1956) and Carslaw and Jaeger (1959).

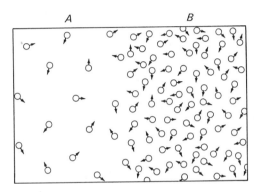

FIGURE 9-3

The motion of diffusing molecules is random. In a given time more atoms will pass from the volume of higher concentration (B) to that of lower concentration (A) than vice versa. In this way, diffusion tends to eliminate concentration differences.

Diffusion in a completely isotropic substance is described by Fick's first law,

$$F = -D\frac{\partial C}{\partial X},\tag{9-1}$$

where F is the rate of transfer of the diffusing molecules across unit area of a plane, $\partial C/\partial X$ is the concentration gradient normal to the plane, and D is the *diffusion coefficient*, a characteristic of the ease of transfer. The negative sign indicates that the net transfer of molecules takes place in the direction opposite to the concentration gradient.

The equation that describes the change of concentration with time is known as Fick's second law,

$$\frac{\partial C}{\partial t} = D\frac{\partial^2 C}{\partial X^2},\tag{9-2}$$

which is for a system in which D is constant and in which there is a concentration gradient in the X direction only.

Equations (9-1) and (9-2) are highly generalized, and in order to use them to obtain reliable calculations, the nature of the physical system of interest must be taken into account. Let us assume that the system to be described is a mineral grain and we are interested in the diffusion of argon out of the grain. Some of the many questions that must be decided in order to find the proper solution are:

1. What is the shape of the grain?

2. What is the nature of the argon concentration within the grain?

3. What is the argon concentration outside of the grain? Will it change with time?

4. Is D constant or does it vary with temperature? With concentration?

5. Is the diffusion isotropic or anisotropic? If anisotropic, what is the description of the anisotropy?

6. Is there only a finite amount of argon in the grain or will more be generated by radioactive decay while diffusion occurs?

Once it has been decided how to describe the system and what the boundary conditions will be, it is possible to derive an appropriate formula. The mathematics are quite difficult, however, and certain simplifying assumptions are usually necessary. In addition, a complete knowledge of the system is seldom possible when dealing with geological materials, so that the description of the system is necessarily oversimplified and inaccurate.

For example, when working with feldspars it is common to assume that:

1. The grains are spherical.

2. The unit of material from which the argon must escape is the grain itself and not something smaller.

3. Diffusion will be isotropic—that is, independent of direction.

4. The amount of argon created by radioactive decay within the crystal is negligible while argon is diffusing.

5. The initial distribution of argon is uniform throughout the crystal.

6. The concentration of argon outside of the crystal is always zero.

7. The diffusion coefficient, D, is independent of everything but temperature.

For these assumptions, the solution is

$$f = 1 - \frac{6}{\pi^2} \sum_{n=1}^{\infty} \frac{1}{n^2} e^{-Dn^2\pi^2 t/a^2}, \tag{9-3}$$

where a is the radius of the spherical grain and f is the fraction of argon lost during a time t and at some constant temperature (Crank, 1956). In addition to the difficulties involved with the validity of the initial assumptions concerning the system, an uncertainty that is seldom stated or discussed is the assumption that the mechanism whereby diffusion of argon occurs can be described by Fick's laws. This is not certain because very little is known about the actual diffusion mechanisms in geological materials.

LABORATORY STUDIES OF DIFFUSION

Because of the importance of argon loss to potassium-argon dating, a great deal of effort has been directed toward determining the argon diffusion characteristics of the rock-forming minerals. Initially, it was hoped that such experiments would lead to a classification of these minerals according to their ability to retain argon. In addition, it was thought that experimentally determined diffusion coefficients might provide a way to correct "apparent" ages for argon loss and to provide a basis for using argon loss to determine the exact geologic conditions (heating, burial, and so forth) that caused the loss. Unfortunately, these goals have not been reached. Although the relative ability of most common minerals to retain argon is known, this knowledge has come largely from geologic studies rather than from diffusion experiments. The quantitative differences in argon retention are still uncertain. One of the main reasons for this is that laboratory measurements are aimed at detecting differences between "zero" diffusion and extremely slow diffusion that nevertheless can add up to a significant loss over millions of years.

Techniques

The usual method of determining diffusion coefficients is to heat a mineral of a given grain size under controlled conditions and measure the amount of argon lost after a given time. Heating is necessary because argon loss at room temperature is too small to measure. Using the information obtained from heating experiments, it is possible to calculate the diffusion coefficient, D, from such equations as equation (9-3).

Generally, the heating is done isothermally and in vacuum; the amount of argon that diffuses from the sample during the chosen time interval is collected, purified, and measured with the addition of an Ar^{38} tracer. This procedure is repeated on the same sample for several progressively higher temperatures, after which the mineral is fused. The sum of the fractions obtained at the different temperatures and at the final fusion temperature gives the total amount of argon in the mineral. It is then easy to calculate the exact fraction of argon lost (f in equation 9-3) at each temperature.

From these data values of D are calculated for each temperature, and these values can be plotted to show the dependence of D on temperature.

Sometimes the heating is done under controlled pressures and atmospheres as well as temperatures. The mineral to be studied is placed in a bomb of the type used for mineral synthesis. The heating is then done isothermally for the desired time. This method has the advantage of allowing the experimenter to control total pressure and P_{H_2O} as well as temperature. Thus the experimental conditions are somewhat more realistic than in vacuum. After the heating is completed, the amount of argon remaining in the mineral is measured and is compared with the amount of argon in an unheated sample of the same mineral to determine the fractional loss. This method requires considerably more equipment, effort, and time than the vacuum-heating method and for this reason is seldom used.

A third method of investigation consists in irradiating the sample with neutrons, producing Ar^{41}, Ar^{39}, and Ar^{37} from K^{41}, K^{39}, and Ca^{40}, respectively. These argon isotopes are radioactive and have short half-lives. The particular isotope produced can be controlled to a considerable degree by regulating the neutron energy. Upon heating in vacuum, the radioactive argon released can be measured with a Geiger counter. This method is very sensitive and can be used to obtain values of D at low temperatures whereas the normal heating-mass spectrometric techniques generally require that the heating be done above 300 to 400°C in order to get enough argon to measure. The disadvantage of this technique is that the neutron irradiation may damage the crystal lattice, altering the diffusion properties of the mineral. The technique is not used widely. For more details and references about the experimental methods, see Fechtig and Kalbitzer (1966).

Presentation of Data

All of the techniques discussed above lead to values of the diffusion coefficient, D, at a series of temperatures. These data are then plotted as the function $\log_{10}D$ versus $1/T$ (Fig. 9-4, a), or if the *diffusion dimension, a,* is not known, as the function $\log_{10}(D/a^2)$ versus $1/T$ (Fig. 9-4, b). The quantity D/a^2 is often called the *diffusion parameter.* The logarithm of D is used because D often ranges through many orders of magnitude. The function $1/T$ is commonly multiplied by 1,000 so that the values along the abscissa will be small whole numbers. The reciprocal of the absolute temperature, $1/T$ (°K), arises from the fact that the ideal temperature dependence of D is given by

$$D = D_o e^{-E/RT}, \tag{9-4}$$

where D_o is a characteristic constant, E is the *activation energy* in kilocalories / mole, R is the universal gas constant, and T is the absolute temperature.

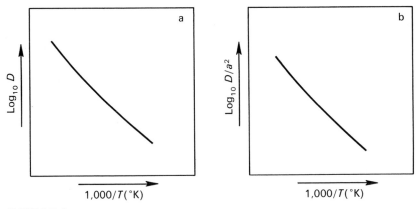

FIGURE 9-4

Diffusion curves are usually plotted either as $\log_{10}D$ versus $1,000/T$ (a) or as $\log_{10}D/a^2$ versus $1,000/T$ if the diffusion dimension is unknown (b).

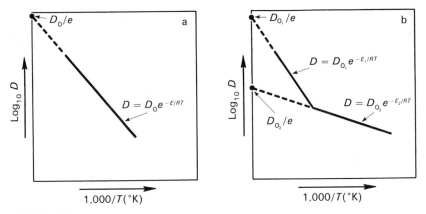

FIGURE 9-5

Schematic ideal diffusion curves for (a) minerals in which diffusion occurs at a single activation energy, E, and (b) minerals in which diffusion occurs at two different activation energies, E_1 and E_2, depending on the temperature range.

The activation energy is the energy required to dislodge and transfer an argon atom from one stable site within the mineral lattice to another. If all of these sites are identical, then all of the diffusion will take place at a single activation energy, which is independent of both temperature and the diffusion coefficient. Because equation (9-4) is exponential, diffusion at any single activation energy results in a straight line on a graph of $\log_{10}D$ versus $1/T$ (Fig. 9-5, a). If argon diffuses at several different activation energies that depend on the temperature range, the graph of $\log_{10}D$ versus $1/T$ ideally will be a series of connected straight lines (Fig. 9-5, b). These changes in activation energy usually are attributed to lattice changes that affect the ease of argon migration. The published diffusion curves suggest, however, that ideal behavior is not common in minerals. Real crystals are far from perfect, and it probably is not correct to assume a single value or even a few discreet values for the activation energy of a mineral.

Validity of Results

The difficulties in obtaining valid results from laboratory diffusion studies probably result from the limitations of the available experimental methods, the lack of an adequate theory for diffusion in minerals, and the complexity of geologic materials and conditions.

The chief objection to laboratory diffusion studies, pointed out by Mussett (in press), is that far too little is known about the actual mechanisms of diffusion and the initial assumptions frequently may be invalid. The diffusion coefficients calculated from a series of experiments are quite sensitive to the model chosen. For example, in the study of micaceous minerals one can assume that diffusion takes place entirely parallel to cleavage, entirely perpendicular to cleavage, or some combination of these two extremes. The choice can make a difference of many orders of magnitude in the diffusion coefficients at a particular temperature (Fig. 9-6).

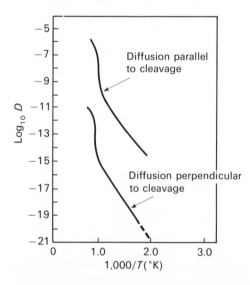

FIGURE 9-6

Argon-diffusion curves for phlogopite (grains 15,000 microns in diameter by 15 microns thick) using two different diffusion models for the same data. Note the strong dependence of the results on the model chosen. [Data from Evernden and others (1960).]

Another complicating factor is that the diffusion mechanisms may change as the mineral is heated. Evernden and others (1960) have interpreted irregularities in their feldspar diffusion curves as being due to structural changes in the mineral lattice. They argue that the exact form of the diffusion curve may be influenced by the manner in which the sample is heated.

Because low-temperature diffusion studies in the laboratory require impractically long periods of time, it is common to conduct the experiments at temperatures above 300 to 400°C and to extrapolate the results to lower temperatures. Mussett (in press), however, has pointed out that diffusion at high temperatures may be due largely to movement of defects in the crystals, a mechanism that is probably inoperative at room temperature. Thus, extrapolation of data obtained at high temperatures may be an invalid approach. The technique of neutron activation has been used to study low-temperature diffusion, but as was previously mentioned this is open to the objection that the neutron irradiation process may damage the crystal lattice, thereby altering the diffusion properties of the mineral.

A final objection to laboratory studies is that most argon diffusion measurements are carried out in vacuum, far out of the stability field of most, if not all, rock-forming minerals. This means that many of the data were gathered under conditions quite different from those that occur in nature. One example that illustrates the importance of this point is the diffusion work on glauconite by Evernden and others (1960). Their results, obtained in vacuum, were quite different from those obtained when the same mineral was heated in the presence of 1,000 to 10,000 p.s.i. of water vapor (Fig. 9-7). The sample heated in vacuum lost argon much more easily than the one heated in the presence of water, and the diffusion did not follow the expected exponential law. They interpreted this difference as due to water loss and accompanying lattice instability in the sample that was heated in vacuum.

FIGURE 9-7

Argon-diffusion curves for glauconite heated in vacuum and under high water-vapor pressure. Note that the sample heated in vacuum lost argon more readily and that the argon diffusion did not follow the exponential law. [After Evernden and others (1960).]

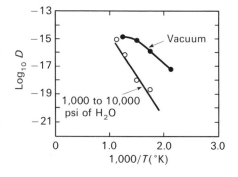

These difficulties in making geologically useful diffusion measurements are illustrated by the results on feldspars (Fig. 9-8). Note that diffusion coefficients for the same kind of feldspar at a particular temperature often differ by several orders of magnitude! This lack of agreement is not surprising in view of the objections listed above and the complexity of the feldspar structure. As Mussett (in press) has emphasized, argon diffusion almost certainly is influenced by the presence of lattice defects. Therefore, there is

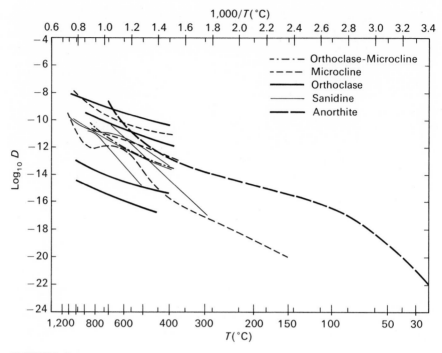

FIGURE 9-8

Argon-diffusion curves for feldspars. Note that the same mineral species often give different results. [After A. E. Mussett (in press).]

no reason why two crystals of the same composition and with the same X-ray and optical properties could not have quite different diffusion characteristics.

Ideally, it should be possible and advantageous to classify minerals by their activation energy, for this parameter describes the ease of argon migration over a broad range of temperature. Yet this too has had only limited success. Figure 9-9 shows a histogram of experimentally determined activation energies for some common minerals. Amphiboles, which are perhaps the best argon retainers, have consistently high activation energies, as would be expected, but the distinctions between the other minerals are not so clear. In practice, microline typically gives lower potassium-argon ages than biotite or muscovite from the same rock, yet this fact is not satisfactorily reflected in the activation energy data. Moreover, diffusion rates are very sensitive to small changes in activation energy, and a difference in E of only a few kilocalories per mole can make a change in D of several orders of magnitude (equation 9-4).

In spite of the difficulties of determining the rates of argon diffusion in the laboratory, the available data still suggest several useful generalizations.

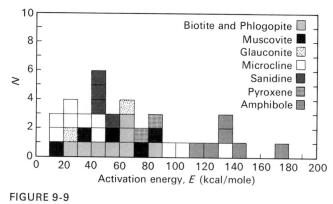

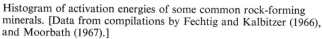

FIGURE 9-9

Histogram of activation energies of some common rock-forming minerals. [Data from compilations by Fechtig and Kalbitzer (1966), and Moorbath (1967).]

Probably the most important of these is that none of the materials commonly used for potassium-argon dating will lose a significant amount of argon at 20°C even over a period of time equivalent to the age of the earth. This is true even for biotite. Minerals that are relatively resistant to argon loss, such as sanidine, could probably be held at temperatures of 150 to 200°C for as much as 10 million years without losing enough argon to appreciably affect the potassium-argon clock. This can be seen from the argon-loss curves plotted in Figure 9-10. These curves were calculated using equation (9-3) and making the usual assumptions for a spherical diffusion model (see p. 150). Diffusion data for two different sanidine samples were used to calculate the amount of argon that would be lost as a function of time for various temperatures. Even the sanidine with the highest diffusion parameter and lowest activation energy (broken lines in Fig. 9-10) would lose only a few percent of its argon in 10 million years. The more resistant sanidine sample (solid lines in Fig. 9-10) would lose less than 5 percent of its argon if held at a temperature of 200°C for 100 million years. Argon loss from hornblende for comparable times and temperatures would be even less. On the other hand, biotite could be expected to lose nearly all of its argon if held at a temperature of 200°C for a million years or less.

The curves shown in Figure 9-10 also demonstrate the futility of using diffusion data in quantitative calculations. For example, the diffusion data for one sanidine suggest that about 4 percent of the argon would be lost in one million years at 250°C, whereas the data for the other sanidine suggest that the loss would be nearly 50 percent for the same time and temperature. Diffusion also is very sensitive to temperature. From the solid curves in Figure 9-10, about 4 percent argon loss would be expected in one million

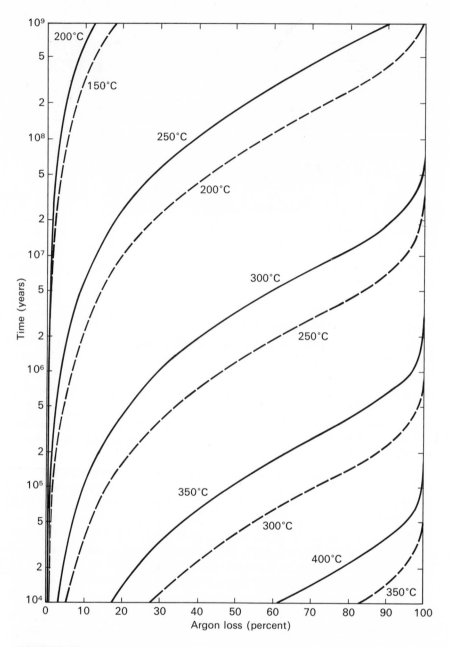

FIGURE 9-10

Argon lost as a function of time and various temperatures for two different sanidines. The curves were calculated for a spherical diffusion model using equation (9-3). Solid curves are for a sanidine with $(D/a^2)_{20°C} = 3 \times 10^{-33}$/sec and $E = 48$ kcal/mole (Frechen and Lippolt, 1965). Broken curves are for a sanidine with $(D/a^2)_{20°C} = 2 \times 10^{-28}$/sec and $E = 40$ kcal/mole (Fechtig and others, 1961).

years at 250°C, but if the temperature were 300°C the loss would be more than 30 percent.

In summary, the experimental determination of diffusion coefficients and activation energies has not been as successful as one might hope, and it is difficult to relate these quantities to geological situations in any really useful way. It seems probable that this will remain the case until a better understanding of diffusion mechanisms in rock-forming minerals is reached.

STUDIES OF ARGON LOSS IN NATURAL SYSTEMS

A great deal of valuable information about the relative ability of minerals to retain argon has been obtained by studying rocks known to have lost argon through natural processes. This approach has the distinct advantage of being directly applicable to real geologic situations. It is not necessary to worry about whether the experimental techniques are realistic. The disadvantage of this method is that it is difficult to make meaningful determinations of diffusion coefficients or activation energies. In addition to the ordinary assumptions that are made in laboratory diffusion studies, it is also necessary to make estimates of the heating conditions. This is not easy because the temperature distribution in and around a cooling rock body changes continuously with time. Thus in spite of the fact that the experimental conditions are completely realistic, it is nearly impossible to know exactly what they are. Activation energies calculated from these studies are typically much lower than those measured in the laboratory, but the reasons for this are not known.

The relative sensitivity of various minerals to post-formation heating is the most valuable information that has been obtained from the study of the distribution of ages as they occur in the field. These experiments are usually done by analyzing various minerals at different distances from an intrusive contact.

The results of a study by S. R. Hart of the Carnegie Institution of Washington (Hart, 1964) are shown in Figure 9-11. For his study, Hart selected an area in the Front Range near Eldora, Colorado, where a Tertiary quartz monzonite stock (the Eldora stock), which has a diameter of about two miles, intrudes gneisses, schists, and amphibolites of the Idaho Springs Formation (Precambrian). Within a few feet of the contact, minerals from the Idaho Springs Formation gave ages similar to samples taken from the stock. Rubidium-strontium ages of potassium feldspar apparently were unaffected beyond about 50 feet from the contact, and potassium-argon ages of hornblende began to give realistic values beyond about 100 feet. Both potassium-argon and rubidium-strontium ages of biotite showed the effects of reheating

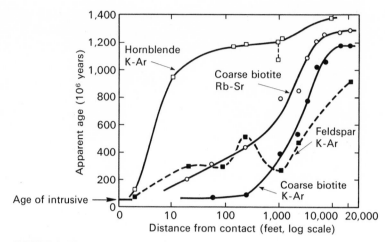

FIGURE 9-11

Change in ages of minerals from Precambrian schists and gneisses as a function of distance from an intrusive contact. [After S. R. Hart, The petrology and isotopic-mineral age relations of a contact zone in the Front Range, Colorado, Jour. Geol., v. 72, p. 493-525. Copyright 1964 by the University of Chicago.]

by the intrusive out to a distance of about 10,000 feet. Four miles from the contact, potassium-argon ages of feldspar were still much too low.

Similar results were obtained by Hanson and Gast (1967) in Minnesota, where the Snowbank stock is intruded by the Precambrian Duluth Gabbro. The Snowbank stock is a granitic body ranging in composition from quartz monzonite to diorite, with dimensions of about 5 kilometers by 8 kilometers. Its age is 2.6×10^9 years, and it was intruded by the Duluth Gabbro about 1.0×10^9 years ago. Hanson and Gast, like Hart, studied samples taken from various distances from the intrusive contact. Their results show the same relative argon retention properties for hornblende, biotite, and feldspar as do those of Hart (Fig. 9-12). In addition, they studied muscovite and found it to be more retentive than biotite but less so than hornblende.

The effects of reheating by smaller bodies, in particular basaltic dikes, have been studied by Hanson and Gast (1967) and by Westcott (1966). Hanson and Gast (1967) measured the ages of hornblende and biotite at various distances from the contact of a dike that is 50 meters thick and which intrudes Precambrian amphibolite of the Beartooth Mountains, Wyoming. Again, their results (Fig. 9-13) show that hornblende was affected by reheating only within a few feet of the contact. At any given distance from the contact, biotite showed much more argon loss than did hornblende. But within less than half the width of the dike from the contact, biotite in the amphibolite no longer showed the effects of reheating. A similar result for biotite was obtained by Westcott (1966), who found that reliable potassium-

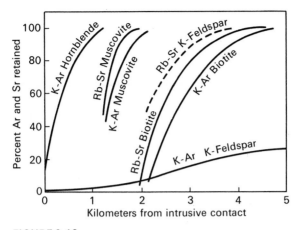

FIGURE 9-12

Generalized curves showing the retention of radiogenic daughter products in minerals from the Snowbank stock as a function of distance from the contact with the Duluth Gabbro. [After G. N. Hanson and P. W. Gast, Geochim. et Cosmochim. Acta, v. 31, p. 1119-1153, 1967.]

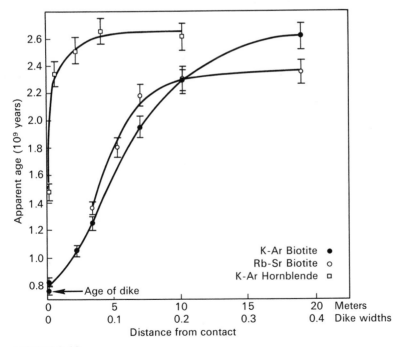

FIGURE 9-13

Change in ages of hornblende and biotite from amphibolite as a function of distance from a basaltic dike. [After G. N. Hanson and P. W. Gast, Geochim. et Cosmochim. Acta, v. 31, p. 1119-1153, 1967.]

argon ages could be obtained at distances of a dike width or more from the contact (Fig. 9-14).

Aldrich and others (1965), in their study of the Iron Mountain region, Michigan, have compared the resistance of various minerals and decay schemes to thermal events. Their approach was to determine ages using a

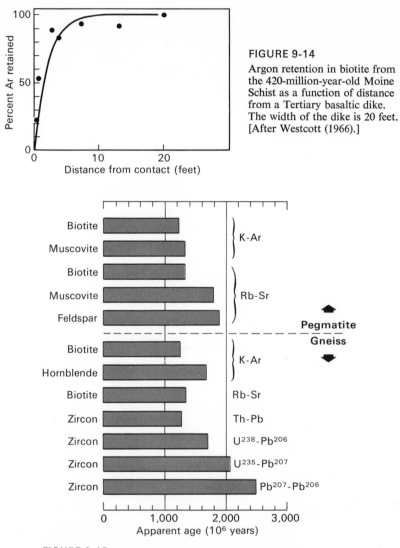

FIGURE 9-14

Argon retention in biotite from the 420-million-year-old Moine Schist as a function of distance from a Tertiary basaltic dike. The width of the dike is 20 feet. [After Westcott (1966).]

FIGURE 9-15

Comparison of mineral ages from the Black Rock pegmatite and its host rock. [After L. T. Aldrich, G. L. Davis, and H. L. James (1965).]

TABLE 9-1

Resistance of various minerals and dating decay schemes to
post-formation thermal events.

Decreasing resistance to thermal event →

K-Ar	Rb-Sr	$U^{238}\text{-}Pb^{206}$	$U^{235}\text{-}Pb^{207}$	$Th^{232}\text{-}Pb^{208}$	$Pb^{207}\text{-}Pb^{206}$
					Zircon
	Feldspar				
Hornblende	Muscovite				
			Zircon		
				Zircon	
		Zircon			
	Biotite				
Muscovite					
Biotite					
Feldspar					

Source: Data from Aldrich and others (1965).

variety of decay schemes on many minerals from one locality. An example
of their results is shown in Figure 9-15.

Such careful studies on natural systems have led to a better understanding of the relative resistance of minerals to the effects of reheating. From
such studies, it is possible to prepare a table (Table 9-1), which compares
the common minerals and decay schemes. Although there will be small
differences that will depend upon the particular geologic conditions, Table
9-1 gives a good idea of what the effects of a thermal event will be on various
minerals.

10

WHAT CAN BE DATED?

In order to be useful for potassium-argon dating, a mineral must meet three basic criteria:

1. It must retain argon at "normal" geologic temperatures—that is, one or two hundred degrees centigrade or less.

2. It must be relatively resistant to alteration and to dissolution by ground water. Nearly all of the silicates meet this criterion, but salts do not.

3. It must contain enough potassium to make the potassium and argon determinations technically feasible. It is not necessary for the mineral to contain potassium as an essential cation; many common "non-potassium" minerals contain sufficient potassium as an impurity to allow age determinations to be made.

TABLE 10-1

Common rock-forming minerals that are generally useful for potassium-argon dating; ⊗ = widely useful, x = sometimes useful.

	Rock type			
	Volcanic	Plutonic	Metamorphic	Sedimentary
Feldspars				
sanidine	⊗			
anorthoclase	⊗			
plagioclase	⊗			
Feldspathoids				
leucite	x			
nepheline	x	x		
Mica				
biotite	⊗	⊗	⊗	
phlogopite			⊗	
muscovite		⊗	⊗	
lepidolite		x		
glauconite				x
Amphibole				
hornblende	⊗	⊗	⊗	
Pyroxene	x	x		
Whole-rock	⊗		x	

SUITABILITY OF VARIOUS MATERIALS

Table 10-1 lists the common rock-forming minerals that are generally considered useful for potassium-argon dating; Figure 10-1 shows their approximate useful range, which is governed by potassium content and characteristic amount of atmospheric argon. To be classified as useful, it is not essential that the mineral give the correct age under all conditions. For example, biotite from metamorphic rocks that have had complex histories frequently gives ages that do not represent the time of formation of the rock. But the biotite ages are useful indicators of post-formation thermal events when combined with data from other minerals and decay schemes. Many minerals that might give perfectly good ages cannot be considered truly useful because they do not occur widely.

Following are some remarks on the suitability of various geologic materials for potassium-argon dating. The reader may wish to consult Chapters 8 and 9 for discussions of the specific problems of extraneous Ar^{40} and argon loss.

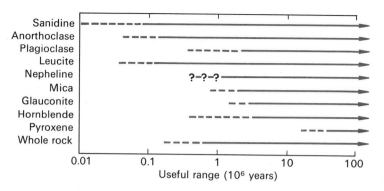

FIGURE 10-1

Approximate useful range of some datable materials.

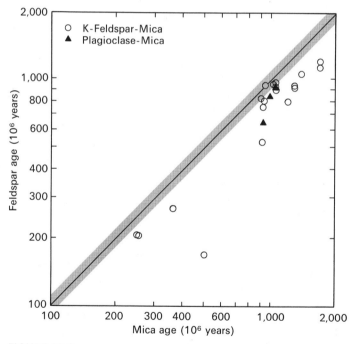

FIGURE 10-2

Comparison of some potassium-argon ages determined from coexisting mica (muscovite or biotite) and "low-temperature" feldspar (microcline, orthoclase, or plagioclase). The outer limits of the shaded band are ±10 percent from perfect agreement (solid line). [Data from Wetherill and others (1955), Wasserburg and others (1956), and Zartman (1964).]

Feldspars

Orthoclase and Microline   These minerals are not suitable for potassium-argon dating because they do not retain argon well even at room temperatures. This appears to be true of all "low-temperature" feldspars. Figure 10-2 shows some results of studies on coexisting mica-feldspar pairs from plutonic and metamorphic rocks. Typically, the feldspars give ages that are 20 to 30 percent too low. The exact reasons for this are not completely clear, but it is probably related to lattice changes that accompany exsolution. Diffusion rates that have been determined in the laboratory for orthoclase and microline are not high enough to account for the observed argon losses, which suggests that the loss of argon from these minerals is due to some phenomenon other than simple diffusion. Sardarov (1957) has investigated the extent of argon loss in microclines as a function of the relative degree of perthitization by comparing the ages of coexisting microcline and mica. His results (Fig. 10-3) clearly show that highly perthitized microclines tend to lose more argon than those that are less perthitized, and that the argon loss is roughly proportional to the degree of perthitization.

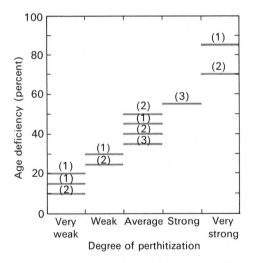

FIGURE 10-3
Potassium-argon age deficiency in microcline as a function of the relative degree of perthitization. Numbers in parentheses indicate the number of samples. [After S. S. Sardarov, Geochemistry, no. 3, p. 233-237, 1957.]

Sanidine and Anorthoclase   In contrast to the "low-temperature" (plutonic and metamorphic) feldspars, the "high-temperature" (volcanic) feldspars appear to retain argon relatively well and thus make good potassium-argon clocks. Ages on coexisting biotite and sanidine from volcanic rocks usually show satisfactory agreement. Some representative examples are shown in Figure 10-4; compare these with the "low-temperature" feldspars shown in Figure 10-2.

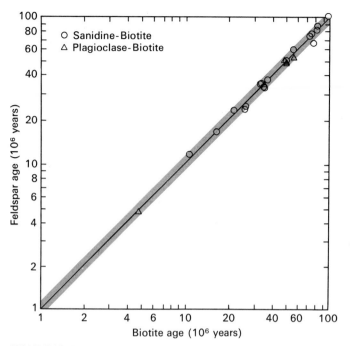

FIGURE 10-4

Comparison of some potassium-argon ages determined from coexisting biotite and volcanic ("high-temperature") feldspar. Outer limits of the shaded band are ± 10 percent from perfect agreement (solid line). [Data from Folinsbee and others (1960, 1961), Dalrymple (1964b), Evernden and others (1964), Hills and Baadsgaard (1967), and unpublished sources of the U.S. Geological Survey.]

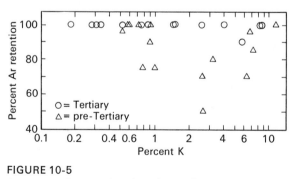

FIGURE 10-5

Argon retention as a function of potassium content for volcanic feldspars. [Data from Evernden and James (1964).]

The use of sanidine and anorthoclase for potassium-argon dating has several distinct advantages: (1) they occur widely in felsic volcanic rocks;

(2) they are easy to separate; (3) they have very high potassium contents (sanidine commonly contains approximately 10 percent K_2O) and can therefore be used to date very young rocks; and (4) the crystals generally contain less atmospheric argon than do other minerals, which makes young rocks easier to date.

There is some question whether pre-Tertiary volcanic feldspars of intermediate potassium content retain argon well. Evernden and Richards (1962) and Evernden and James (1964) have studied the retentivity of "high-temperature" feldspars as a function of potassium content and age. Their approach was to compare feldspar ages with ages on coexisting minerals or ages determined by fossil control. Their results, which are shown graphically in Figure 10-5, suggest the following conclusions:

1. Volcanic feldspars with less than about 0.8 percent K_2O or more than about 8 percent K_2O will retain argon completely for several hundred million years.

2. Tertiary feldspars of nearly any potassium content appear to retain argon completely.

3. Pre-Tertiary feldspars of intermediate potassium content lose argon. The reasons for this are not known, but the loss may be related to unmixing. Feldspars of mixed or intermediate composition may unmix (separate into two feldspars) if they are given enough time. This unmixing process apparently is accompanied by argon loss (see preceding discussion of orthoclase and microcline). In contrast, Tertiary feldspars of intermediate potassium content, which have had insufficient time to unmix, appear to retain most or all of their argon.

Plagioclase   As with the potassium feldspars, "high-temperature" plagioclase, found in volcanic rocks, usually retains argon completely, whereas "low-temperature" plagioclase, found in plutonic and metamorphic rocks, does not (see Figs. 10-2 and 10-4). Therefore, plagioclase from volcanic rocks can be used for potassium-argon dating. Volcanic plagioclase typically contains from a few tenths of a percent up to about 1 percent of K_2O. Although plagioclase has been used successfully to date rocks less than 1 million years old, it is most useful on rocks of Pliocene age or older. There is some evidence that plagioclase with more than about 0.8 percent K_2O does not retain all of its argon over periods of 10^8 years or more (see discussion in preceding section and Fig. 10-5).

Feldspathoids

Leucite   Leucite has been used successfully to date volcanic rocks (see, for example, Evernden and Curtis, 1965a). It appears to retain argon well,

TABLE 10-2
Comparison of potassium-argon ages of nepheline
with coexisting biotite and amphibole.

Biotite	Amphibole	Nepheline
900		904
852		891
858		998
900		1,007
	982	1,156

Source: Data from Macintyre and others (1966).

at least in rocks of Cenozoic age. Leucite may contain 18 to 20 percent or more of K_2O and thus can be used to date young rocks with a minimum of material. Unfortunately, it does not occur widely, so its use in dating is not common.

Nepheline Nepheline, a common feldspathoid mineral, occurs in volcanic, plutonic, and metamorphic rocks. Its use for potassium-argon dating has been investigated by Macintyre and others (1966), who studied samples from the Grenville Province of the Precambrian Shield of Canada and found that nepheline retains argon well for periods of 10^9 years or more. In several of the samples tested by them, nepheline gave significantly higher ages than coexisting biotite and amphibole (Table 10-2). In none of their samples, however, did a nepheline age exceed typical potassium-argon ages for the Grenville Province (800 to $1,200 \times 10^6$ years); in fact, the nepheline ages agree closely with those determined by rubidium-strontium and uranium-lead methods. Macintyre and his co-workers concluded that the discrepancies were due to argon loss in biotite and amphibole rather than to excess argon in nepheline. Shanin and others (1967) also found good argon retentivity in nepheline when ages were compared with potassium-argon and uranium-lead ages on coexisting mica and zircon. It appears, then, that nepheline is suitable for potassium-argon dating. Potassium contents typically range from about 3 to 10 percent. It should be useful over a wide age range, although it has not been tested on young rocks. Like other feldspathoids, the use of nepheline for dating is limited because it occurs only in certain subsilicic alkaline rocks.

Sodalite and Other Feldspathoids Excess Ar^{40} in sodalite and cancrinite has been reported by York and others (1965) and by Macintyre (Univ. Toronto Ph.D. Thesis, 1966), but the details of their investigations have not been published. With the exception of leucite and nepheline, feldspathoids occur so rarely that they cannot be considered very useful for potassium-argon dating.

Quartz

Few attempts have been made to use quartz for dating. It probably will retain argon well because of its tight lattice structure, but potassium contents are so low (typically less than 0.1 percent K_2O) that accurate analyses are difficult. Rama and others (1965) found excess Ar^{40} in the fluid inclusions of vein quartz (see Table 8-1).

Mica

Biotite Biotite is one of the most useful of all minerals for potassium-argon dating. It occurs commonly in volcanic, plutonic, and metamorphic rocks and has a relatively high potassium content (typically from 7 to 9 percent of K_2O). Under normal geologic conditions biotite retains argon well (see Figs. 7-8 and 7-9), but argon is easily lost from biotite by reheating above a few hundred degrees centigrade (Figs. 9-11 through 9-14). In complex metamorphic terranes biotite ages often are too low, but for this very reason biotite is quite useful as a sensitive indicator of post-formation thermal events.

Muscovite Muscovite occurs in plutonic and metamorphic rocks and has a very high potassium content (generally from 8 to 12 percent of K_2O). It has somewhat better argon retention properties than biotite (Figs. 9-12 and 9-15), and is widely used for potassium-argon determinations. Sericite (fine-grained muscovite) has been used to determine the age of hydrothermal deposits; an example is given in Chapter 11 (p. 205–207). See also the remarks under "Biotite" above.

Phlogopite and Lepidolite Phlogopite has properties similar to biotite and occurs in metamorphic rocks. Lepidolite is found commonly in pegmatites but is not as widely used as the other micas because of its somewhat limited occurrence. Lepidolite usually contains about 8 to 10 percent K_2O, and phlogopite contains about the same amount of K_2O as biotite. Both of these minerals are useful for dating. See the remarks under "Biotite" above.

Glauconite Glauconite is the only mineral that can be used routinely to date sedimentary rocks directly. It apparently forms shortly after deposition and thus gives an age that represents approximately the time of formation of the rock. Most glauconites contain between about 4 and 7 percent of K_2O and are easily dated. It has been used successfully to date rocks from a few million to more than a billion years old.

Glauconite loses argon more easily than other micas, perhaps because of its extremely small grain size. A temperature of about 150°C is sufficient to cause argon loss if the temperature is prolonged. Because of this, burial of a few thousand feet may result in ages that are too low. Evernden and others (1961) found a progressive lowering of glauconite ages with sample depth in the Eocene and Oligocene Kreyenhagen Formation of California (Fig. 10-6). Because the geologic time-scale is based primarily upon sedimentary rocks rather than any other type, the importance of glauconite as a geochronometer is considerable. For this reason, potassium-argon dating of glauconite has received a great deal of attention. Generally, it has been found that glauconite gives ages that are either reasonable or a bit too low (Fig. 10-7). This is not surprising in view of the ease with which it loses argon.

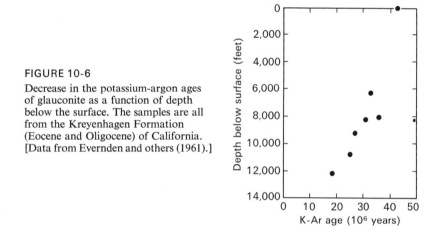

FIGURE 10-6
Decrease in the potassium-argon ages of glauconite as a function of depth below the surface. The samples are all from the Kreyenhagen Formation (Eocene and Oligocene) of California. [Data from Evernden and others (1961).]

As was mentioned in Chapter 8, glauconite occasionally contains a detrital component that can contribute inherited (contamination) Ar^{40} to the sample and result in an apparent age that is too high. This detrital component is usually illite, which can be very difficult to detect by either optical or X-ray techniques. The data in Figure 10-7, however, suggest that argon loss is a more serious problem in potassium-argon dating of glauconite than is inherited (contamination) Ar^{40}.

In summary, glauconite is a very useful mineral for potassium-argon dating and is about the only mineral that can be used to date sedimentary rocks directly. The post-depositional history of the sample is critical, however, for burial of a few thousand feet or the slightest thermal event may cause argon loss. For additional discussion concerning the dating of glauconite, consult the review by Hurley (1966).

Amphibole

Hornblende   A very useful mineral for potassium-argon dating, hornblende occurs commonly in volcanic, plutonic, and metamorphic rocks and usually contains between about 0.2 and 1 percent of K_2O. Hornblende is most

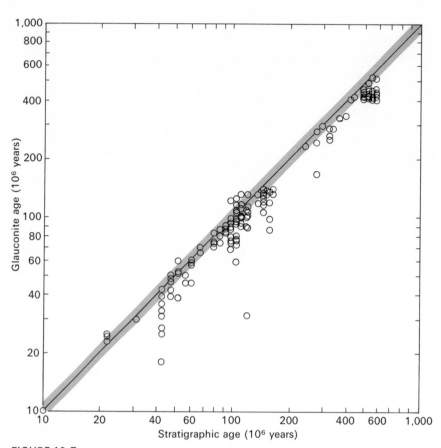

FIGURE 10-7

Glauconite potassium-argon ages plotted against stratigraphic ages. Outer limits of the shaded band are ±10 percent from perfect agreement (solid line). [Data from a compilation by Hurley (1966).]

useful for dating rocks of middle Tertiary age or older. It is the most resistant of the common minerals to argon loss (Figs. 9-11, 9-12, and 9-13, and Table 9-1). Because of this, potassium-argon ages determined from coexisting hornblende and biotite provide a sensitive indicator of thermal events. In rocks that have simple histories, hornblende and biotite ages frequently are concordant (Fig. 10-8).

Other Amphiboles Other amphiboles appear to have argon retention properties similar to hornblende, but because of their restricted occurrence are not as often used for dating. Riebeckite from plutonic rocks has given reasonable ages (Lanphere and others, 1964) as have actinolite and glaucophane from metamorphic rocks (Fig. 10-8). It seems reasonable to suspect

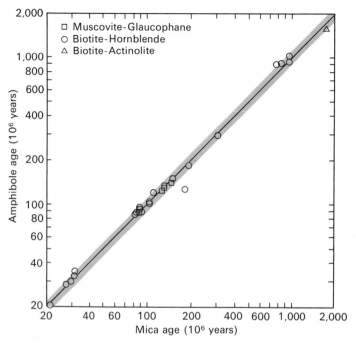

FIGURE 10-8

Comparison of some potassium-argon ages determined from amphibole with ages for coexisting mica. Outer limits of the shaded band are ±10 percent from perfect agreement (solid line). [Data from Hart (1961), Lee and others (1964), Kistler and Dodge (1966), and unpublished sources of the U.S. Geological Survey.]

that probably all of the amphiboles could satisfactorily be used for potassium-argon dating, but few amphiboles other than hornblende have been tested adequately.

Pyroxene

Pyroxene occurs commonly in volcanic, plutonic, and metamorphic rocks, but there are several major difficulties with using it for dating. One is its extremely low potassium content. Pyroxenes usually contain less than 0.1 percent of K_2O, which makes accurate analyses very difficult and limits its use mostly to rocks of Mesozoic age or older. The second difficulty is the apparently frequent occurrence of significant amounts of excess Ar^{40}, which leads to anomalously high ages (see Chapter 8, especially Table 8-2). McDougall (1961, 1963) and McDougall and Rüegg (1966) have found that pyroxenes from diabase rather consistently give ages that are concordant with ages on coexisting plagioclase (Fig. 10-9). In contrast, Kistler and

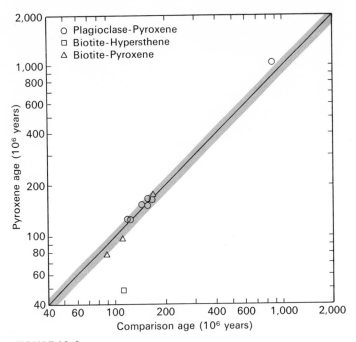

FIGURE 10-9

Comparison of potassium-argon ages determined from pyroxene with ages
for coexisting biotite and plagioclase. Outer limits of shaded band are
±10 percent from perfect agreement (solid line). [Data from McDougall
(1961, 1963), McDougall and Rüegg (1966), and Kistler and Dodge
(1966).]

Dodge (1966) found that three pyroxenes from plutonic rocks gave ages
that were too low compared with ages determined from coexisting biotite.
One of these, a hypersthene, had apparently lost more than 50 percent of
its argon. In view of the uncertainties regarding the suitability of pyroxene
for dating and the analytical difficulties of measuring potassium and argon
in these minerals, it is not recommended that pyroxene be used routinely
for potassium-argon dating.

Glass

The suitability of volcanic glass for potassium-argon dating is somewhat
uncertain. There is no reason why massive, unhydrated obsidian should not
retain argon well. The few obsidians that have been analyzed gave reasonable
ages, although there are seldom any coexisting minerals with which they can
be compared. Other glasses from felsic rocks give mixed results (Fig. 10-10).
It is clear that some glasses retain argon well whereas others do not, but it

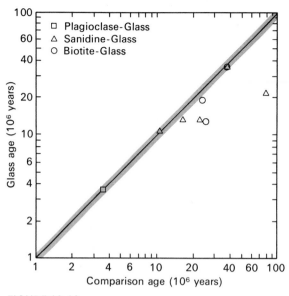

FIGURE 10-10

Comparison of some potassium-argon ages for silicic volcanic glass with ages for coexisting biotite or feldspar. Outer limits of shaded band are ±10 percent from perfect agreement (solid line). [Data from Schaeffer and others (1961), Evernden and others (1964), Hills and Baadsgaard (1967), and unpublished sources of the U.S. Geological Survey.]

is not yet possible to distinguish between the reliable and unreliable glasses. The argon loss may be related to the degree of hydration, for if water can diffuse in, argon can certainly diffuse out. At present, however, the use of glass for dating has not been studied adequately, and generally it should be considered an unreliable material for dating. For a discussion of basaltic glasses, refer to the section on "Whole-rock Samples" (p. 180).

Clay Minerals

Because of the obvious importance of dating sedimentary rocks, several attempts have been made to utilize clay minerals, especially illite, for potassium-argon dating, but these attempts have met with little success. Illite commonly contains from 6 to 10 percent K_2O. It forms as a product of weathering of other silicates, and is a very common constituent of shales. Illite can be separated quite easily by modern ultracentrifuge techniques and thus would be a good mineral for dating. Like the other clay minerals, however, illite is frequently detrital, having been recycled in the process of weathering of older sedimentary rocks.

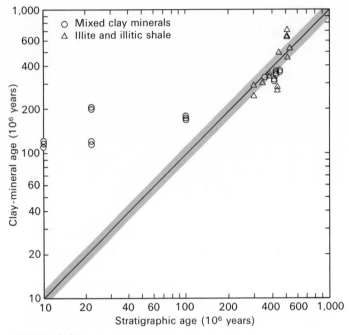

FIGURE 10-11

Potassium-argon ages for clay minerals compared with their stratigraphic ages. Outer limits of shaded band are ± 10 percent from perfect agreement (solid line). [Data from a compilation by Hurley (1966).]

Hurley and others (1961, 1963) have made extensive investigations on the clay fractions of shales and recent river sediments. Except for a few early Paleozoic samples, these clay fractions all gave potassium-argon ages much older than the stratigraphic age of the rock (Fig. 10-11). Samples of recent river sediments gave ages from 100 million years to more than 800 million years. Presumably, a large proportion of the clay minerals in shales are detrital and reflect, at least partly, the age of the source material. As discouraging as this is for direct dating, it does suggest the possibility of using potassium-argon "ages" on sedimentary rocks as an aid in determining provenance. An example of this is given in Chapter 11 (p. 213). Evernden and others (1961) investigated the possibility of dating illitic shales, and although many of their determinations agreed reasonably well with the known stratigraphic ages, some gave ages that were too high or too low by 25 percent or more (Fig. 10-11).

In summary, clay minerals in sedimentary rocks appear to have both detrital and authigenic components. In older rocks, the authigenic component often dominates, for they frequently give reasonable ages. Nevertheless,

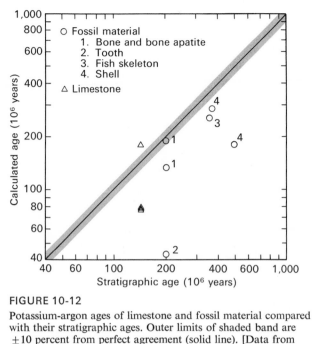

FIGURE 10-12

Potassium-argon ages of limestone and fossil material compared with their stratigraphic ages. Outer limits of shaded band are ±10 percent from perfect agreement (solid line). [Data from Lippolt and Gentner (1962, 1963).]

dating of clay minerals is subject to such large uncertainties that their use for routine dating is not recommended.

Fossil Material

The few attempts to date fossil material directly have yielded disappointing results. Lippolt and Gentner (1962, 1963) measured the argon and potassium contents of bone, teeth, and mollusk shells and found radiogenic argon in six specimens. All but one of the ages, however, were significantly less than the known stratigraphic age (Fig. 10-12). Diffusion experiments on two of the specimens indicate that radiogenic argon is easily lost from bone. It does not seem probable that meaningful potassium-argon ages can be obtained on fossil material.

Limestone

Limestone can contain up to several percent of K_2O. The few attempts to date limestone have not been encouraging, but this is at least partly because of the uncertain history of the samples used. Of four European Jurassic limestones dated, three gave ages that were too low, and one gave an age that was too high (Fig. 10-12). It is possible that future research will make limestones datable by the potassium-argon method, but at present the effects of detrital components and the argon-retention properties of these materials have not been tested adequately.

Sylvite

Sylvite is a potassium salt (KCl) that is sometimes found in evaporite deposits. Because of its high potassium content, it is an ideal candidate for potassium-argon dating. As with most salts, however, sylvite is soluble in water and thus is not particularly stable under geologic conditions. Attempts to date sylvite have yielded mixed results, but frequently the calculated ages are too low. For example, Smits and Gentner (1950) calculated ages of 20 million years and 200 million years for sylvite samples of Oligocene and Permian age, respectively. Because sylvite is not common and may be subject to argon loss, it is not very useful for dating. Less common potassium salts (for example, carnallite, langbeinite, polyhalite) would also probably be unsatisfactory because of their susceptibility to argon loss by dissolution and recrystallization.

Other Minerals

Several other minerals have been tried as geochronometers. The cyclosilicates beryl, tourmaline, and cordierite commonly have large amounts of excess Ar^{40} and thus are highly unsatisfactory. Lippolt and Gentner (1963) found excess Ar^{40} in the fluid inclusions of fluorite from hydrothermal deposits (see Table 8-1). Macintyre (Univ. Toronto Ph.D. Thesis, 1966) found that a sample of scapolite gave a potassium-argon age that was consistent with geological evidence, whereas a zeolite that he tested yielded an apparent age that was nearly two orders of magnitude too low.

Whole-rock Samples

In principle, a rock that contains only components that are good potassium-argon geochronometers should give a valid age. In practice, this has proved to be true, and as a result whole-rock dating of mafic volcanic rocks, especially basalt, has become an important part of potassium-argon research. Basalt is useful chiefly because of its wide occurrence and frequent association with geologic features of interest. Several examples of the validity of potassium-argon ages determined from carefully selected basalts are given in Chapter 7 (see Tables 7-6 and 7-7 and the accompanying discussion in the text). For examples of the use of whole-rock basalt dating, see McDougall (1964) and Chapter 11.

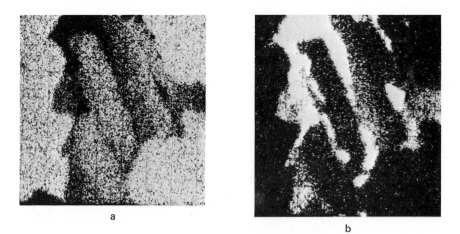

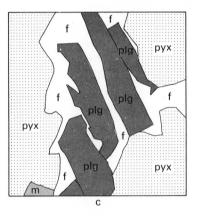

FIGURE 10-13

Electron microprobe scans, showing location (light areas) of (a) calcium and (b) potassium in a holocrystalline late Cenozoic basalt from California. The sketch (c) shows the identity of the principal mineral grains: pyx = pyroxene, m = iron-titanium oxide, plg = plagioclase, f = interstitial potassium feldspar. The field of view is about 80 microns square. [Electron microprobe scans courtesy of Bernard W. Evans.]

The procedure for evaluating whole-rock samples for dating can be stated quite simply. Because the rock is to be dated by the decay of K^{40}, the investigator should ask himself, "Where is the potassium, and is it in components that will have retained the argon that has been generated since the rock crystallized?"

From geochemical considerations, most of the potassium in basalt should reside in the last components to solidify—for example, in interstitial material, which is usually glass or fine-grained feldspar. Observations with electron microprobes on the potassium distribution in basalts have confirmed this expectation. Miller and Mussett (1963) found that potassium in a sample of the Whin sill, a Carboniferous or Permian diabase, was concentrated in the fine-grained groundmass and not in the plagioclase laths. Figure 10-13 shows the location of potassium in a Cenozoic basalt flow from California. Clearly, the potassium is concentrated in the interstitial feldspar, which probably is anorthoclase or sanidine. Similar electron microprobe studies on basalts that contain glass have shown that the interstitial glass contains most of the potassium. For this reason, a careful evaluation of the condition and composition of the interstitial material is very important for whole-rock dating.

The ability of basaltic glass to retain argon is somewhat uncertain, but there is evidence that suggests that some glass loses argon rather easily. Table 10-3 presents a few examples of hyalocrystalline basalts and basaltic glasses whose potassium-argon ages are too low when compared with their known age. Most of these basalts have rather large amounts of glass. On the other hand, some basalts with smaller amounts of fresh interstitial glass give ages that appear reasonable. For example, McDougall and others (1966) obtained satisfactory results on whole-rock samples that contained up to 15 percent of fresh glass. Eventually, it may be possible to distinguish between retentive and nonretentive basaltic glasses, but for the present it is wise to reject for routine dating any whole-rock samples that contain glass. (See also the discussion of rhyolitic glasses on page 176).

The degree of alteration is another criterion to consider when evaluating whole-rock samples for dating. Alteration may have released radiogenic argon from the crystal lattices of the potassium-containing minerals and result in an age that is too low. Miller and Mussett (1963) studied the potassium-argon ages of samples of a diabase dike as a function of the relative degree of alteration and found that the most altered samples gave the lowest ages (Fig. 10-14). Webb and McDougall (1967) compared potassium-argon ages on basalts with sanidine ages from closely associated trachytes and found that argon leakage had not occurred in spite of slight alteration of the plagioclase and the groundmass in the basalts. More strongly altered specimens, however, gave potassium-argon ages that were 15 to 20 percent low. Alteration of minerals that contain a negligible amount of potassium, such as the deuteric alteration of olivine to iddingsite, should have no effect on the age as long as the potassium-bearing components are unaltered.

Whole-rock samples that contain minerals whose time of origin is in question, such as the minerals that occur as amygdaloidal fillings, or whose argon retention properties are questionable, such as zeolites or most feldspathoids, also should be considered unreliable for whole-rock dating. Xenoliths and xenocrysts are another problem in whole-rock dating because they can contribute significant amounts of inherited (contamination) Ar[40]. (See the discussion on inherited (contamination) Ar[40] in Chapter 8.)

In summary, whole-rock samples can give perfectly reliable results if the samples are selected carefully. Ideally, the sample should be relatively coarse-

TABLE 10-3
Examples of low potassium-argon ages determined from basaltic glass and basalts that contain glass.

Description	Calculated age (10^6 years)	Control age	Reference
Chilled diabase, mostly devitrified glass	148	164 million years, determined from separated plagioclase	McDougall (1961)
100 percent fresh, undevitrified glass	126	Upper Triassic (180 to 200 million years), determined from fossil evidence	Brew and Muffler (1965)
20 percent fresh glass, 5 percent altered glass	11.5	Overlain by 22-million-year-old rhyolite	Dalrymple (1964b)
30 percent fresh glass, 5 percent altered glass	11.6	Overlain by 22-million-year-old rhyolite	Dalrymple (1964b)
15 percent fresh glass, 5 percent altered glass	13.6	Overlain by 22-million-year-old rhyolite	Dalrymple (1964b)
25 percent fresh glass, 5 percent altered glass	3.5	Overlain by 22-million-year-old rhyolite	Dalrymple (1964b)
Basalt matrix (> 50 percent glass), plagioclase phenocrysts removed	1.6	7.4 million years, determined from separated plagioclase	Unpublished

184

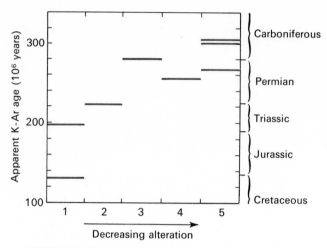

FIGURE 10-14

Potassium-argon age as a function of the relative degree of alteration for whole-rock diabase samples from the Whin sill (Carboniferous to Permian). [Data from Miller and Mussett (1963).]

grained so that every component present can be identified easily with a normal petrographic microscope. It should be completely unweathered and unaltered and contain no glass, devitrified glass, clay minerals, foreign inclusions, zeolites, or secondary mineralization. In many mafic volcanic rocks the groundmass is so clouded by opaque mineral inclusions that the material of which it is composed cannot be identified. Such samples should not be dated. Of course, it is always possible that a rock that does not meet these criteria might give a good age, but if the reliability of the sample is not certain beforehand, then the results will be ambiguous.

HOW MUCH IS NEEDED?

The amount of sample needed for an argon determination depends on the argon concentration, which in turn depends on the potassium content and age of the sample; the amount required decreases with increasing age and potassium content. For the mass spectrometric analysis, it is convenient to have the Ar^{40}/Ar^{38} ratio near one, although ratios between about 0.3 and 3 are easily handled. Figure 10-15 shows the amount of mineral or rock required to give an Ar^{40}/Ar^{38} ratio of unity for the approximate tracer size used in the U.S. Geological Survey laboratories and many others. The graph was calculated on the assumption that the atmospheric Ar^{40} concentration was negligible. This assumption is generally satisfactory for Mesozoic or older rocks, but for younger rocks the atmospheric Ar^{40} concentration may be appreciable, and thus increase the Ar^{40}/Ar^{38} ratio.

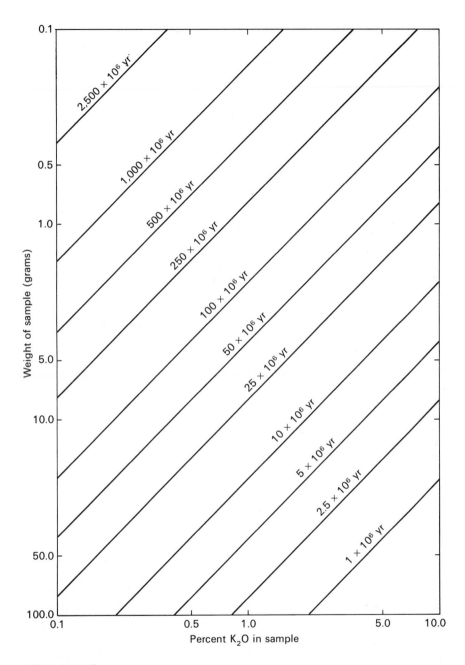

FIGURE 10-15

Ideal amount of sample for an argon analysis as a function of potassium content and age. Calculated to give an Ar^{40}/Ar^{38} ratio of 1 for a tracer size of 3.0×10^{-10} mole Ar^{38} and assuming the atmospheric Ar^{40} is zero.

It is not advisable to analyze samples that weigh less than about 0.2 gram, regardless of their age, because of the difficulty of obtaining a representative sample. It is also difficult to handle more than about 15 to 20 grams of material in the extraction process, so very young samples must be dated using considerably smaller sample sizes than Figure 10-15 indicates.

For a potassium measurement the amount of material needed is a function of potassium content but not of age. This is because the amount of potassium is very large compared to K^{40}, and its change with time is negligible. Depending on the analytical technique used, 0.2 to 0.5 gram is generally enough (see Chapter 6 on methods of potassium determination). Unless the sample is extremely homogeneous it is not wise to use amounts less than about 0.2 gram, because of the problems of obtaining a representative aliquant with small amounts of sample.

PURITY OF MINERAL CONCENTRATES

The ideal concentrate would, of course, be 100 percent pure, but complete purity is seldom attainable. But with a little care and effort most minerals can be concentrated to 99 percent or greater purity. The primary reason for using nearly pure mineral concentrates is to lessen the problems encountered when the sample is split into separate fractions for potassium measurement and argon analysis. The measurement of potassium and the analysis of argon must be done on entirely separate aliquants of the sample, so it is very important that each aliquant is representative. This problem is not encountered in rubidium-strontium dating, where the sample is first dissolved and then the solution is divided into separate fractions for the rubidium and strontium measurements.

The effect of impurities depends considerably upon the potassium contents of the sample and of the impurity. To illustrate, consider a sample that consists of 1,000 grains of feldspar, of which 100 grains will be used for a potassium measurement. If the sample is pure, then the 100-grain split will be representative and its potassium content will be the same as the potassium content of the entire sample. Now suppose that the feldspar is mostly plagioclase (1.0 percent K_2O) with one grain of sanidine (10 percent K_2O). If that grain ends up in the 100-grain split, it will increase the potassium content by slightly more than 9 percent of the measured value. On the other hand, if the feldspar is sanidine with one grain of plagioclase as an impurity, the effect will be negligible. There are thus two ways to lessen these undesirable effects of splitting a mineral concentrate for dating: use very pure concentrates and use large numbers of grains. This discussion has been concerned with the effects of impurities that are of the same age as the sample. If the impurities are foreign inclusions (xenocrysts) and contain inherited Ar^{40}, then the problem is even more serious and complex. For a discussion of inherited Ar^{40}, see Chapter 8.

SIZE FRACTIONS

The size of the mineral grains used for dating should be within close limits; that is, a wide variety of grain sizes is not desirable in a mineral concentrate. This is because different size grains of the same mineral commonly form within the rock at different times and they may have quite different potassium contents. Thus a wide range of grain sizes can easily lead to an inhomogeneous sample, from which representative aliquants are difficult to obtain. The size selected for analysis should be governed by the natural grain size of the mineral in the rock. Concentrates with Tyler sieve-scale ranges of 28 to 60 mesh, 40 to 80 mesh, or 60 to 100 mesh are most convenient to work with, but 100 to 150 mesh is also satisfactory. If the grain size is too large, the number of grains in a sample will be small, which introduces sample splitting problems. If the grain size is much smaller than 150 mesh, electrostatic charges make the material somewhat difficult to handle, and the relative mobility of very small grains in a vacuum becomes a problem.

SAMPLE PREPARATION

The preparation of samples for potassium-argon dating often is one of the most time-consuming steps in the entire dating procedure. This is especially true when, as is most often the case, the potassium-containing mineral(s) must be separated from the rock. Haste and carelessness in the preparation of samples may lead directly to inaccurate and unsatisfactory results. It is especially important that the equipment that comes in contact with the sample be cleaned thoroughly beforehand. It is often necessary to spend several hours or more cleaning an entire room before beginning work on the crushing or separation of a new sample.

Mineral Separation

The separation of minerals from rocks is done by taking advantage of physical properties, such as specific gravity, magnetic susceptibility, or shape. Magnetic methods and heavy-liquid gravity separation are usually sufficient to separate minerals for dating. It has been our experience that electrostatic, high-tension, elutriation, or flotation techniques are unnecessary except in rare circumstances. For separating mica, any technique that takes advantage of the flatness of the mineral grains is useful. Faul and Davis (1959) have described an asymmetric vibrator that is very useful and efficient for mica separation. Separation by shape is not very successful for other minerals.

In this section we will describe briefly the general procedures that we have found most efficient for preparing samples for dating. We assume that the reader is already familiar with the equipment and techniques for heavy-liquid and magnetic separation. If not, we suggest consulting some of the numerous papers and books that deal with these subjects—for example, Browning (1961), Dean and Davis (1941), Harris and others (1967), or Zussman (1967). An excellent selected bibliography of mineral separation techniques has been compiled by Harmon and Greenwood (1968).*

Crushing and Sieving   The rock is crushed and sieved into several size fractions (Tyler mesh sizes 28 to 60, 60 to 100, and 100 to 150 are usually satisfactory), from which the fraction that will give the highest yield of pure mineral grains is selected for further concentration. It is always better to do the crushing gradually by making repeated passes through the crushers at progressively finer settings; this prevents large amounts of material from being pulverized into an unusable powder. The selected size fraction is then washed with water to remove the fine dust, and dried. For most minerals, drying may be done quickly in an oven at a temperature of slightly more than 100°C.

Magnetic Separation   Many common minerals—for example, biotite and hornblende—are paramagnetic and may be concentrated with magnetic separators. Frequently, nonmagnetic minerals, such as feldspar, can be separated in this way by removing magnetic impurities. For example, it is easy to separate feldspar and quartz from glass and mafic minerals in a rhyolite.

Heavy-liquid Separation   Final concentration and purification are usually accomplished with liquids of high but variable specific gravity. Bromoform $(G=2.85)$ and acetylene tetrabromide $(G=2.96)$ are the most satisfactory liquids for this purpose. Their density can be decreased by controlled dilution with ethyl alcohol or acetone, and the exact specific gravity can be measured quite accurately with a Westphal balance or similar instrument. Methylene iodide $(G=3.33)$ works well if a heavier liquid is needed, but it is expensive. It too may be diluted with acetone. A clean separation of biotite

---

*Available on request from Lunar and Earth Sciences Division, NASA, Manned Spacecraft Center, Houston, Texas 77058.

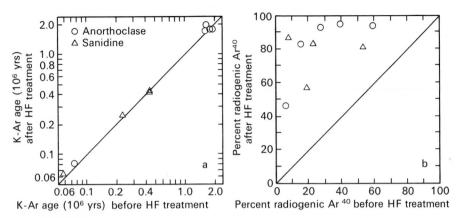

FIGURE 10-16

Comparisons of potassium-argon age data for sanidine and anorthoclase before and after treatment with HF. (a) Calculated ages. (b) Radiogenic argon percentage. [Data from Evernden and Curtis (1965a).]

and hornblende commonly can be made using methylene iodide of intermediate specific gravity (3.15 to 3.20).

HF *Treatment*   Feldspars, both sanidine and plagioclase, can be treated with a warm solution of 5 to 10 percent HF for 10 to 20 minutes to remove small glass or mineral particles attached to the grains. After removing the sample from the HF, it should be rinsed and then cleaned with an ultrasonic vibrator and distilled water to remove small particles that usually adhere to the grains. After treatment, the concentrate can be treated with heavy liquids again to remove the remaining impurities.

This procedure has two important advantages: first, it helps to obtain a very pure mineral concentrate; second, it significantly reduces the atmospheric argon contamination. Evernden and Curtis (1965a) investigated the effect of the HF treatment on the potassium-argon ages of feldspars and found no undesirable effects. The ages of samples after treatment were either the same as before treatment or slightly higher, presumably because the HF removed adhering particles of nonretentive glass (Fig 10-16,a). They found also that the potassium content was frequently higher for the same reason. In every sample they treated, the percentage of radiogenic argon was dramatically increased (Fig. 10-16,b). Apparently the HF removes only the outer layers of the crystals and removes potassium and argon in equal amounts.

To reduce the atmospheric argon contamination to a minimum for dating very young feldspars, the sample may again be treated with HF immediately before it is placed into the argon extraction line. The HF procedure has been tested only for feldspars and should never be used on any of the mafic minerals.

Whole-rock Samples

A block about 1 to 1.5 cm square and 2 to 3 cm long is cut from the part of the hand specimen immediately adjacent to the part used for the thin section. Two thin slices (about 2 mm thick) are then cut from the ends or sides of the block. These slices are pulverized and analyzed for potassium, and the remainder of the block (usually 5 to 15 grams, depending upon age and K_2O content) is used for the argon measurement. An alternative procedure, described by McDougall (1964), consists in crushing the hand specimen into fragments about 0.5 to 1 cm in diameter and splitting the crushed material into aliquants for the potassium and argon measurements.

The problem of obtaining a representative sample is often more serious for whole-rock samples than it is for mineral separates, especially if the rock is coarse grained or has large phenocrysts. Fortunately, most basalts are sufficiently fine grained so that the problem is minimized when a block of several cubic centimeters is used. Dalrymple and Hirooka (1965) found a variation in potassium content of about 3 percent within one single hand specimen of fine-grained basalt and of 22 percent within a single flow (see Table 7-6). This demonstrates the importance of using immediately adjacent pieces for the argon and potassium measurements.

AGE LIMITS OF THE METHOD

Upper Limit

For all practical purposes the potassium-argon method has no upper limit. Because of the long half-life of K^{40}, the potassium-argon method can be (and is) used to date the oldest dateable objects in the solar system—meteorites. The oldest meteorites give potassium-argon and rubidium-strontium ages of 4.5 to 5.0×10^9 years, which is only a few half-lives of K^{40}. For examples and discussion of potassium-argon dating of meteorites see Krankowsky and Zahringer (1966), Reynolds (1967), and Bogard and others (1968).

Lower Limit

With present techniques, it would be possible to measure precisely the age of a 20-gram sample of sanidine (10 percent K_2O) that was only 100 years old, if it were not for the interference of contaminating atmospheric argon. As was discussed in Chapter 7, the atmospheric Ar^{40} must be subtracted from the total Ar^{40} in order to find the amount of radiogenic Ar^{40}. When the quantity of atmospheric Ar^{40} is large relative to the amount of radiogenic

Ar^{40}, then precision and accuracy are decreased because of the problem of subtracting one large number from another to find the small remainder (see Fig. 7-3).

The radiogenic Ar^{40} component of very young rocks is relatively small even when great care is taken to reduce the atmospheric Ar^{40} to a minimum. Some atmospheric argon can be removed by baking the sample in vacuum on the argon extraction line, but a small amount always remains in the equipment used for the measurements and in the sample itself. Frechen and Lippolt (1965) have showed that some of the atmospheric argon in sanidine, biotite, and basalt is firmly held within the crystal lattice and can be removed only at the risk of losing significant quantities of radiogenic argon (Fig. 10-17). Mussett and Dalrymple (1968) discovered that basalt and sanidine samples whose surfaces had never been exposed to the atmosphere still contained significant quantities of atmospheric argon. At present it seems impossible to eliminate completely the atmospheric argon contamination.

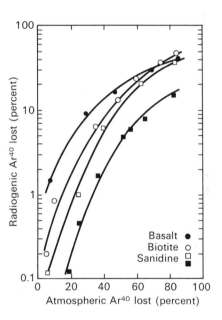

FIGURE 10-17

Loss of radiogenic argon as a function of the amount of atmospheric argon removed. [After Frechen and Lippolt (1965).]

Within broad ranges, different materials appear to have characteristic amounts of atmospheric Ar^{40}. Figure 10-18 shows histograms of the amounts of contaminating atmospheric Ar^{40} per gram of sample for 615 samples measured in our laboratory. For a given material, the atmospheric Ar^{40} varies over a range of one order of magnitude or more. Yet there do appear to be noticeable differences between one kind of sample material and another. Biotite nearly always contains more atmospheric Ar^{40} than either horn-

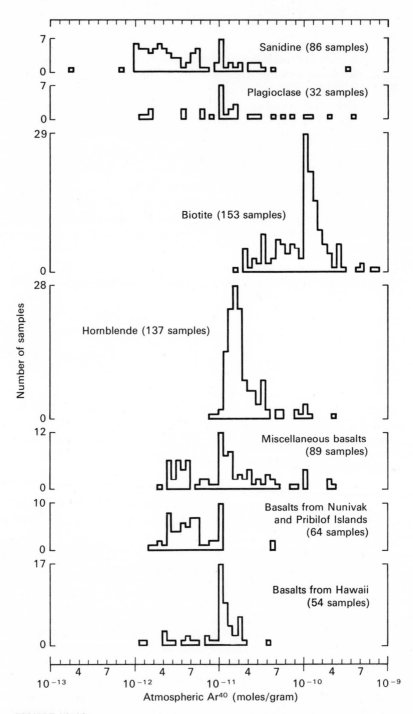

FIGURE 10-18

Histograms of the amount of atmospheric Ar⁴⁰ contamination in various materials used for potassium-argon dating.

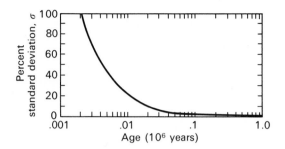

FIGURE 10-19

Error in age as a function of age for 20 grams of sanidine with 10 percent of K_2O. Calculated using equation (7-1), $\sigma_{38}^{36} = 2$ percent, and total $Ar_A^{40} = 3 \times 10^{-11}$ mole.

blende or plagioclase. Sanidine typically contains less atmospheric Ar^{40} than other minerals, especially when treated with HF. Most of the sanidine samples shown in Figure 10-18 were so treated. Basalt usually has less atmospheric Ar^{40} than hornblende, biotite, or plagioclase. In addition, basalts may exhibit regional differences. For example, basalts from Nunivak Island and the Pribilof Islands, Alaska, are generally "cleaner" than basalts from Hawaii.

For dating very young rocks, it is desirable to have material that is both high in potassium and naturally low in atmospheric argon. Hornblende and plagioclase can be used for rocks a half-million or so years old under ideal conditions, but their low potassium contents preclude their use for much younger rocks. Potassium contents of typical pyroxenes are so low that their use is precluded even on rocks as young as middle Tertiary. In spite of its high potassium content, biotite is generally not useful below about 1 to 2 million years because of its naturally high content of atmospheric argon. Whole-rock samples (including obsidians) can sometimes be used for ages as low as 10^5 years under favorable conditions. The most satisfactory mineral for dating very young rocks is sanidine because of its high potassium content and its naturally low content of atmospheric argon, which can be reduced still further by using the HF treatment discussed on p. 189.

Figure 10-19 shows the estimated precision for potassium-argon age measurements on young sanidine samples of various ages. The curve was calculated from equation (7-1) for a 20-gram sample with 10 percent K_2O using a value of 2 percent for σ_{38}^{36} and a total atmospheric Ar^{40} contamination of 3×10^{-11} mole, which is a realistic figure for sanidine under moderately good experimental conditions. From the curve it is evident that it should be possible to date 10,000-year-old sanidine with a standard deviation of precision of about ± 20 percent. In a recent test of this hypothesis, Dalrymple (1968) determined potassium-argon ages for a series of rhyolite domes in

TABLE 10-4

Potassium-argon ages of some Holocene rhyolites of the Mono and Inyo Craters, California. The measurements were made on sanidine samples with K_2O contents of about 11 percent. The $\pm$ figures are estimated standard deviations of analytical precision. Determinations made on samples with less than 5 percent radiogenic argon are not shown in the table. The broken horizontal lines separate measurements on single rhyolite domes.

Sample no.	Radiogenic Ar^{40} (percent)	K-Ar age (years)	Ionium age (years)
5G201	24.4	$7,700 \pm 400$	
	9.3	$6,900 \pm 1,000$	$1,000 \pm 3,000$
6G005	8.4	$8,700 \pm 1,400$	
5G202	6.4	$6,800 \pm 1,400$	
	7.0	$6,100 \pm 1,200$	
5G203	5.0	$6,800 \pm 2,000$	$1,800 \pm 2,000$
5G204	6.1	$6,900 \pm 1,600$	
	6.3	$6,300 \pm 1,400$	
6G006	5.7	$11,500 \pm 2,900$	
	7.1	$9,000 \pm 1,800$	
6G016	12.3	$8,200 \pm 900$	$4,700 \pm 2,500$
	10.0	$10,400 \pm 1,400$	
6G017	5.1	$8,400 \pm 2,400$	$10,500 \pm 1,800$
	11.6	$9,100 \pm 1,000$	

Source: Dalrymple (1968). Ionium ages from Taddeucci and others (1968).

eastern California and obtained the results shown in Table 10-4. In general, the agreement between replicate determinations and the internal consistency of the results are, as a whole, encouraging. Furthermore, the measured ages agree relatively well with ionium ages measured by Taddeucci and others (1968) on the same samples. It is difficult to evaluate the accuracy of such young ages because very small amounts of extraneous Ar^{40} could have a considerable influence on the results. Even so, the experiment did demonstrate that potassium-argon dating of rocks on the order of 10^3 to 10^4 years old is analytically feasible.

11

PUTTING THE CLOCK TO WORK

A frequent problem for the geochronologist and for the geologist who uses geochronologic data is the evaluation of ages. It is always desirable to be able to make some judgment about the quality and "reasonableness" of a radiometric age rather than to accept it on face value. For any single date whose validity cannot be checked against other geological or geophysical evidence, there is always a finite probability, although small, that it might be wrong by as much as several orders of magnitude. For a date of 100 million years with an estimated error of ± 5 million years at the two-thirds confidence level, there is, statistically, 1 chance out of 20 that the age could be off by 10 million years, and 1 chance out of 333 that the age could be off by 15 million years. This all depends, of course, on the assumption that the errors are distributed normally and that the estimated error is approximately correct. Because geologic systems are imperfect and the measurements are difficult, the odds that a single age determination is wrong by some unspeci-fied amount should never be discounted completely unless there is some independent evidence to substantiate the age. This is one very good reason why single, isolated measurements are of limited value.

EVALUATION OF AGE DATA

There are three ways in which age data may be evaluated, all of which rely to some extent upon subjective judgments. Data may be compared directly with independent physical evidence from the same unit, they may be compared with physical evidence from stratigraphically related units, or they may be compared, by inference, with indirectly related evidence. The relative power of these different tests will be discussed briefly.

Direct Comparison with Other Radiometric Ages

Concordance of ages determined with different decay schemes on the same unit is usually good evidence that the ages are correct. This type of comparison essentially eliminates large analytical errors. In most situations it also decreases the likelihood of errors due to unrecognized geologic factors. For example, it is improbable that reheating will affect the daughter products of two decay schemes in such a way as to give concordant ages, particularly if the two ages are determined from different minerals. It is possible, however, to get concordant but incorrect rubidium-strontium and potassium-argon ages from biotite, because strontium and argon seem to show similar diffusion behavior in biotite under some conditions (see, for example, Figs. 9-11 and 9-12).

Concordance of potassium-argon ages determined for two different minerals from the same rock also constitutes powerful evidence that the ages are correct. Very few minerals respond in exactly the same way to geologic conditions that are capable of affecting potassium-argon dates, because the loss of argon, in general, proceeds at different rates in different minerals for any given set of conditions.

Duplicate determinations made on the same mineral concentrate minimize any serious analytical errors in either determination but do not rule out errors due to such geologic factors as reheating. A slightly stronger comparison would be one between two dates determined from the same mineral but from different samples of the rock. This not only minimizes analytical errors, but also guards against sampling and labeling errors as well as any source of error that might be introduced at the time of mineral separation, such as contamination from the crushing equipment.

Direct Comparison with Fossils

Agreement between an age determination and a fossil or fossil assemblage from the same unit is a positive evaluation of both the fossil age assignment and the radiometric age. For any given geologic situation an evaluation must usually be made to decide whether the radiometric dating method or the fossils possess better resolution—the capability of distinguishing between geologic events that are closely spaced in time.

Stratigraphic Sequence

If the potassium-argon ages of a group of rocks agree with the stratigraphic sequence determined on the basis of physical relationships or fossil evidence, then the probability is good that the radiometric ages are reliable. An example of this are the data in Table 7-7. For single age measurements of units that either overlie or underlie beds containing fossils, the fossil evidence only places an upper or lower limit on the age determination.

Inference

In this category we place any evaluations that involve lithologic correlations, as well as correlations with tectonic events thought to have taken place in the area. We also include what may best be termed "geologic accordance"— the degree to which the radiometric age agrees with the overall geologic field relationships. The evaluation of a radiometric age on the basis of geologic accordance is almost entirely subjective and should be done only in the absence of any other means of evaluating the age.

Lithologic correlations over either great or small distances generally do not form a sound basis for evaluating radiometric dates. Rather, dating is often used to test the validity of such correlations. Some dated units, however, can be correlated reasonably with a unit of known age elsewhere, and when this can be done the correlation serves at least as a partial test of the validity of the age determination.

Correlation of a dated unit with a tectonic event can sometimes give useful information about whether the date is reasonable. For example, if an age determination is made on a rock that is thought to have formed during the Laramide orogeny, then one should expect to get a "Laramide date." As a rule, however, this type of comparison is not a good way to evaluate an age determination, because the chance for error is often greater in the correlation than in the age measurement.

In Precambrian terranes the absence of other time-stratigraphic evidence has led to the use of radiometric ages as a means of correlating metamorphic and igneous events. But because the possibility that mineral ages have been affected by subsequent heating events is much greater for Precambrian rocks than for younger rocks, correlations involving radiometric ages should be made with caution and, ideally, should be based on a geologically accordant array of ages measured for different minerals using different decay schemes.

TABLE 11-1

Checklist of possible causes of apparently anomalous potassium-argon ages. Improbable mechanisms are in parentheses.

Random errors (ages appear either too old or too young)	Ages appear too young	Ages appear too old
Analytical error	Unsatisfactory material	Excess Ar^{40}
Incorrect geologic age assignment	Post-formation heating	Inherited Ar^{40}
Faulty sampling	Alteration or weathering	(Potassium loss)
Mislabeled sample	(Potassium gain)	

POSSIBLE CAUSES OF ANOMALOUS AGES

When age determinations do not agree with other evidence, it is usually desirable to pinpoint the cause. This is not always possible, but often some of the hypothesized causes can be eliminated either because steps have been taken to minimize the probability that they will affect the age determination or because the history of the sample rules them out. In the discussion that follows, "anomalous age" means an age determination that appears obviously discordant; the term does not apply to an age that is influenced by the small random errors that affect analytical accuracy and precision as discussed in Chapter 7.

Most of the possible causes of apparently anomalous ages are listed in Table 11-1 and discussed below. This outline can serve as a checklist for tracking down possible sources of discrepant data. Note that some of these causes are not directly related to the potassium-argon method, but are due either to human error or to incomplete knowledge of the history of the sample. The latter is the most common cause of apparently anomalous potassium-argon ages. If evidence of a past geologic event or process goes undetected when the sample is collected or is not well enough understood to be minimized by appropriate precautionary measures, then anomalous ages can be expected. But human error accounts for its share of anomalies, simply because the determination of a potassium-argon age is such a technically complicated process. There is always a chance of incorrect measurements unless precautions, such as making duplicate determinations, have been taken to reveal them. Most of the causes of anomalous ages, summarized below, have been discussed and illustrated in Chapters 7, 8, and 9, which present the subjects of precision and accuracy, extraneous Ar^{40}, and argon loss in more detail.

Random Errors

Random errors can lead to an apparent age that seems either too old or too young when compared with other evidence. Essentially, all random errors fall into the category of human error—mistakes made during collection, preparation, or analysis of the sample.

Analytical Error in the Age Determination   Mistakes made in the analytical procedure are usually detected before the age is calculated. For example, if an investigator realizes that he forgot to close a high-vacuum valve during the argon extraction, he can repeat the analysis. But occasionally a mistake will slip by unnoticed, and the result will be an age that is incorrect. One way to avoid this sort of error is to do all measurements in duplicate, and this is often done. Another form of safeguard is to measure ages of several minerals from the same rock and rely on concordant results to provide a check on the measurements as well as on the post-formation history of the rock sample. (See Chapters 5 and 6 for descriptions of the procedures for analyzing argon and measuring potassium.)

Incorrect Geologic or Paleontologic Age Assignment   When a potassium-argon age does not agree with geologic or paleontologic evidence, it is not necessarily the age determination that is at fault. Often the conflict is due to an incorrect correlation or paleontologic age assignment.

Faulty Sampling   Probably an unnecessarily large percentage of the conflicts between potassium-argon ages and other geologic evidence is due to incorrect sampling procedures. For this reason, it is not wise to rely at all upon correlations or upon the boulder that has rolled down the hill from the outcrop. Samples for dating should be collected from the outcrop of interest. An example of confusion caused by faulty sampling is given on pages 208–213.

Mislabeled Sample   It is easy to mislabel samples, especially when they are continually being relabeled as they progress from the field through the laboratory. This probably happens more often than one would like to admit and the only remedy is extra care.

Ages That Seem Too Young

Ages that seem too young are usually attributable to geologic conditions that have caused argon loss and to lack of knowledge about the argon retention of the materials involved. Such ages can often be avoided if the available knowledge and experience are used wisely.

Unsuitable (*nonretentive*) *Sample Material*   Some minerals generally give reliable potassium-argon ages, but others do not. The relative retentivity of most of the common rock-forming minerals is known, and there is no reason to use unsuitable material. If there is any doubt about the argon retention properties of a sample, it is unwise to use it until it has been thoroughly tested. (See Chapter 10 for a discussion of the suitability of various minerals and rocks for potassium-argon dating.)

Post-formation Heating   Reheating of a rock after its initial crystallization results in the loss of argon from most minerals, and this loss results in ages that are too young. Because most minerals lose argon at quite different rates, post-formation heating events can usually be detected by measuring the ages of different minerals from the same rock. Biotite and hornblende are a convenient mineral pair for this purpose because hornblende is extremely retentive whereas biotite loses argon rather easily. Concordance of potassium-argon ages on coexisting hornblende and biotite is almost a sure indication that partial argon loss has not occurred since the rock formed. Measuring the age of the same mineral by two different techniques is another check for argon loss, but it is not always foolproof. For example, strontium and argon can be lost from biotite at nearly the same rate, and the potassium-argon and rubidium-strontium ages would be concordant but incorrect. (See Chapter 9 for a discussion of the effects of post-formation heating events on potassium-argon ages.)

Alteration   Both alteration and weathering break down the mineral lattice and cause partial or complete loss of argon. Usually alteration can be recognized in hand specimen or thin section, and the sample can be discarded before any analytical work is started.

Potassium Gain   It is very probable that any geologic conditions that would lead to a net gain in potassium also would cause considerable disruption of the mineral lattice and give the sample the appearance of having been altered. It is also likely that the process of potassium gain would be accompanied by considerable loss of argon from the mineral. Potassium gain is a very improbable cause of anomalous ages.

Ages That Seem Too Old

Excess Ar^{40} Any excess Ar^{40} is radiogenic Ar^{40} that is incorporated into the mineral lattice during or after formation of the rock. There are a number of well-documented examples of excess Ar^{40}, and there can be no doubt that it occurs, although infrequently. For a more complete discussion of this, see Chapter 8.

Inherited (*contamination*) Ar⁴⁰   Inherited (contamination) Ar⁴⁰ is due to contamination by older inclusions. This is most serious in younger rocks but the effect depends on the amount, composition, and age of the contamination as well as on the age of the sample (Fig. 8-7). Inherited (contamination) Ar⁴⁰ is a serious and continual problem in dating ash-flow tuffs because of their turbulent emplacement. Older contaminating material also can be introduced into a sample at the time of crushing and mineral separation if care is not taken. Inherited Ar⁴⁰ is discussed more completely in Chapter 8.

Potassium Loss   As with potassium gain (see comments above), potassium loss would probably result from some form of alteration that would be recognizable and would also cause argon loss. One laboratory study of potassium loss by base exchange showed that potassium loss was equally accompanied by argon loss. Up to 80 percent of the potassium was removed from the biotite without affecting the potassium-argon age (see p. 51 and Fig. 4-4); beyond 80 percent potassium loss the calculated age decreased. Potassium loss is a possible but improbable cause of ages that are older than the emplacement age.

EXAMPLES OF POTASSIUM-ARGON DATING STUDIES

The remainder of this chapter will be devoted to seven examples, selected to show both the kinds of problems that potassium-argon dating can help to solve and some of the troubles that are frequently encountered. These examples are not just abstracts of the work, but are descriptions of specific phases of important research studies. A special effort has been made to point out the faults as well as the merits of each study. It should be emphasized that they are all the result of cooperation between investigators in different disciplines, and are not just the work of a geochronologist dating rocks. Without this cooperation, the importance of the results would have been greatly diminished. In addition, all were rather complete and large-scale studies. It is rare that a single isolated age determination by itself yields truly important results.

Zinjanthropus

The discovery, by Dr. and Mrs. Louis S. B. Leakey in 1959, of fossil hominid remains of great antiquity at Olduvai Gorge, Tanzania, was one of the most exciting archeological finds of modern times. The remains were closely associated with volcanic deposits that were dated by J. F. Evernden and

G. H. Curtis of the University of California, Berkeley, using the potassium-argon method. A brief summary of this important research and the controversy that surrounded the initial results will serve to illustrate three important points: (1) the use of potassium-argon dating to determine, more or less directly, the age of important fossil material and of young volcanic rocks; (2) the importance of a correct geologic framework, in this case a carefully established stratigraphy, for geochronological studies; and (3) the necessity for selecting samples carefully.

Olduvai Gorge, in equatorial East Africa, cuts through Pleistocene beds that consist of interbedded volcanic flows and tuffs and continental sedimentary deposits. The sequence has been divided into five units called, from oldest to youngest, Beds I through V. Beds I and II contain some of the oldest known hominid remains and an extensive sequence of Paleolithic artifacts and living sites that apparently were concentrated along the shores of a perennial alkaline-saline lake.

In 1959, Dr. and Mrs. Leakey discovered a fossil hominid skull, which they called *Zinjanthropus boisei*, associated with Stone Age culture material in Bed I (Leakey, 1959). This was followed a year later by the excavation of still older remains of a pre-*Zinjanthropus* child, which were found approximately 2 feet stratigraphically below *Zinjanthropus* (Leakey, 1961). Fortunately, these important finds were closely associated with material that could be dated by the potassium-argon method, for Bed I consists largely of trachytic pyroclastic deposits and flows of trachyandesite and basalt.

From the associated faunal assemblage, it was known that *Zinjanthropus* was probably early Pleistocene. Preliminary potassium-argon age determinations by J. F. Evernden and G. H. Curtis (Leakey and others, 1961) led them to the conclusion that the fossils were about 1.75 million years old—an age far older than had been suspected, for the Pleistocene was then thought to be only about 1 million years long. They had determined ages ranging from 1.57 to 1.89 million years for anorthoclase separated from the series of tuffs most closely associated with the hominid remains, and ages on biotite and plagioclase ranging from 1.02 to 1.38 million years for samples collected near the top of Bed I.

The controversy concerning the correct age of *Zinjanthropus* arose primarily over two points. First, von Koenigswald and others (1961) determined potassium-argon ages of 1.3 million years for the basalt near the base of Bed I and ages of 2.25 and 1.67 million years for two basalt pebble tools supposedly from Bed I. These data seemed to conflict with the older age of about 1.75 million years for the overlying hominid-bearing tuffs. Second, the ages determined by Evernden and Curtis for Bed I* indicated that Bed I

---

*These early debates concerned only the part of Bed I above the basalt flows. Hay (1963) later redefined Bed I to include the basalts and some of the underlying deposits.

was formed during a period of 0.7 million years or more, whereas the pale-ontological and geological evidence suggested a much shorter interval of formation.

The controversy concerning the length of time represented by Bed I was resolved when careful stratigraphic studies by Hay (1963, 1967a, 1967b) revealed that the sample that gave the younger age of 1.02 million years and was first reported by Leakey and others (1961) to have come from the top of Bed I almost certainly came from a sample of Bed V, which locally unconformably overlies Bed II. The sample that gave the age of 1.38 million years was found to have come from a level well below the top of Bed I, and upon redating gave an age of 1.57 million years. This eliminated the apparently long interval of formation for Bed I.

The controversy over the age of the basalt was not so easily resolved. The entire problem was mostly due to the fact that the samples of the basalt flows were highly weathered, altered, and extremely fine-grained (Leakey and others, 1962), and thus were unsuitable for dating. In response to the basalt dates of von Koenigswald and his colleagues, Curtis and Evernden determined potassium-argon ages for two additional basalt specimens from the Olduvai flows. These gave ages of 1.7 and 4.0 to 4.4 million years, which Curtis and Evernden considered to be minimum ages because of the unsuitable nature of the material. Thus, early ages on the basalt, all apparently on unsuitable material, ranged from 1.3 to more than 4 million years. To add to the confusion, the pebble tools dated by von Koenigswald and his colleagues could have come from any of Beds I through IV (Leakey and others, 1962), and therefore their ages were largely irrelevant to the problem.

Since the time of these early controversies, Evernden and Curtis (1965a) have published the results of an extensive program of potassium-argon dating of the volcanic material with which the hominids of Olduvai Gorge are associated. Their work, combined with the stratigraphic studies of Hay and the archeologic work of Leakey, has established without question that *Zinjanthropus* and the other associated hominid remains in Bed I are about 1.75 million years old. The stratigraphy of part of Bed I, as reconstructed by Hay (Grommé and Hay, 1967), is presented in Figure 11-1 along with the age determinations most closely related to the *Zinjanthropus* site. All determinations on samples from tuff beds were made on anorthoclase except for KA1047 and KA1088, which were made on plagioclase. Sample KA1047 came from 12 inches above *Zinjanthropus*, KA850 from only 1 inch above the living floor (KA1051 is a repeat determination), and KA1180 from 81 inches below. Samples KA1043, KA1053, KA1057, KA1058, and KA1179 are from an unwelded ignimbrite that is stratigraphically above a related hominid site. Determinations for samples KA924A, KA966, and KA1039 are considered unreliable by Evernden and Curtis (1965a) because of subsequent improvements in their analytical technique.

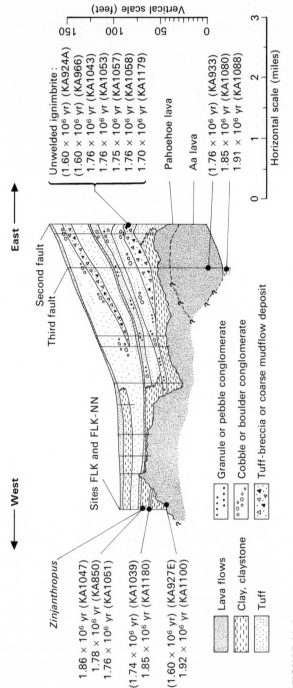

FIGURE 11-1
Stratigraphy of Bed I, Olduvai Gorge, Tanzania, showing the locations of the fossil hominid
Zinjanthropus and of radiometrically dated samples. Vertical lines indicate positions of measured
sections. The sequence is reconstructed as it would have appeared at the end of Bed I time. Ages
in parentheses are considered unreliable by Evernden and Curtis (1965a). [After C. S. Grommé and
R. L. Hay, Earth Planet. Sci. Letters, v. 2, p. 111-115, 1967.]

The age of the basalt near the bottom of Bed I is now firmly established as approximately 1.85 million years by the dates of about 1.75 million years for samples above the basalt and of 1.85 and 1.91 million years for samples below it (KA1080, KA1088). But efforts to date the basalt directly have proved largely futile. Determinations of 1.6 to more than 4 million years have been discarded by Evernden and Curtis (1965a) as unreliable because of technical problems and the unsuitability of the basalt for dating. The one measurement considered by them to be reliable (KA1100, 1.92 million years) was made on a sample that was treated with HF and HCl to remove altered material and glass. Because this procedure has not been adequately tested, it is difficult to see why this age should be considered any better than the others. The controversy over the age of the basalt clearly illustrates the futility of trying to obtain reliable ages on unsuitable material. It should be mentioned that these basalts are the original basis for the Olduvai normal polarity event (see Fig. 11-2).

One of the most serious problems encountered by Evernden and Curtis in dating the Olduvai sequence was that of contamination, for much of the material has been reworked by streams. Evidence of detrital components and of redeposition by fluvial action eventually led Evernden and Curtis to discard a large proportion of their age measurements because of the possibility that they had been made on contaminated samples. This left them open to the criticism, whether justified or not, that some of the ages had been discarded on the basis of the results rather than on some more objective criteria (for example, see the *Current Anthropology Comments* appended to the paper by Evernden and Curtis, 1965a). This criticism could have been avoided if both the reworked and the obviously contaminated samples had been rejected *before* they were dated.

In summary, the dating of *Zinjanthropus* is an extremely important piece of research that involved close cooperation by scientists in several disciplines. The results indicate conclusively that man as a tool-making animal is at least 1.75 million years old. This age has been confirmed independently by a fission-track date of 2.03 ± 0.28 million years on pumice from Bed I (Fleischer and others, 1965). Many of the problems that arose with this work could have been minimized and perhaps avoided completely if Hay's stratigraphy had been available earlier and if more care had been used in selecting material for dating.

Age of Mineralization at Marysvale, Utah

Knowing the age of mineralization relative to the ages of other geologic units can be a valuable aid in the exploration for new mineral resources. In spite of this, relatively little has been published concerning the use of potassium-argon dating in this type of research. One of the few published

TABLE 11-2

Potassium-argon ages from Marysvale, Utah (Bassett and others, 1963). Units are listed in stratigraphic order. Brackets enclose samples from the same flow.

Unit	Sample no.	Material	No. of determinations	Calculated age (10^6 years) K-Ar	Calculated age (10^6 years) U-Pb
Mineralization	—	uraninite	1		13
	KA60	sericite	2	13.5	
Mount Belknap Rhyolite	⎡KA28	glass	2	19.5	
	⎣KA29	glass	1	20.0	
	KA31	glass	2	15.6	
	KA34	glass	3	13.7	
	KA14	glass	2	17.8	
	KA15	glass	2	19.0	
Glassy dikes and diatremes	KA20	glass	3	22.0	
		biotite	2	19.1	
	KA12	glass	3	14.2	
		biotite	4	21.0	
Quartz monzonite	KA2	biotite	3	23.6	
	KA11	biotite	2	26.0	
	KA17	biotite	2	24.3	
Bullion Canyon Volcanics	KA7	sanidine	2	29.5	

accounts is that of Bassett and others (1963), which concerns the age of the mineralization in the Marysvale area of Utah. This example shows the way in which potassium-argon dating can be used to determine the age of mineralization, and that minimum ages, in this case on volcanic glass, can sometimes be useful.

The Marysvale area comprises volcanic and intrusive rocks of post-Oligocene, pre-Pleistocene age that rest on a basement of Paleozoic to Mesozoic sedimentary rocks. The three principal units are, from oldest to youngest, the Bullion Canyon Volcanics, quartz monzonite and related granitic rocks, and the Mount Belknap Rhyolite. Glassy dikes and diatremes in the area petrographically resemble the Mount Belknap Rhyolite, but their contemporaniety is not certain from geologic evidence. Uranium mineralization occurs along the margins of the intrusive masses, and lead-zinc-silver ore (with traces of uranium), associated with hydrothermal alteration along fractures, occurs in Paleozoic sedimentary rocks. The relative ages of the two types of mineralization apparently were not known before the dating studies.

Bassett and his co-workers made potassium-argon measurements on samples of sanidine, biotite, glass, and sericite and obtained the results shown in Table 11-2. Several points are clear from these determinations. First, the potassium-argon ages are consistent with the known stratigraphy. The Bullion Canyon Volcanics give the oldest ages, the granitic intrusive rocks are slightly younger, and the Mount Belknap Rhyolite gives still younger ages. Potassium-argon ages determined from sericite are concordant with uranium-lead ages determined from uraninite and are younger than the ages of rocks cut by the mineralization. Second, some of the ages on glass are low relative to ages on coexisting biotite and on other glass samples from the same unit. Bassett and others (1963) used coexisting biotite and glass from two samples to test the applicability of the potassium-argon method to volcanic glass. They found that the glass in sample KA12, which is extensively altered, gave an age that was low relative to the biotite age whereas the unaltered glass in KA20 gave a more reasonable age. For the glass samples from the Mount Belknap Rhyolite, Bassett and his co-workers found that KA31 and KA34, which were highly altered, gave the lowest ages and that unaltered samples (KA28 and KA29) gave the highest. The remaining two samples (KA14 and KA15), which were only mildly altered, gave ages slightly younger than the unaltered ones. From these data they concluded that the variation of the apparent ages was a function of alteration, that the most probable age of the Mount Belknap Rhyolite was approximately 20 million years, and that the Mount Belknap flows and the diatremes were correlative.

Because the criteria for selecting reliable volcanic glasses for dating have not been developed and because apparently unaltered glasses can give ages that are too low (see Chapter 10, p. 176), the ages on the Mount Belknap Rhyolite should all be considered minimum ages. The maximum permissible age of these rocks is limited by the underlying quartz monzonite. Thus the age of the Mount Belknap flows is bracketed between about 20 million years and 25 million years. Furthermore, the presence of an erosional hiatus between the intrusive rocks and the Mount Belknap Rhyolite suggests that these two units are not the same age. Therefore, even though the glass ages probably should be interpreted as minimum ages, the conclusion of Bassett and others (1963) that the Mount Belknap flows are approximately 20 million years old is still valid. Note that the concordance of the ages of the older glass from the Mount Belknap flows and the biotite from the glassy dikes and diatremes is by itself insufficient evidence for their correlation, because the reliability of the glass is uncertain.

Finally, another interesting result to come from this work is that the age determined from sample KA11, in which the biotite is extensively altered, agrees well with the ages determined from the two unaltered samples. This is another example of the observation that altered and weathered biotites often give reasonable results (p. 51).

Geomagnetic Reversals

The proof of the hypothesis that the earth's magnetic field has undergone reversals in polarity, together with the development of a potassium-argon time-scale for these geomagnetic reversals, constitutes one of the most exciting and important developments in modern geophysics. Shortly after the publication of early versions of this time-scale, these reversals were found recorded in the magnetic anomalies of the sea floor (see, for example, Vine, 1966, or a recent review by Heirtzler and others, 1968), which gave new impetus to the theory of sea-floor spreading and ultimately led to new ways of looking at global tectonics (see, for example, Isacks and others, 1968). Reversals also have been found recorded in deep-sea sediments (see the recent paper by Glass and others, 1967), thereby providing a means for worldwide correlation of Pleistocene marine sequences. The development of the time-scale for geomagnetic reversals is a good example of (1) the use of the potassium-argon method to test a geophysical hypothesis and to date worldwide events connected with the earth's interior, (2) the importance of proper sampling procedures, and (3) the necessity to evaluate data and to take into account the resolution of the dating method. Reviews of the reversal problem are given by Cox and others (1964b, 1967) and McDougall and Chamalaun (1966). The most recent compilation of data and references is that of Cox and others (1968).

When igneous rocks solidify and the magnetic minerals cool through their Curie point, they become magnetized in the direction of the earth's field; exceptions to this are rare. This magnetism, although very weak, is extremely stable, and its direction can be measured easily to within a few degrees. Because the earth's magnetic field is a global phenomenon and is more or less symmetrical, it is possible to calculate the ancient position of the north and south magnetic poles from this magnetic direction. Thus most igneous rocks retain a record of the nature of the magnetic field at the time and place the rock was formed, provided, of course, that the rock has not been reheated or altered.

In 1906, the French physicist Bernard Brunhes discovered that some lava flows in France were magnetized in a direction exactly opposite to the present field. From this he concluded that the earth's field in France must have been reversed in times past. This hypothesis went unchallenged, and largely unnoticed, until about 1950, when John Graham, then of the Carnegie Institution of Washington, proposed that reversed magnetism in rocks might not be due to reversals of the earth's magnetic field but instead be due to a property of the rock itself. Louis Néel, a French physicist, soon discovered several ways in which rocks theoretically might acquire a magnetism that was opposite to the ambient field, and shortly thereafter S. Uyeda and T. Nagata of the University of Tokyo discovered a volcanic rock that was reproducibly self-reversing. Thus by the mid-1950s there had evolved two hypotheses to explain reversed magnetism in rocks; the field-reversal hypothesis, which attributed reversed magnetism to worldwide reversals of the earth's magnetic field, and the self-reversal hypothesis, which attributed it to a property of certain rocks.

One way to resolve this problem was to determine both the polarity and the ages of a large number of lava flows of diverse composition from different localities around the world. If the self-reversal hypothesis was valid, then the polarity of rocks should show no correlation with their age. If, on the other hand, the field reversal hypothesis was valid, then normal and reversed rocks should fall into definite time intervals, and a valuable by-product of the experiment would be a time-scale of the reversals. This approach was followed vigorously, primarily by two research groups—Allan Cox, Richard R. Doell, and G. Brent Dalrymple of the U.S. Geological Survey in Menlo Park, California, and Ian McDougall, D. H. Tarling, and F. H. Chamalaun of the Australian National University in Canberra. The eventual results are shown in Figure 11-2, which are worldwide data from a recent compilation by Cox and others (1968). As can be seen from the figure, rocks with normal and reversed magnetic directions fall into definite time groupings, thereby confirming field reversal. Times during which the field was predominantly of one polarity are called geomagnetic polarity epochs and are named for scientists who have made significant contributions to geomagnetic field studies. Within these epochs are shorter intervals, during which the field returned briefly to the opposite polarity. These shorter intervals are called polarity events and are named for the locality at which they were first discovered.

During its early development, the reversal time-scale underwent numerous modifications, most of which were necessitated by new data. At least one modification, however, is the result of a conflict that arose because of careless sampling procedures. The first reversal time-scale based on potassium-argon ages was proposed by Cox and others (1963a) in June of 1963 and was based on only nine data. Four months later, two additional time-scales were published almost simultaneously, one by McDougall and Tarling (1963) and another by Cox and others (1963b) (Fig. 11-3). The time-scale of Mc-Dougall and Tarling was based on a total of 21 data and that of Cox and his colleagues on 20 data. Of these, each had the previously published 9 data in common. The two scales were not in agreement, especially concerning the age of the second reversal boundary. It was soon discovered that two of the data used by Cox and his co-workers were incorrect because the units studied had been carelessly sampled (Cox and others, 1964a). The samples for potassium-argon dating were collected by Dalrymple, and the samples for paleomagnetic study were collected by Cox and Doell at a later date. Because of an inadequate description of a sample location (inadequate only

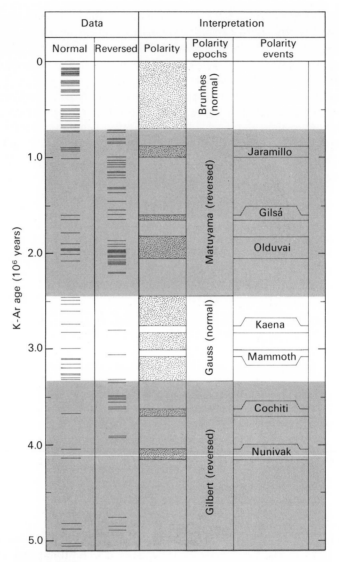

FIGURE 11-2

Time-scale geomagnetic reversals. Stippled areas in center column indicate normal field polarity; unstippled areas, reversed field polarity. [Data from a compilation by Cox and others (1968).]

by about 5 to 6 feet!) and an incorrect (but reasonable) geologic correlation, the dated samples and the magnetic samples were collected from different flows! Once these errors were cleared up and some new data were made available, the true picture of geomagnetic reversals began to emerge, and future modifications were mainly due to the appearance of new data and the realization that the reversal time scale was complicated by the existence of short events.

From the conflict described above came the realization that if unnecessary confusion was to be minimized, the data used to define the time-scale would have to meet some criteria for reliability. As a result, the following minimum standards were developed (Doell and others, 1966; McDougall and Chamalaun, 1966; Cox and Dalrymple, 1967): (1) the samples used for dating and magnetic study must come from the same rock unit, (2) laboratory tests must confirm the stability of magnetization, (3) the standard deviation of the age determination must be ≤ 0.1 million years for rocks less than 2.0 million years old and ≤ 5 percent for older rocks, and (4) the material used for dating must be a reliable potassium-argon geochronometer. At present, there are nearly 200 data that satisfy these criteria and these data are the basis for the time-scale shown in Figure 11-2. It is worth mentioning that the majority of the ages are on whole-rock basalts. No doubt additional data will call for further revisions, but they will probably be minor, for most of the unreliable data have already been weeded out.

Finally, it would be of interest if the reversal time-scale could be extended back in time beyond 5 million years, but two questions arise: (1) does the

FIGURE 11-3
Early versions of the time-scale of geomagnetic reversals by (a) Cox and others (1963b), and (b) McDougall and Tarling (1963). The conflict over the reversal boundary placed at 1.8 million years by Cox and others and at 2.5 million years by McDougall and Tarling was due partly to careless sampling by Cox and others (1963b).

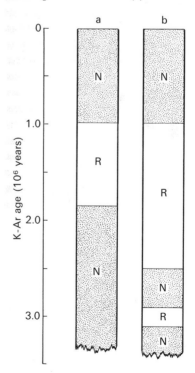

potassium-argon method have sufficient resolution to do this considering the length of the epochs and events, and (2) could it be done with a reasonable amount of data? Unfortunately, the answer to both of these questions is negative. Cox and Dalrymple (1967) have shown statistically that at present potassium-argon dating does not have the resolution required to identify events much beyond about 5 to 6 million years. This is illustrated by Figure 11-4, which shows the decreasing ability of potassium-argon dating to

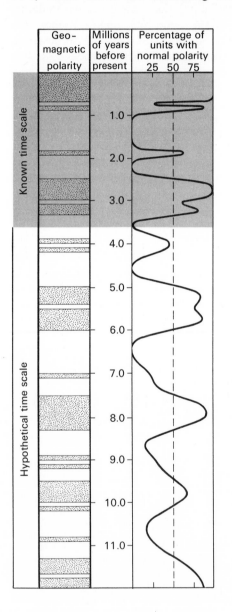

FIGURE 11-4

Percentage of samples that would have normal polarity as a function of their potassium-argon ages, assuming a dating precision of 3 percent standard deviation and an infinite sample density. The left-hand column shows the assumed polarity of the magnetic field (stippled is normal, unstippled is reversed). The polarities earlier than 3.6 million years are entirely hypothetical and are intended only to show the loss of resolving power of the potassium-argon method with increase in age of samples. [After G. B. Dalrymple, A. Cox, R. R. Doell, and C. S. Grommé, Earth Planet. Sci. Letters, v. 2, p. 163-173, 1967. Based on the probability model of Cox and Dalrymple (1967).]

resolve epoch boundaries and events with increasing age. For example, an error of 3 percent corresponds to an error of 0.3 million years for rocks that are 10 million years old—an error that is larger than the duration of polarity events. Even epoch boundaries would be difficult to identify much beyond 5 to 6 million years ago unless an impractically large number of data were available. An empirical test of this prediction has proven the difficulty involved in working with older polarity data. In spite of the availability of more than 40 new late Miocene and Pliocene polarity data, Dalrymple and others (1967) were able to identify only two polarity features more than 5 million years old; these were reversal boundaries that could be identified only because datable rocks of opposite polarity occurred in stratigraphic succession. This illustrates the importance of a quantitative approach to the questions of precision and resolving power of the dating method. To have ignored this approach might have resulted in years of pointless data gathering.

Provenance of Triassic Sedimentary Rocks

As with many other physical properties, the radiometric age of detrital components can be used as an indicator of provenance. The use of potassium-argon data as an aid in determining the source of detritus is based on the simple principle that the apparent age of a detrital mineral will be equal to or less than the age of the oldest source rock. Although very little use has been made of potassium-argon dating in such applications, it will probably become more and more important in the future. Therefore, it will be worthwhile to describe briefly the results of an important and careful study by F. J. Fitch (Birkbeck College), J. A. Miller (University of Cambridge), and D. B. Thompson (University of Manchester) that concerns the use of potassium-argon ages of detrital micas as indicators of the provenance of some Triassic sedimentary rocks from the Stockport-Macclesfield district, Cheshire, England.

The rocks studied by Fitch and his co-workers (Fitch and others, 1966) are primarily micaceous sandstones, siltstones, and shales of the Bunter and Keuper groups, each of which is divided into several formations:

> Keuper Group
> Keuper Marl
> Keuper Waterstones
> Lower Keuper Sandstone
>
> Bunter Group
> Bunter Upper Mottled Sandstone
> Bunter Pebble Beds
> Manchester Marls
> Collyhurst Sandstone
> Lower Mottled Sandstones

These continental fluvial deposits are part of a succession that was formed by infilling of the Cheshire Basin during Permian and Triassic times. The Bunter and Keuper Groups are Triassic on the basis of fossil evidence. Samples for study were collected from boreholes and from outcrops of the two uppermost formations of the Bunter Group and the two lowermost formations of the Keuper Group. Both biotite and muscovite were separated from mica-rich horizons and used for the potassium-argon measurements.

As Fitch and others (1966) point out, it is not possible to evaluate satisfactorily the results from potassium-argon studies of detrital minerals without carefully evaluating (1) the accuracy of the geological age of the sedimentary deposits; (2) the adequacy of the sampling; and (3) the possible extent of argon loss due to weathering, erosion, sedimentation processes, and post-depositional events. It is, of course, also necessary to have adequate information about the potassium-argon ages of minerals from all of the possible source areas. In critically evaluating these factors for their investigation, they conclude briefly (1) that close contemporaneity of the deposits studied (and, presumably, the fossil evidence) cannot be absolutely assured because of the nature of fluvial continental deposits; (2) that it would have been advantageous to obtain a more complete set of samples, which means that a final stratigraphic analysis would require further sampling; and (3) that some argon loss, largely due to diagenesis, could be expected, especially in the biotites.

Fitch and his colleagues plotted their biotite and muscovite data from the Keuper and Bunter Groups on histograms* and discussed the value of such an approach. First, this technique makes it possible to evaluate the statistical spread of apparent potassium-argon ages in the source area. Second, by plotting the biotite and muscovite ages separately, it is possible to evaluate the extent of argon loss, because muscovite is somewhat more resistant to argon loss than biotite. For example, sharp single modes indicate a homogeneous source area (that is, homogeneous insofar as the potassium-argon ages are concerned), whereas a more diffuse distribution suggests an inhomogeneous source. If the biotite and muscovite modes do not coincide, it could mean either that argon loss has occurred in one of the minerals (biotite would be the more likely of the two to lose argon) or that the biotite and muscovite come from rocks of different ages. In addition, the use of histograms or frequency-distribution curves allows data from different areas to be compared easily. Note that the choice of an appropriate class interval is important if the histograms are to have any meaning. If the class interval is too large, the data will tend to cluster into an artificial and probably misleading mode. On the other hand, the interval should not be smaller

---

*Actually, they used "frequency polygons" or "frequency distribution curves," but they referred to them as histograms.

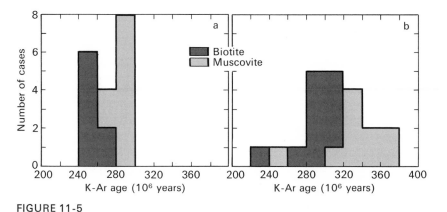

FIGURE 11-5

Histograms showing potassium-argon ages of detrital micas from the Bunter (a) and Keuper (b) groups (Triassic). [Data from Fitch and others (1966).]

than the resolution of the method (see the last part of Chapter 7), otherwise differences that are unreal may appear. For these data a class interval of about 20 million years seems appropriate. Fitch and others (1966) appear to have used a class interval of 10 million years, which at 300 million years implies a resolution that is probably optimistic.

Histograms of the Keuper and Bunter mica ages are shown in Figure 11-5. From these data Fitch and others (1966) were able to draw several important conclusions. First, the Bunter micas were derived from a homogeneous source area, whereas the source area for the Keuper micas was probably somewhat heterogeneous. Second, the source area of the Bunter micas was composed of crystalline rocks with mica ages in the range of 280 to 300 million years, the biotites having lost a small amount of argon, as was expected. These workers then compared their results with mica ages from the seven possible source areas and, by a process of elimination, concluded that the Bunter sediments had to come from the south via a river that drained the Variscan mountains of France and southern Britain. The most likely source of the Keuper micas is thought by them to include the Bunter source as well as older crystalline rocks and local sources. Their conclusions agree with petrographic evidence of provenance and permit a considerably firmer conclusion than was previously possible.

There are several important points about the study of Fitch and his co-workers that are worth emphasizing. First, they were extremely careful to evaluate all of the factors that might influence the validity of their conclusions and were quick to point out the shortcomings as well as the merits of their study. Second, their study did not consist of simply a few age measurements but of more than forty determinations on two different minerals.

In addition, their data were used to supplement, not replace, other evidence of provenance, particularly petrographic studies. Finally, they chose for study a compact area in which there was some realistic chance of arriving at a solution. All in all, their study was well designed and is a good example of a new and potentially important use of potassium-argon dating.

Dating the Sierra Nevada Batholith

A large number of age determinations have been made on minerals from granitic plutons. This is natural because the age of plutonism is vital information in the geologic analysis of an area, and only on rare occasions are plutonic rocks bracketed by stratified deposits that provide adequate fossil data. The application of potassium-argon dating to plutonic rocks, however, is not always straightforward. As discussed in Chapter 4, the potassium-argon clock is an accumulation clock, and in the complex evolution of a large batholith many factors may cause the clock to read incorrect geologic time. The results of combined field studies and radiometric dating of the Sierra Nevada batholith of California provide a good example of both the power and the weakness of potassium-argon dating of plutonic rocks.

The geology of the Sierra Nevada has been studied for more than a hundred years, but F. C. Calkins' mapping in the Yosemite region during the period 1913–1915 was the first attempt to distinguish the various intrusive bodies that constitute the batholith on the basis of relative ages determined from field relations (Calkins, 1930). Subsequent field studies, including the early results of a major investigation by the U.S. Geological Survey aimed at synthesizing the structure and history of the Sierra Nevada batholith, have been summarized by Bateman and others (1963). We will discuss here only some of the evidence concerning the age of emplacement of the batholith.

The Sierra Nevada batholith has been assigned a Jurassic or Cretaceous age on the basis of geologic relations (Bateman and others, 1963). In the western foothills of the Sierra Nevada, Upper Cretaceous strata unconformably overlie the Upper Jurassic strata that are intruded by the batholith. Granitic rocks in the eastern part of the Sierra Nevada intrude Lower Jurassic strata, and in the Inyo Mountains, which are east of the Sierra Nevada, granitic rocks intrude Middle Triassic strata.

The first systematic attempt to determine the age of the Sierra Nevada batholith using radioactive dating methods was by G. H. Curtis, J. F. Evernden, and Joseph Lipson of the University of California, Berkeley, who used the potassium-argon method (Curtis and others, 1958). They measured ages on biotite from granitic rocks in the western foothills and in the central part of the batholith in the vicinity of Yosemite National Park. They deter-

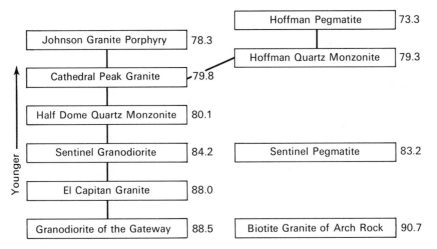

FIGURE 11-6

Intrusive sequence in the Yosemite region according to Calkins (1930) and R. L. Rose (Univ. California, Berkeley, Ph.D. thesis, 1957). Relative ages from field relationships are shown by solid lines connecting the boxes. Potassium-argon ages of biotite, in millions of years, are recalculated from the data of Curtis and others (1958) using the decay constants in Appendix A. Subsequent work has shown that many of these ages are too young because of reheating by the younger intrusions.

mined ages ranging from 124.2 to 136.2 million years* for samples from individual plutons in the western foothills, and ages ranging from 73.3 to 90.7 million years for a suite of plutonic rocks in the Yosemite region. The intrusive sequence in the Yosemite area, determined from field relations, is shown in Figure 11-6 together with these early potassium-argon ages. The agreement between the potassium-argon ages and the intrusive sequence is remarkable.

These Yosemite data pose two important questions: Is the agreement between the geologic evidence and the potassium-argon ages fortuitous? Do the potassium-argon ages indicate the time of crystallization of individual plutons, or do the ages represent some time subsequent to crystallization?

McIntyre (1963), in an evaluation of the precision of the Yosemite data, made some pertinent points about the first question; in particular he said that the precision of the potassium-argon ages was not good enough to claim that the method measured the age of crystallization of individual plutons. Curtis and others (1958) gave no estimate of precision for their data, but in another paper (Evernden and others, 1957) they stated that their analytical technique had an inherent probable error of less than 1.5 percent. It is not

*We have recalculated the ages reported by Curtis and other (1958) using the decay constants given in Appendix A.

clear whether this error was meant to apply to both the potassium and argon data or only to the argon data. They also stated that replicate determinations substantiated the error estimate, but the data were not reported. In spite of these unknown factors, let us assume that the results of Curtis and others (1958) have a probable error of 1.5 percent, which is equivalent to a standard deviation of 2.2 percent for a single age determination. Then we can apply the critical value test (page 120) to decide whether the apparent age differences represent real differences in the potassium-argon ages. Using equation (7-3) for single potassium-argon age determinations on each rock with $\sigma_1 = \sigma_2 = 2.2$ percent, then the critical value for 95-percent confidence is 6.1 percent, or 4.9 and 5.5 million years for rocks 80 and 90 million years old, respectively. Thus it is not possible to claim, with 95-percent confidence, that any real age difference was detected between many of the Yosemite plutons. In his evaluation, McIntyre (1963) concluded that there was a 70-percent probability that the range of potassium-argon ages obtained for the Yosemite rocks is due to random analytical errors; that is, the agreement between potassium-argon ages and intrusive sequence is fortuitous. But McIntyre, lacking reliable published data on reproducibility, estimated the precision (σ) of a potassium-argon determination as 10 percent, which is certainly too large (see Chapter 7). We can now say, on the basis of much more information on precision that was available to McIntyre, that there is a real difference in apparent potassium-argon age between the oldest and youngest rocks in the Yosemite region, but that the remarkable correlation between intrusive sequence and calculated potassium-argon ages is probably largely accidental.

In answer to the second question, whether the apparent potassium-argon ages indicated the time of crystallization of individual plutons, we can say that many of the ages do not. Subsequent dating studies of larger portions of the batholith have demonstrated that reheating of older plutons has occurred. Recall that Curtis and others (1958) used only micas, mostly biotite, for their age measurements, and that at the time of their study the serious problem of argon loss from biotite under conditions of reheating was not appreciated fully. The proximity of some of the older Yosemite plutons to the younger central core of the batholith suggests that some of the measured ages on the older rocks are much younger than the actual age of crystallization.

The next systematic potassium-argon dating in the Sierra Nevada batholith was done by R. W. Kistler, P. C. Bateman, and W. W. Brannock of the U.S. Geological Survey, who measured ages on a series of plutons in a belt across the batholith south of the Yosemite region (Kistler and others, 1965). The found that granitic rocks in the central Sierra Nevada are characterized by concordant ages on coexisting biotite and hornblende, and that the plutons that flank this central core on the east and on the west, and which are older on the basis of field relations, yield discordant mineral ages—the apparent ages of hornblende are greater than those of biotite. Kistler and others (1965) interpreted this pattern of discordant mineral ages as the result of reheating (see Chapter 9) produced by intrusion of the younger plutons of the central core.

Several hundred potassium-argon ages have now been measured on granitic rocks of the Sierra Nevada batholith, and the picture is beginning to unfold. Kistler and others (1965) showed that some of the rocks along the east side are as old as Early Jurassic. McKee and Nash (1967) reported a potassium-argon age of 213 million years (Triassic) for a pluton in the Inyo Mountains. Plutons of Jurassic or Cretaceous age are present in the western foothills of the Sierra Nevada, and the central core of the batholith contains rocks as young as Late Cretaceous. Thus, it is now apparent that the intrusion of the younger plutons has caused reheating of the older plutons. This, in many cases, has resulted in argon loss from the older rocks and has produced hybrid ages, of the type shown in Figure 4-2, that do not represent rock-forming events. For example, it is now known that the potassium-argon biotite ages of 78 to 80 million years obtained by Curtis and others (1958) for the Johnson Granite Porphyry and the Cathedral Peak Granite represent approximate crystallization ages, but the ages of 88 million years for the El Capitan Granite and the Biotite Granite of Arch Rock probably are too young by more than 50 percent because of reheating by the later intrusions. For a detailed discussion of the geochronology of the Sierra Nevada batholith the reader is referred to the paper by Evernden and Kistler (in press).

The Sierra Nevada studies show that the intrusive history of a large batholith can be worked out using detailed field relationships and a large number of age determinations. They also make apparent that a few isolated age measurements on plutonic bodies may be of little value or, even worse, may provide misleading information. Patterns of discordant mineral ages may not make it easy to determine the age of emplacement of individual plutons, but these discordant patterns may instead provide even more valuable information on geologic processes, such as cooling history.

Dating the Precambrian of Arizona

The dating of Precambrian rocks was a major objective of potassium-argon measurements during the early development of the method. It was natural to concentrate on the Precambrian, which constitutes nearly 90 percent of earth history, because in the absence of fossils radiometric dating methods could possibly make significant contributions to Precambrian history. Unfortunately, this early concentration on Precambrian problems had some serious disadvantages, because the dating methods were then in the initial stages of development and because metamorphic rocks are among the most complicated rock systems. It was found that some minerals—for example, feldspars—could not be expected to retain all of their argon over a period of 10^9 years (see Fig. 10-2). Subsequent work also showed that later metamorphic events, some of which were not recognized easily, could cause partial or complete loss of radiogenic argon from minerals, biotite in particular. Both of these factors result in potassium-argon ages that are too young, and commonly this is the situation in areas that have been affected by multiple heating or metamorphic events.

The prospect of getting meaningful potassium-argon ages from Precambrian terranes is not as gloomy as the potential problems outlined above might indicate. In fact, potassium-argon ages agree well with ages determined by other dating methods in regions that have had simple geologic histories. Even in regions that have had complex histories potassium-argon ages are very valuable in outlining problems as well as supplementing other dating methods. Investigations of the Precambrian of the southwestern United States provide a good example of the application of potassium-argon dating, in combination with geologic studies and other dating methods, to Precambrian problems.

In the far southwestern United States, particularly in Arizona, geologists for many years have assigned Precambrian rocks to two informal age groups, older Precambrian and younger Precambrian. "Older" Precambrian has been used in a provincial sense to distinguish the metamorphic and plutonic rocks of Precambrian age from the presumably "younger" Precambrian nonmetamorphosed sedimentary sequences that were deposited on the older basement complex. A major period of deformation and metamorphism of the older Precambrian rocks, accompanied by intrusion of large volumes of granitic rocks, occurred before the younger Precambrian rocks were deposited. This major period of metamorphism and intrusion was named the Mazatzal Revolution by E. D. Wilson on the basis of his studies in central Arizona (Wilson, 1939). This terminology was subsequently extended by geologists far beyond the area Wilson studied, even though it is not possible, on the basis of field relationships, to prove whether metamorphism and intrusion occurred at the same time throughout the region. The extended use of both the concept and the term "Mazatzal Revolution" led to significant disagreement among geologists and geochronologists working in the far southwestern United States, and it has taken some ten years since the first measurement of radiometric ages in the region to sort out the confusion. Why does confusion arise from terminology and nomenclature? We have seen that careless sampling resulted, at one time, in conflicting time scales for geomagnetic reversals (see p. 208). In the geochronologic studies of the Arizona Precambrian, three factors contributed to the general confusion: (1) incomplete sampling of a complex metamorphic terrane, (2) differences in the behavior of minerals and isotope systems in response to post-formation metamorphism, and (3) preconceived ideas, based at least in part on nomenclature, about the geologic environment of the region.

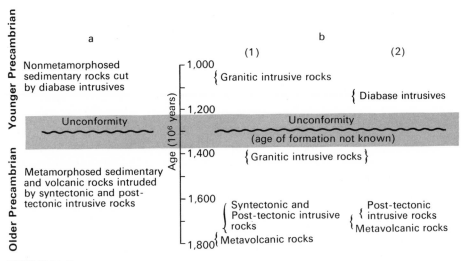

FIGURE 11-7

(a) Highly generalized stratigraphic relations of Precambrian rocks of Arizona before any isotopic ages were measured. (b) Current status of stratigraphic relations and time-scale of Precambrian rocks of (1) northern Arizona and southern Nevada, and (2) southern Arizona. [Data from Wasserburg and Lanphere (1965), Silver (1967, 1968), and Livingston and Damon (1968).]

Geology, perhaps more than most sciences, requires a good deal of nomen-clature and classification in order to handle the vast amount of descriptive information so a certain amount of confusion really is not surprising.

The first isotopic ages determined in the region were potassium-argon and rubidium-strontium ages of mica from pegmatites and granitic rocks. These ages were measured by L. T. Aldrich, G. W. Wetherill, and G. L. Davis of the Carnegie Institution of Washington. They suggested a period of intrusion of granite plutons approximately 1,350 million years ago in Arizona, New Mexico, Colorado, and Wyoming (Aldrich and others, 1957). Giletti and Damon (1961), who measured additional ages on micas from granitic rocks and relatively older metamorphic rocks in northwestern Arizona, correlated this "1,350 million-year orogeny" with the Mazatzal Revolution of Wilson. Subsequent work has shown that neither of these studies was really detailed enough to determine whether the measured ages defined a rock-forming event or reflected a later disturbance that affected older rocks. The pattern of measured ages suggested that the latter possibility was true in some areas.

The next development resulted from studies of the older Precambrian of eastern California, where several workers employing potassium-argon, rubidium-strontium, and isotopic uranium-lead dating methods showed that the basement complex contains metamorphic and intrusive rocks 1,600 to 1,800 million years old and intrusive rocks 1,400 million years old (see review by Wasserburg and Lanphere, 1965). The obvious questions, then, were, did these same age groups also occur further east in Arizona and adjacent states, and did the 1,350 million-year orogeny of Giletti and Damon in Arizona really represent a thermal disturbance rather than a true rock-forming event? As a result of information developed by many workers using all available dating methods, the answer to both questions is, in general, "Yes," though a much more complex Precambrian history has now been documented. Effort has been concentrated in Arizona because there the Precambrian is extensively exposed and contains a large variety of rock types. The current status of the stratigraphic relations and the time-scale of the Precambrian rocks of Arizona are shown in Figure 11-7, where they are compared with the stratigraphic relations known before any isotopic ages were measured.

It should be noted in Figure 11-7 that there were three distinct periods of granitic plutonism in Arizona during the Precambrian. Confusion about the use of the term "Mazatzal Revolution" was caused largely by disagreement over whether the revolution is characterized by granitic rocks intruded about 1,400 million years ago or by those intruded about 1,700 million years ago. In studies of the type area in the Mazatzal Mountains, Silver (1967) measured isotopic uranium-lead ages of 1,650 million years on post-tectonic granitic rocks. This means that the Mazatzal Revolution of Wilson corresponds to the oldest rock-forming event shown in Figure 11-7.

One might ask, how much did potassium-argon dating contribute to our knowledge of the Precambrian of the Southwest? In some of the other examples of early potassium-argon studies, the ages were low because of argon loss during post-formation heating events. In the Southwest, however, potassium-argon ages for hornblende from metamorphic and igneous rocks and for muscovite from pegmatites have nearly always proved reliable. In contrast, both potassium-argon and rubidium-strontium ages on biotite were commonly low. In summary, all of the major Precambrian events in Arizona can be documented using only potassium-argon ages, particularly those on hornblende, but the Precambrian time-scale shown in Figure 11-7 represents the integrated effort of several investigators who, collectively, used all of the available dating methods. There is no question that the various isotopic uranium-thorium-lead methods have been more successful in enabling geologists to look back through the overprint of post-formation metamorphic events than either the potassium-argon or rubidium-strontium methods. Uranium-lead isotopic analyses of zircon have enabled L. T. Silver and his colleagues from the California Institute of Technology to develop a fine structure of Precambrian history in Arizona that would not have been possible by means of other dating methods.

We have discussed the problems inherent in applying the potassium-argon method to Precambrian metamorphic rocks, but these problems are not limited only to Precambrian rocks. The same problems occur in regions that have been affected by metamorphic events of any age. The potassium-argon clock is an accumulation clock, and any metamorphic event that affects the region can cause loss of radiogenic argon and result in incorrect measurements of geologic time.

Geologic Time-scale

Time has been one of the fundamental considerations in studies of the earth since geology became a science. During the eighteenth and nineteenth centuries time-scales for geologic events were constructed on the basis of stratigraphic and paleontologic evidence. Standard geologic columns that gave the relative order of geologic events were produced in this way, but no quantitative measurement of elapsed time was possible. The next stage in geochronology was the development of "hour-glass" methods, which depend upon measuring the cumulative effect of a geological process whose rate is known. The two most common hour-glass methods were based on the increase in salinity of the oceans and on the rate of accumulation of sediments. These hour-glass methods are crude approximations at best, but they provided the first reasonably objective time-scales.

To illustrate the problems inherent in hour-glass methods, it is interesting to compare the assumptions made in using the sedimentation method with those made in potassium-argon dating (see Chapter 4) or other radiometric dating techniques. Only rarely can the rate of sedimentation be estimated directly, such as in annual varves. Generally, the maximum thickness of sediments deposited during a given interval of geologic time is used to determine the sedimentation rate. This leads to immediate trouble because the length of the time interval is uncertain. In addition to this difficulty, the approach has other obvious disadvantages. First, the rate of sedimentation must be constant; second, there must be no breaks during the accumulation of sediments; and third, all of the sedimentary record must be preserved. These three assumptions are similar in kind to those made in radioactive dating (constant decay, no daughter loss, and so forth), but since they are almost certainly never met completely in sedimentation, no quantitative time-scale can be developed using this approach. Nevertheless, cumulative maximum thicknesses of sedimentary rocks have been valuable in interpolating between radiometric control points, particularly in the time-scales developed early in the twentieth century.

Only with the development of radioactive dating methods did it become possible to construct a truly quantitative geologic time-scale, and even this approach is not as simple as it may seem at first because it requires a critical evaluation of the analytical accuracy and stratigraphic relevance of each datum. The history of attempts to establish a quantitative time-scale were reviewed recently by L. R. Wager (1964), so we will not attempt to recount them here. It is instructive, however, to note how many ages were used to construct these time-scales and which dating methods were used.

In 1913 Arthur Holmes proposed the first time-scale based on radiometric data. Holmes used one uranium-helium age and three uranium-lead ages in this first time-scale. In 1937 Holmes proposed another time-scale, this one based on 18 uranium-helium ages and 12 uranium-lead ages. Ten years later Holmes published a time-scale for Phanerozoic (post-Precambrian) time using only five selected uranium-thorium-lead ages. These five were among the first isotopic ages available and were a significant improvement over the chemical ages used in his previous time-scales. Unfortunately, the stratigraphic position of three of the ages is somewhat ambiguous, and it has since been shown that one of the remaining samples has not been a closed geochemical system since crystallization. Nevertheless, the 1947 time-scale of Holmes was very valuable and was used for many years.

The development of the potassium-argon and rubidium-strontium dating methods led to a rapid accumulation of radiometric ages in the 1950's, and these enabled Holmes (1960) and J. L. Kulp (1961) to publish new geologic time-scales. The relative explosion in the amount of available radiometric ages has made it possible to utilize a large amount of data in the most recent time-scales. A group of Russian scientists headed by G. D. Afanassyev published a time-scale in 1964 based on 222 age determinations—14 rubidium-strontium ages, 37 uranium-thorium-lead ages, and 171 potassium-argon ages. Also in 1964, at a symposium dedicated to Arthur Holmes, a time-scale based on 337 age determinations was published (Harland and others, 1964). Of these ages, 286 were determined using the potassium-argon method, 27 using the rubidium-strontium method, and 24 using seven other methods, principally uranium-lead methods. This time-scale is shown in Figure 11-8.

Thus far we have discussed only time-scales for the Paleozoic, Mesozoic, and Cenozoic eras, which together constitute Phanerozoic time. What about the Precambrian, which constitutes nearly 90 percent of the time that has elapsed since the earth was formed? The purpose of a quantitative time-scale is to place units of time on a scale that defines the relative order of events as well as their age. Such a time-order scale, applicable to the entire Earth, has been established for Phanerozoic time based on the progressive development and correlation of plants and animals. No world-wide order of events has been established for Precambrian time because, in the absence or scarcity of fossils upon which to base long-range correlations, it has not been possible to correlate local sequences. Although radioactive ages have been instrumental in enabling geologists to decipher the complex history of regions of Precambrian rocks, the subdivision of Precambrian time has been strictly arbitrary, and no scheme for a satisfactory worldwide time-scale for the Precambrian has been agreed upon. This is why no geologic periods are shown in Figure 11-8 for the Precambrian.

The most detailed quantitative time-scale is the one for the Cenozoic Era, the Tertiary and Quaternary Periods, which constitutes the interval of time between the present and about 65 million years ago. A large number of age determinations are available, and almost all of these are potassium-argon ages. In an extensive study, J. F. Evernden, D. E. Savage, G. H. Curtis, and G. T. James, all of the University of California at Berkeley, were able to develop a Cenozoic time-scale relating the sequence of fossil mammals in North America to the potassium-argon ages of interbedded volcanic rocks (Evernden and others, 1964). It has been rather difficult, however, to relate this land-mammal time-scale to the Tertiary marine sequences upon which the classic geologic time-scale is based. Moreover, the relative scarcity of datable material has made it more difficult to date the marine sequences directly. On the basis of potassium-argon dating, Turner (in press) recently assigned radiometric ages to the boundaries between four Pacific Coast Miocene foraminiferal stages. Additional progress is being made on the

FIGURE 11-8

Geologic time-scale based on data compiled at the 1964 symposium held in honor of the late Arthur Holmes (Harland and others, 1964).

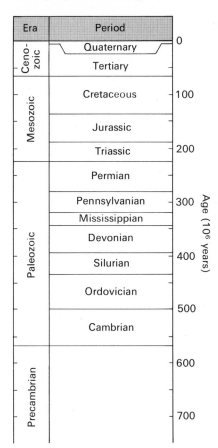

construction of a quantitative time-scale for the marine Cenozoic, and when this is done it should be possible to correlate the land-mammal and marine time-scales.

Before an age determination is used for time-scale purposes, three factors must be evaluated critically: (1) the precision and accuracy of the analyses, (2) the condition of the system—that is, whether the mineral or rock sample has remained a closed system to parent-daughter gain or loss since crystallization of the rock, and (3) the exact stratigraphic position of the dated sample. The first factor generally is not troublesome. Nevertheless, it is important to note that although an analytical uncertainty of 3 percent has only a small effect on the age of late Tertiary samples, it would amount to about one-third of the length of a typical geologic period for a 500-million-year-old sample. In order to evaluate the other two factors, a great deal of experience and expert judgment is required. In particular, the third criterion is essential to a successful time-scale. Ideally, the material dated should occur in the same geologic unit as the fossils that determine the stratigraphic age. Fossiliferous strata containing glauconite would be ideal, except that, as noted in Chapter 10, glauconite loses argon easily and often does not give reliable ages. Intrusive igneous rocks generally provide good material for dating, but intrusive rocks are seldom bracketed closely enough by fossiliferous units to allow assignment of a precise stratigraphic age. Lava flows and volcanic ash beds that either contain fossils or are interbedded with fossiliferous strata are probably the best kinds of material for time-scale work.

In summary, geological time-scales are dynamic, not static documents. The ages of many of the boundaries between geologic periods are not well established, and, as new data are acquired, the ages of these boundaries will be revised. For example, data acquired since the Phanerozoic time-scale (Fig. 11-8) was compiled in 1964 suggest that the ages assigned to the Devonian-Mississippian, Silurian-Devonian, Triassic-Jurassic, and Tertiary-Quaternary boundaries should be revised. This evolution can be expected to continue as the radiometric and stratigraphic data are further refined. Because of its wide applicability, potassium-argon dating research will continue to contribute greatly to future time-scales.

REFERENCES CITED

Abbey, S., and Maxwell, J. A., 1960, Determination of potassium in micas, a flame photometric study: Chemistry in Canada, v. 12, p. 37-41.

Aldrich, L. T., Davis, G. L., and James, H. L., 1965, Ages of minerals from metamorphic and igneous rocks near Iron Mountain, Michigan: Jour. Petrology, v. 6, p. 445-472.

Aldrich, L. T., and Nier, A. O., 1948a, Argon 40 in potassium minerals: Phys. Rev., v. 74, p. 876-877.

Aldrich, L. T., and Nier, A. O., 1948b, The occurrence of He^3 in natural sources of helium: Phys. Rev., v. 74, p. 1590-1594.

Aldrich, L. T., and Wetherill, G. W., 1958, Geochronology by radioactive decay: Ann. Rev. Nuclear Sci., v. 8, p. 257-298.

Aldrich, L. T., Wetherill, G. W., and Davis, G. L., 1957, Occurrence of 1350 million-year-old granitic rocks in western United States: Geol. Soc. America Bull., v. 68, p. 655-656.

Aller, L. H., 1961, *The Abundance of the Elements:* New York, Interscience Publishers, Inc., 283 p.

Allsopp, H. L., 1965, Rb-Sr and K-Ar age measurements on the Great Dyke of Southern Rhodesia: Jour. Geophys. Research, v. 70, p. 977-984.

Alpert, D., and Buritz, R. S., 1954, Ultra-High Vacuum. II. Limiting factors on the attainment of very low pressures: Jour. Applied Physics, v. 25, p. 202-209.

Amirkhanoff, K. I., Brandt, S. B., and Bartnitsky, E. N., 1961, Radiogenic argon in minerals and its migration: Annals N. Y. Acad. Sci., v. 91, p. 235-275.

Armstrong, R. L., 1966, K-Ar dating using neutron activation for Ar analysis: granitic plutons of the eastern Great Basin, Nevada and Utah: Geochim. et Cosmochim. Acta, v. 30, p. 565-600.

Aston, F. W., 1919, A positive ray spectrograph: Phil. Mag., ser. 6, v. 38, p. 707-714.

Aston, F. W. 1920a, The constitution of atmospheric neon: Phil. Mag., ser. 6, v. 39, p. 449-455.

Aston, F. W., 1920b, The mass-spectra of chemical elements: Phil. Mag., ser. 6, v. 39, p. 611-625.

Aston, F. W., 1921, The mass spectra of the alkali metals: Phil. Mag., ser. 6, v. 42, p. 436-441.

Aston, F. W., 1923, Atomic weights and isotopes: Smithsonian Inst. Rept. for 1921, Pub. 2679, p. 181-196.

Bainbridge, K. T., Goldhaber, M., and Wilson, E., 1951, Influence of the chemical state on the lifetime of an isomer: Phys. Rev., v. 84, p. 1260-1261.

Baksi, A. K., York, D., and Watkins, N. D., 1967, Age of the Steens Mountain geomagnetic polarity transition: Jour. Geophys. Research, v. 72, p. 6299-6308.

Bassett, W. A., Kerr, P. F., Schaeffer, O. A., and Stoenner, R. W., 1963, Potassium-argon dating of the late Tertiary volcanic rocks and mineralization of Marysvale, Utah: Geol. Soc. America Bull., v. 74, p. 213-220.

Bateman, P. C., Clark, L. D., Huber, N. K., Moore, J. G., and Rinehart, C. D., 1963, The Sierra Nevada batholith, a synthesis of recent work across the central part: U.S. Geol. Survey Prof. Paper 414-D, p. D1-D46.

Bieri, R. H., and Koide, Minoru, 1967, Valve for precise pipetting of small amounts of gases: Rev. Sci. Instruments, v. 38, p. 1159-1160.

Bleakney, Walker, 1930, Ionization potentials and probabilities for the formation of multiply charged ions in helium, neon and argon: Phys. Rev., v. 36, p. 1303-1308.

Boato, G., Careri, G., and Santangelo, M., 1952, Argon isotopes in natural gases: Nuovo Cimento, ser. 9, v. IX, p. 44-49.

Bogard, D., Burnett, D., Eberhardt, P., and Wasserburg, G. J., 1968, ^{40}Ar-^{40}K ages of silicate inclusions in iron meteorites: Earth Planet. Sci. Letters, v. 3, p. 275-283.

Bohr, N., 1913, On the constitution of atoms and molecules: Phil. Mag., ser. 6, v. 26, p. 1-25, 476-502, 857-875.

Boltwood, B. B., 1907, On the ultimate disintegration products of the radio-active elements. Part II. The disintegration products of uranium: Am. Jour. Sci., ser. 4, v. 23, p. 77-88.

Bramley, Arthur, 1937, The potassium-argon transformation: Science, v. 86, p. 424-425.

Brandt, S. B., Petrov, B. V., and Kriventsov, P. P., 1966, Migration of radiogenic argon from sylvinite under the influence of stress: Geokhimiya, no. 11, p. 1365.

Brew, D. A., and Muffler, L. J. P., 1965, Upper Triassic undevitrified volcanic glass from Hound Island, Keku Strait, Southeastern Alaska: U.S. Geol. Survey Prof. Paper 525-C, p. C38-C43.

Brewer, A. K., 1935, Further evidence for the existence of K^{40}: Phys. Rev., v. 48, p. 640.

Brewer, A. K., 1938, Isotopes of potassium: Ind. and Eng. Chemistry, v. 30, p. 893-896.

Browning, J. S., 1961, Heavy liquids and procedures for laboratory separation of minerals: U.S. Bur. Mines Inf. Circ. 8007, 14 p.

Burnett, D. S., Lippolt, H. J., and Wasserburg, G. J., 1966, The relative isotopic abundance of K^{40} in terrestrial and meteoritic samples: Jour. Geophys. Research, v. 71, p. 1249-1269.

Calkins, F. C., 1930, The granitic rocks of the Yosemite region, p. 120-129 *in*

Matthes, F. E., Geological history of the Yosemite Valley: U.S. Geol. Survey Prof. Paper 160, 137 p.

Campbell, N. R., 1908, The radioactivity of potassium, with special reference to solutions of its salts: Proc. Cambridge Phil. Soc., v. 14, p. 557-567.

Campbell, N. R., and Wood, Alexander, 1906, The radioactivity of the alkali metals: Proc. Cambridge Phil. Soc., v. 14, p. 15-21.

Carslaw, H. S., and Jaeger, J. C., 1959, *Conduction of Heat in Solids:* London, Oxford Univ. Press, 510 p.

Chadwick, J., 1932, The existence of a neutron: Proc. Roy. Soc. London, ser. A, v. 136, p. 692-708.

Cluley, H. J., 1955, The determination of potassium by precipitation as potassium tetraphenylboron and its application to silicate analysis: The Analyst, v. 80, p. 354-364.

Cook, Kenneth L., 1943, The relative abundance of the isotopes of potassium in Pacific kelps and in rocks of different geologic age: Phys. Rev., v. 64, p. 278-293.

Cooper, J. A., 1963, The flame photometric determination of potassium in geological materials used for potassium-argon dating: Geochim. et Cosmochim. Acta, v. 27, p. 525-546.

Cooper, J. A., Martin, I. D., and Vernon, M. J., 1966, Evaluation of rubidium and iron bias in flame photometric potassium determination for K-Ar dating: Geochim. et Cosmochim. Acta, v. 30, p. 197-205.

Cox, Allan, and Dalrymple, G. B., 1967, Statistical analysis of geomagnetic reversal data and the precision of potassium-argon dating: Jour. Geophys. Research, v. 72, no. 10, p. 2603-2614.

Cox, Allan, Dalrymple, G. B., and Doell, R. R., 1967, Reversals of the earth's magnetic field: Scientific American, v. 216, p. 44-54.

Cox, Allan, Doell, R. R., and Dalrymple, G. B., 1963a, Geomagnetic polarity epochs and Pleistocene geochronometry: Nature, v. 198, p. 1049-1051.

Cox, Allan, Doell, R. R., and Dalrymple, G. B., 1963b, Geomagnetic polarity epochs—Sierra Nevada II: Science, v. 142, p. 382-385.

Cox, Allan, Doell, R. R., and Dalrymple, G. B., 1964a, Geomagnetic polarity epochs: Science, v. 143, p. 351-352.

Cox, Allan, Doell, R. R., and Dalrymple, G. B., 1964b, Reversals of the earth's magnetic field: Science, v. 144, p. 1537-1543.

Cox, Allan, Doell, R. R., and Dalrymple, G. B., 1968, Radiometric time-scale for geomagnetic reversals: Quarterly Jour. Geol. Soc. London, v. 124, p. 53-66.

Crank, J., 1956, *The Mathematics of Diffusion:* London, Oxford Univ. Press, 347 p.

Curtis, G. H., 1966, The problem of contamination in obtaining accurate dates of young geologic rocks: p. 151-162 *in* Schaeffer, O. A., and Zahringer, J., eds., *Potassium-Argon Dating*, New York, Springer-Verlag, 234 p.

Curtis, G. H., Evernden, J. F., and Lipson, J., 1958, Age determination of some granitic rocks in California by the potassium-argon method: Calif. Div. Mines Sp. Rept. 54, 16 p.

Dalrymple, G. B., 1964a, Argon retention in a granitic xenolith from a Pleistocene basalt, Sierra Nevada, California: Nature, v. 201, p. 282.

Dalrymple, G. B., 1964b, Cenozoic chronology of the Sierra Nevada, California: Univ. Calif. Pub. in Geol. Sci., v. 47, p. 1-41.

Dalrymple, G. B., 1968, Potassium-argon ages of Recent rhyolites of the Mono and Inyo Craters, California: Earth Planet. Sci. Letters, v. 3, p. 289-298.

Dalrymple, G. B., 1969, ^{40}Ar/^{36}Ar analyses of historic lava flows: Earth Planet. Sci. Letters, v. 6, p. 47-55.

Dalrymple, G. B., Cox, Allan, and Doell, R. R., 1965, Potassium-argon age and paleomagnetism of the Bishop Tuff, California: Geol. Soc. America Bull., v. 76, p. 665-674.

Dalrymple, G. B., Cox, Allan, Doell, R. R., and Grommé, C. S., 1967, Pliocene geomagnetic polarity epochs: Earth Planet. Sci. Letters, v. 2, p. 163-173.

Dalrymple, G. B., and Hirooka, Kimio, 1965, Variation of potassium, argon, and calculated age in a late Cenozoic basalt: Jour. Geophys. Research, v. 70, p. 5291-5296.

Dalrymple, G. B., and Moore, J. G., 1968, Argon 40: Excess in submarine pillow basalts from Kilauea Volcano, Hawaii: Science, v. 161, p. 1132-1135.

Damon, P. E., ed., 1965, Correlation and chronology of ore deposits and volcanic rocks: Geochemical Section, Geochronology Laboratories, Univ. Arizona Ann. Prog. Rept. No. C00-689-50 to the Research Div., U.S.A.E.C. (various paging).

Damon, P. E., 1968, Potassium-argon dating of igneous and metamorphic rocks with applications to the basin ranges of Arizona and Sonora: p. 1-71 in Hamilton, E. I., and Farquhar, R. M., eds., Radiometric Dating for Geologists, New York, Interscience Publishers, Inc., 506 p.

Damon, P. E., and Kulp, J. L., 1957, Argon in mica and the age of the Beryl Mountain, New Hampshire, pegmatite: Am. Jour. Sci., v. 255, p. 697-704.

Damon, P. E., and Kulp, J. L., 1958, Excess helium and argon in beryl and other minerals: Am. Min., v. 43, p. 433-459.

Damon, P. E., Laughlin, A. W., and Percious, J. K., 1967, Problem of excess argon-40 in volcanic rocks: p. 463-481 in Radioactive Dating and Methods of Low-level Counting, Vienna, Internat. Atomic Energy Agency, 744 p.

Davidson, C. F., 1964, On diamantiferous diatremes: Econ. Geol., v. 59, p. 1368-1380.

Dean, R. S., and Davis, C. W., 1941, Magnetic separation of ores: U.S. Bur. Mines Bull. 425, 417 p.

Dempster, A. J., 1918, A new method of positive ray analysis: Phys. Rev., v. 11, p. 316-325.

Dobrosserdow, D., 1925, Einige Erwägungen über die Eigenschaften des Elementes Nr. 87, des Dwicäsiums (Dc = 224), und über die mögliche Ursache der Radio-aktivität von K und Rb: Jour. Chimique de l'Ukraine 1, S.491-497. (Abs. given in Phys. Ber. 7, p. 1414-1415, 1926.)

Doell, R. R., Dalrymple, G. B., and Cox, Allan, 1966, Geomagnetic polarity epochs—Sierra Nevada Data, 3: Jour. Geophys. Research, v. 71, p. 531-541.

Doell, R. R., Dalrymple, G. B., Smith, R. L., and Bailey, R. A., 1968, Paleomag-netism, potassium-argon ages and geology of volcanic rocks from the Valles Caldera, New Mexico: p. 211-248 in Coats, R. R., Hay, R. L., and Anderson, C. A., eds., Studies in Volcanology—A Memoir in Honor of Howell Williams, Geol. Soc. America Memoir 116, 678 p.

Duckworth, H. E., 1960, Mass Spectroscopy: Cambridge Univ. Press, 206 p.

Dushman, Saul, 1962, *Scientific Foundations of Vacuum Technique* (2nd ed.): J. M. Lafferty, ed., New York, John Wiley & Sons, Inc., 806 p.

Ellestad, R. B., and Horstman, E. L., 1955, Flame photometric determination of lithium in silicate rocks: Analytical Chemistry, v. 27, p. 1229-1231.

Engelkemeir, D. W., Flynn, K. F., and Glendenin, L. E., 1962, Positron emission in the decay of K^{40}: Phys. Rev., v. 126, p. 1818-1822.

Errock, G. A., 1965, Mass spectrometry design—magnetic deflexion instruments: p. 1-35 *in* Reed, R. I., ed., *Mass Spectrometry*, New York, Academic Press, 463 p.

Evernden, J. F., and Curtis, G. H., 1965a, Potassium-argon dating of late Cenozoic rocks in East Africa and Italy: Current Anthropology, v. 6, p. 343-385.

Evernden, J. F., and Curtis, G. H., 1965b, The present status of potassium-argon dating of Tertiary and Quarternary rocks: INQUA, Report of the VIth International Congress on Quaternary, Warsaw, 1961, v. 1, p. 643-651.

Evernden, J. F., Curtis, G. H., and Kistler, R. W., 1957, Potassium-argon dating of Pleistocene volcanics: Quaternaria, v. IV, p. 1-5.

Evernden, J. F., Curtis, G. H., Kistler, R. W., and Obradovich, J., 1960, Argon diffusion in glauconite, microcline, sanidine, leucite, and phlogopite: Am. Jour. Sci., v. 258, p. 583-604.

Evernden, J. F., Curtis, G. H., and Lipson, J., 1957, Potassium-argon dating of igneous rocks: Am. Assoc. Petroleum Geologists Bull., v. 41, p. 2120-2127.

Evernden, J. F., Curtis, G. H., Obradovich, J., and Kistler, R. W., 1961, On the evaluation of glauconite and illite for dating sedimentary rocks by the potassium-argon method: Geochim. et Cosmochim. Acta, v. 23, p. 78-99.

Evernden, J. F., and James, G. T., 1964, Potassium-argon dates and the Tertiary floras of North America: Am. Jour. Sci., v. 262, p. 945-974.

Evernden, J. F., and Kistler, R. W., Chronology of emplacement of Mesozoic batholiths in California and western Nevada: U.S. Geol. Survey Prof. Paper 623. (In press.)

Evernden, J. F., and Richards, J. R., 1962, Potassium-argon ages in eastern Australia: Jour. Geol. Soc. Australia, v. 9, p. 1-50.

Evernden, J. F., Savage, D. E., Curtis, G. H., and James, G. T., 1964, Potassium-argon dates and the Cenozoic mammalian chronology of North America: Am. Jour. Sci., v. 262, p. 145-198.

Farrar, E., Macintyre, R. M., York, D., and Kenyon, W. J., 1964, A simple mass spectrometer for the analysis of argon at ultra-high vacuum: Nature, v. 204, p. 531-533.

Faul, H., and Davis, G. L., 1959, Mineral separation with asymmetric vibrators: Am. Min., v. 44, p. 1076-1082.

Fechtig, H., Gentner, W., and Kalbitzer, S., 1961, Argonbestimmungen un Kaliummineralien—IX. Messungen zu den verschiedenen Arten der Argon diffusion: Geochim. et Cosmochim. Acta, v. 25, p. 297–311.

Fechtig, H., and Kalbitzer, S., 1966, The diffusion of argon in potassium-bearing solids: p. 68-107 *in* Schaeffer, O. A., and Zahringer, J., eds., *Potassium-Argon Dating*, New York, Springer-Verlag, 234 p.

Ferrara, G., Gonfiantini, R., and Pistoia, P., 1963, Isotopic composition of argon from steam jets of Tuscany: p. 267-275 *in* Tongiorgi, E., ed., *Nuclear Geology on Geothermal Areas*, Spoleto, Consiglio Nazionale della Ricerche Laboratorio di Geologia Nucleare, Pisa, 284 p.

Fitch, F. J., Miller, J. A., and Thompson, D. B., 1966, The palaeogeographic significance of isotopic age determinations on detrital micas from the Triassic of the Stockport-Macclesfield district, Cheshire, England: Palaeogeography, Palaeoclimatology, Palaeoecology, v. 2, p. 281-312.

Fleischer, R. L., Price, P. B., Walker, R. M., and Leakey, L. S. B., 1965, Fission-track dating of Bed I, Olduvai Gorge: Science, v. 148, p. 72-74.

Folinsbee, R. E., Baadsgaard, H., and Lipson, J., 1960, Potassium-argon time scale: 21st Internat. Geol. Cong., Copenhagen, 1960, Pt. III, p. 7-17.

Folinsbee, R. E., Baadsgaard, H., and Lipson, J., 1961, Potassium-argon dates of Upper Cretaceous ash falls, Alberta, Canada: Annals N.Y. Acad. Sci., v. 91, p. 352-363.

Frechen, J. von, and Lippolt, H. J., 1965, Kalium-Argon-Daten zum Alter des Laacher Vulkanismus, der Rheinterrassen und der Eiszeiten: Eiszeitalter und Gegenwart, v. 16, p. 5-30.

Funkhouser, J. G., 1966, The determination of a series of ages of a Hawaiian volcano by the potassium-argon method: Ph.D. Thesis, University of Hawaii, 168 p.

Fyfe, W. S., Lanphere, M. A., and Dalrymple, G. B., Experimental introduction of excess Ar^{40} into a granitic melt: Contrib. to Min. and Pet. (In press.)

Gentner, W., and Kley, W., 1957, Argon bestimmungen an Kaliummineralien—IV. Die Frage der Argonverluste in Kalifeldspaten und Glimmermineralien: Geochim. et Cosmochim. Acta, v. 12, p. 323-329.

Gerling, E. K., Ermolin, G. M., Baranovskaya, N. V., and Titov, N. E., 1952, First experience with the application of the argon method for the determination of the age of minerals: Doklady Akad. Nauk. S.S.S.R., v. 86, p. 593-596.

Gerling, E. K., Morozova, I. M., and Kurbatov, V. V., 1961, The retentivity of radiogenic argon in ground micas: Annals N.Y. Acad. Sci., v. 91, p. 227-234.

Giletti, B. J., and Damon, P. E., 1961, Rubidium-strontium ages of some basement rocks from Arizona and northwestern Mexico: Geol. Soc. America Bull., v. 72, p. 639-644.

Glass, B., Ericson, D. B., Heezen, B. C., Opdyke, N. D., and Glass, J. A., 1967, Geomagnetic reversals and Pleistocene chronology: Nature, v. 216, p. 437-442.

Goodman, Clark, and Evans, R. D., 1941, Age measurements by radioactivity: Geol. Soc. America Bull., v. 52, p. 491-544.

Grasty, R. L., and Miller, J. A., 1965, The omegatron: a useful tool for argon isotope investigation: Nature, v. 207, p. 1146-1148.

Grommé, C. S., and Hay, R. L., 1967, Geomagnetic polarity epochs: new data from Olduvai Gorge, Tanganyika: Earth Planet. Sci. Letters, v. 2, p. 111-115.

Hamilton, E. I., 1965, *Applied Geochronology:* New York, Academic Press, 267 p.

Hanson, G. N., and Gast, P. W., 1967, Kinetic studies in contact metamorphic zones: Geochim. et Cosmochim. Acta, v. 31, p. 1119-1153.

Hanson, G. N., and Himmelberg, G. R., 1967, Ages of mafic dikes near Granite Falls, Minnesota: Geol. Soc. America Bull., v. 78, p. 1429-1432.

Harland, W. B., Smith, A. G., and Wilcock, B., eds., 1964, *The Phanerozoic Time-scale:* Quarterly Jour. Geol. Soc. London, v. 120 S, 458 pp.

Harmon, R. S., and Greenwood, W. R., 1968, Mineral separation—techniques, processes, and applications. A selected bibliography, 1920-1968: Open file report, Lunar and Earth Sciences Division, NASA, Manned Spacecraft Center, Houston, Texas, 16 p.

Harris, P. M., Hollick, C. T., and Wright, R., 1967, Mineral separation for age determination: Inst. Mining and Metallurgy Bull. 732, p. 181-189.

Hart, S. R., 1961, The use of hornblendes and pyroxenes for K-Ar dating: Jour. Geophys. Research, v. 66, p. 2995-3001.

Hart, S. R., 1964, The petrology and isotopic-mineral age relations of a contact zone in the Front Range, Colorado: Jour. Geol., v. 72, p. 493-525.

Hart, S. R., 1966, A test for excess radiogenic argon in micas: Jour. Geophys. Research, v. 71, p. 1769-1770.

Hart, S. R., and Dodd, R. T., Jr., 1962, Excess radiogenic argon in pyroxenes: Jour. Geophys. Research, v. 67, p. 2998-2999.

Hay, R. L., 1963, Stratigraphy of Beds I through IV, Olduvai Gorge, Tanganyika: Science, v. 139, p. 829-833.

Hay, R. L., 1967a, Hominid-bearing deposits of Olduvai Gorge: NAS-NRC Symposium on Time and Stratigraphy in the Evolution of Man: NAS-NRC Publ. 1469, p. 30-42.

Hay, R. L., 1967b, Revised stratigraphy of Olduvai Gorge: p. 221-228 in Bishop, W. W., and Clark, J. D., eds., 1967, Background to Evolution in Africa, Univ. Chicago Press, 935 p.

Heirtzler, J. R., Dickson, G. O., Herron, E. M., Pitman, W. C., III, and LePichon, X., 1968, Marine magnetic anomalies, geomagnetic field reversals, and motions of the ocean floor and continents: Jour. Geophys. Research, v. 73, p. 2119-2136.

Herzog, R., 1934, Ionen-und elektronenoptische Zylinderlinsen und Prismen I: Zeitschr. Physik, v. 89, p. 447-473.

Hillebrand, W. F., Lundell, G. E. F., Bright, H. A., and Hoffman, J. I., 1953, Applied Inorganic Analysis (2nd ed.): New York, John Wiley & Sons, Inc., 1034 p.

Hills, L. V., and Baadsgaard, H. 1967, Potassium-argon dating of some lower Tertiary strata in British Columbia: Bull. Canadian Petroleum Geology, v. 15, p. 138-149.

Hintenberger, Heinrich, 1962, High-sensitivity mass spectroscopy in nuclear studies: Ann. Rev. Nuclear Sci., v. 12, p. 435-506.

Holmes, Arthur, 1960, A revised geological time-scale: Trans. Edinburgh Geol. Soc., v. 17, p. 183-216.

Houtermans, F. G., 1966, History of the K/Ar method of geochronology: p. 1-6 in Schaeffer, O. A., and Zahringer, J., eds., Potassium-Argon Dating, New York, Springer-Verlag, 234 p.

Hurley, P. M., ed. 1962, Variations in isotopic abundances of strontium, calcium, and argon and related topics: 10th Ann. Prog. Rept. to A.E.C., NYO-3943, 153 p.

Hurley, P. M., 1966, K-Ar dating of sediments: p. 134-151 in Schaeffer, O. A., and Zahringer, J., eds., Potassium-Argon Dating, New York, Springer-Verlag, 234 p.

Hurley, P. M., Brookins, D. G., Pinson, W. H., Hart, S. R., and Fairbairn, H. W., 1961, K-Ar age studies of Mississippi and other river sediments: Geol. Soc. America Bull., v. 72, p. 1807-1816.

Hurley, P. M., Hunt, J. M., Pinson, W. H., and Fairbairn, H. W., 1963, K-Ar age values on the clay fractions in dated shales: Geochim. et Cosmochim. Acta, v. 27, p. 279-284.

Ingamells, C. O., 1962, Determination of major and minor alkalies in silicates by differential flame spectrophotometry: Talanta, v. 9, p. 781-793.

Inghram, M. G., 1954, Stable isotope dilution as an analytical tool: Ann. Rev. Nuclear Sci., v. 4, p. 81-92.

Inghram, M. G., and Hayden, R. J., 1954, A handbook on mass spectroscopy: NAS-NRC Nuclear Sci. Ser., Rept. no. 14, 51 p.

Isacks, Bryan, Oliver, Jack, and Sykes, Lynn R., 1968, Seismology and the new global tectonics: Jour. Geophys. Research, v. 73, p. 5855-5899.

Karpinskaya, T. B., 1967, Synthesis of argon muscovite: Internat. Geol. Rev., v. 9, p. 1493-1495.

Karpinskaya, T. B., Ostrovskiy, I. A., and Shanin, L. L., 1961, Synthetic introduction of argon into mica at high pressures and temperatures: Akad. Nauk S.S.S.R., Geol. Ser., no. 8, p. 87-89.

Kendall, B. R. F., 1960, Isotopic composition of potassium: Nature, v. 186, p. 225-226.

Kirsten, T., 1966, Determination of radiogenic argon: p. 7-39 in Schaeffer, O. A., and Zahringer, J., eds., Potassium-Argon Dating, New York, Springer-Verlag, 234 p.

Kirsten, T., 1968, Incorporation of rare gases in solidifying enstatite melts: Jour. Geophys. Research, v. 73, p. 2807-2810.

Kistler, R. W., Bateman, P. C., and Brannock, W. W., 1965, Isotopic ages of minerals from granitic rocks of the central Sierra Nevada and Inyo Mountains, California: Geol. Soc. America Bull., v. 76, p. 155-164.

Kistler, R. W., and Dodge, F. C. W., 1966, Potassium-argon ages of coexisting minerals from pyroxene-bearing granitic rocks in the Sierra Nevada, California: Jour. Geophys. Research, v. 71, p. 2157-2161.

Klemperer, Otto, 1935, On the radioactivity of potassium and rubidium: Proc. Roy. Soc. London, ser. A, v. 148, p. 638-648.

Kölhorster, Werner Von, 1930, Gammastrahlen an Kaliumsalzen: Zeitschr. Geophysik, v. 6, no. 4, p. 341-357.

Krankowsky, D., and Zahringer, J., 1966, K-Ar ages of meteorites: p. 174-200 in Schaeffer, O. A., and Zahringer, J., eds., Potassium-Argon Dating, New York, Springer-Verlag, 234 p.

Kraushaar, J. J., Wilson, E. D., and Bainbridge, K. T., 1953, Comparison of the values of the disintegration constant of Be^7 in Be, BeO, and BeF_2: Phys. Rev., v. 90, p. 610-614.

Kulp, J. L., 1961, Geologic time scale: Science, v. 133, p. 1105-1114.

Kulp, J. L., and Engels, Joan, 1963, Discordances in K-Ar and Rb-Sr Isotopic ages: p. 219-238 in Radioactive Dating, Vienna, Internat. Atomic Energy Agency, 440 p.

Lanphere, M. A., and Dalrymple, G. B., 1965, P-207—An interlaboratory standard muscovite for argon and potassium analyses: Jour. Geophys. Research, v. 70, p. 3497-3503.

Lanphere, M. A., and Dalrymple, G. B., 1966, Simplified bulb tracer system for argon analyses: Nature, v. 209, p. 902-903.

Lanphere, M. A., and Dalrymple, G. B., 1967, K-Ar and Rb-Sr measurements on P-207, the U.S.G.S. interlaboratory standard muscovite: Geochim. et Cosmochim. Acta, v. 31, p. 1091-1094.

Lanphere, M. A., Irwin, W. P., and Hotz, P. E., 1968, Isotopic age of the Nevadan orogeny and older plutonic and metamorphic events in the Klamath Mountains, California: Geol. Soc. America Bull., v. 79, p. 1027-1052.

Lanphere, M. A., MacKevett, E. M., Jr., and Stern, T. W., 1964, Potassium-argon and lead-alpha ages of plutonic rocks, Bokan Mountain area, Alaska: Science, v. 145, p. 705-707.

Laznitzki, A., and Oeser, E. A., 1937, The radioactivity of potassium prepared from animal tissue: Jour. Chem. Soc. London, Part II, p. 1090-1091.

Leakey, L. S. B., 1959, A new fossil skull from Olduvai: Nature, v. 184, p. 491-493.

Leakey, L. S. B., 1961, New finds at Olduvai Gorge: Nature, v. 189, p. 649-650.

Leakey, L. S. B., Curtis, G. H., and Evernden, J. F., 1962, Age of basalt underlying Bed I, Olduvai: Nature, v. 194, p. 610-612.

Leakey, L. S. B., Evernden, J. F., and Curtis, G. H., 1961, Age of Bed I, Olduvai Gorge, Tanganyika: Nature, v. 191, p. 478-479.

Lee, D. E., Thomas, H. H., Marvin, R. F., and Coleman, R. G., 1964, Isotopic ages of glaucophane schists from the area of Cazadero, California: U.S. Geol. Survey Prof. Paper 475-D, p. D105-D107.

Lippolt, H. J., and Gentner, W., 1962, Argon bestimmungen an Kalium-Mineralien-X. Versuche der Kalium-Argon-Datierung von Fossilien: Geochim. et Cosmochim. Acta, v. 26, p. 1247-1253.

Lippolt, H. J., and Gentner, W., 1963, K-Ar dating of some limestones and fluorites (Examples of K-Ar ages with low Ar-concentrations): p. 239-244 *in Radioactive Dating*, Vienna, Internat. Atomic Energy Agency, 440 p.

Livingston, D. E., and Damon, P. E., 1968, The ages of stratified Precambrian rock sequences in central Arizona and northern Sonora: Canadian Jour. Earth Sci., v. 5, p. 763-772.

Livingston, D. E., Damon, P. E., Mauger, R. L., Bennett, Richmond, and Laughlin, A. W., 1967, Argon 40 in cogenetic feldspar-mica mineral assemblages: Jour. Geophys. Research, v. 72, p. 1361-1375.

Lovering, J. F., and Richards, J. R., 1964, Potassium-argon age study of possible lower-crust and upper-mantle inclusions in deep-seated intrusions: Jour. Geophys. Research, v. 69, p. 4895-4901.

McDougall, Ian, 1961, Determination of the age of a basic igneous intrusion by the potassium-argon method: Nature, v. 190, p. 1184-1186.

McDougall, Ian, 1963, Potassium-argon age measurements on dolerites from Antarctica and South Africa: Jour. Geophys. Research, v. 68, p. 1535-1545.

McDougall, Ian, 1964, Potassium-argon ages from lavas of the Hawaiian Islands: Geol. Soc. America Bull., v. 75, p. 107-128.

McDougall, Ian, Allsopp, H. L., and Chamalaun, F. H., 1966, Isotopic dating of the newer volcanics of Victoria, Australia, and geomagnetic polarity epochs: Jour. Geophys. Research, v. 71, p. 6107-6118.

McDougall, Ian, and Chamalaun, F. H., 1966, Geomagnetic polarity scale of time: Nature, v. 212, p. 1415-1418.

McDougall, Ian, and Green, D. H., 1964, Excess radiogenic argon in pyroxenes and isotopic ages on minerals from Norwegian eclogites: Norsk Geologisk Tidsskrift, v. 44, pt. 2, p. 183-196.

McDougall, Ian, and Rüegg, N. R., 1966, Potassium-argon dates on the Serra Geral Formation of South America: Geochim. et Cosmochim. Acta, v. 30, p. 191-195.

McDougall, Ian, and Tarling, D. H., 1963, Dating of polarity zones in the Hawaiian Islands: Nature, v. 200, p. 54-56.

McIntyre, D. B., 1963, Precision and resolution in geochronometry: p. 112-134 in Albritton, C. C., ed., The Fabric of Geology, Reading, Mass., Addison-Wesley, 372 p.

McKee, E. H., and Nash, D. B., 1967, Potassium-argon ages of granitic rocks in the Inyo batholith, east-central California: Geol. Soc. America Bull., v. 78, p. 669-680.

Macintyre, R. M., 1966, Studies in potassium-argon dating: Ph.D. Thesis, University of Toronto, 191 p.

Macintyre, R. M., York, Derek, and Gittins, J., 1966, Argon retentivity of nephelines: Nature, v. 209, p. 702-703.

Mason, Brian, 1958, Principles of Geochemistry (2nd ed.): New York, John Wiley & Sons, Inc., 310 p.

Meyer, Stefan, and Schweidler, Egon, 1927, Radiöaktivität: Leipzig and Berlin, B. G. Teubner, 721 p.

Miller, J. A., and Mussett, A. E., 1963, Dating basic rocks by the potassium-argon method—The Whin sill: Geophys. Jour., v. 7, p. 547-553.

Mitchell, J. G., 1968, The argon-40/argon-39 method for potassium-argon age determination: Geochim. et Cosmochim. Acta, v. 32, p. 781-790.

Moorbath, S., 1967, Recent advances in the application and interpretation of radiometric age data: Earth Science Reviews, v. 3, p. 111-133.

Morgan, J. W., and Goode, A. D. T., 1966, Potassium abundances in some ultrabasic and basic rocks: Earth Planet. Sci. Letters, v. 1, p. 110-112.

Müller, O., 1966, Potassium Analysis: p. 40-67 in Schaeffer, O. A., and Zahringer, J., eds., Potassium-Argon Dating, New York, Springer-Verlag, 234 p.

Mullins, L. J., and Zerahn, Karl, 1948, The distribution of potassium isotopes in biological material: Jour. Biol. Chemistry, v. 174, p. 107-113.

Mussett, A. E., Diffusion measurements and the potassium-argon method of dating: Geophysical Jour. (In press.)

Mussett, A. E., and Dalrymple, G. B., 1968, An investigation of the source of air Ar contamination in K-Ar dating: Earth Planet. Sci. Letters, v. 4, p. 422-426.

Naughton, J. J. 1963, Possible use of argon-39 in the potassium-argon method of age determination: Nature, v. 197, p. 661-663.

Newman, F. H., and Walke, H. J., 1935, The radioactivity of potassium and rubidium: Phil. Mag., ser. 7, v. 19, p. 767-773.

Nier, A. O., 1935, Evidence for the existence of an isotope of potassium of mass 40: Phys. Rev., v. 48, p. 283-284.

Nier, A. O., 1947, A mass spectrometer for isotope and gas analysis: Rev. Sci. Inst., v. 18, p. 398-411.

Nier, A. O., 1950, a redetermination of the relative abundances of the isotopes of carbon, nitrogen, oxygen, argon, and potassium: Phys. Rev., v. 77, p. 789-793.

Noble, C. S., and Naughton, J. J., 1968, Deep-ocean basalts—Inert gas content and uncertainties in age dating: Science, v. 162, p. 265-267.

Pearson, R. C., Hedge, C. E., Thomas, H. H., and Stern, T. W., 1966, Geochronology of the St. Kevin Granite and neighboring Precambrian rocks, northern Sawatch Range, Colorado: Geol. Soc. America Bull., v. 77, p. 1109-1120.

Rama, S. N. I., Hart, S. R., and Roedder, Edwin, 1965, Excess radiogenic argon in fluid inclusions: Jour. Geophys. Research, v. 70, p. 509-511.

Ramsay, William, and Soddy, Frederick, 1903, Experiments in radioactivity, and the production of helium from radium: Proc. Roy. Soc. London, v. 72, p. 204-207.

Rankama, Kalervo, 1954, *Isotope Geology:* London, Pergamon Press Ltd., 535 p.

Reynolds, J. H., 1956, High sensitivity mass spectrometer for noble gas analysis: Rev. Sci. Inst., v. 27, p. 928-934.

Reynolds, J. H., 1967, Isotopic abundance anomalies in the solar system: Ann. Rev. Nuclear Sci., v. 17, p. 253-316.

Reynolds, J. H., and Spira, Robert, 1966, Individual tracers for isotope dilution analysis of rare gases: Nuclear Instruments and Methods, v. 42, p. 225-228.

Rittenberg, D., 1942, Some applications of mass spectrometric analysis to chemistry: Jour. Applied Physics, v. 13, p. 561-569.

Rose, H. J., Jr., Adler, Isidore, and Flanagan, F. J., 1963, X-ray fluorescence analysis of the light elements in rocks and minerals: Applied Spectroscopy, v. 17, p. 81-85.

Rose, R. L., 1957, Geology of the May Lake area, Yosemite National Park, California: Ph.D. Thesis, University of California, 219 p.

Rutherford, E., 1906, *Radioactive Transformations:* New York, Charles Scribner's Sons, 287 p.

Rutherford, E., 1911, The scattering of α and β particles by matter and the structure of the atom: Phil. Mag., ser. 6, v. 21, p. 669-688.

Rutherford, E., and Soddy, Frederick, 1902a, The cause and nature of radioactivity. Pt. I: Phil. Mag., ser. 6, v. 4, p. 370-396.

Rutherford, E., and Soddy, Frederick, 1902b, The cause and nature of radioactivity. Pt. II: Phil. Mag., ser. 6, v. 4, p. 569-585.

Rutherford, E., and Soddy, Frederick, 1902c, The radioactivity of thorium compounds. I. An investigation of the radioactive emanation: Jour. Chem. Soc. London, v. 81, p. 321-350.

Rutherford, E., and Soddy, Frederick, 1902d, The radioactivity of thorium compounds. II. The cause and nature of radioactivity: Jour. Chem. Soc. London, v. 81, p. 837-860.

Sardarov, S. S., 1957, Retention of radiogenic argon in microcline: Geochemistry, no. 3, p. 233-237.

Schaeffer, O. A., Stoenner, R. W., and Bassett, W. A., 1961, Dating of Tertiary volcanic rocks by the potassium-argon method: Annals N.Y. Acad. Sci., v. 91, p. 317-320.

Schumb, W. C., Evans, R. D., and Leaders, W. M., 1941, Radioactive determination of the relative abundance of the isotope K^{40} in terrestrial and meteoric potassium: Jour. Am. Chem. Soc., v. 63, p. 1203-1205.

Segré, E., and Wiegand, C. E., 1949, Experiments on the effect of atomic electrons on the decay constant of Be^7: Phys. Rev., v. 75, p. 39-43.

Shanin, L. L., Kononova, V. A., and Ivanov, I. B., 1967, On the use of nepheline in K-Ar dating: Akad. Nauk. S.S.S.R. Izv. Ser. Geol., no. 5, p. 19-30.

Shapiro, Leonard, and Brannock, W. W., 1962, Rapid analysis of silicate, carbonate, and phosphate rocks: U.S. Geol. Survey Bull. 1144-A, 56 p.

Sharp, R. P., 1968, Sherwin Till-Bishop Tuff geological relationships, Sierra Nevada, California: Geol. Soc. America Bull., v. 79, p. 351-363.

Silver, L. T., 1967, Apparent age relations in the older Precambrian stratigraphy of Arizona (abs.): Program Conf. on Geochronology of Precambrian Stratified Rocks, Edmonton, Canada, p. 87.

Silver, L. T., 1968, Precambrian batholiths of Arizona (abs.): Geol. Soc. America, Program Ann. Meeting Cordilleran Section, p. 109-110.

Smits, F., and Gentner, W., 1950, Argonbestimmungen an Kalium-Mineralien. I. Bestimmungen an tertiären Kalisalzen: Geochim. et Cosmochim. Acta, v. 1, p. 22-27.

Smythe, W. R., and Hemmendinger, A., 1937, The radioactive isotope of potassium: Phys. Rev., v. 51, p. 178-182.

Strutt, R. J., 1908, Helium and radio-activity in rare and common minerals: Proc. Roy. Soc. London, ser. A, v. 80, p. 572-594.

Suhr, N. H., and Ingamells, C. O., 1966, Solution technique for analysis of silicates: Analytical Chemistry, v. 38, p. 730-734.

Taddeucci, A., Broecker, W. S., and Thurber, D. L., 1968, ^{230}Th dating of volcanic rocks: Earth Planet. Sci. Letters, v. 3, p. 338-342.

Taylor, T. I., and Urey, H. C., 1938, Fractionation of the lithium and potassium isotopes by chemical exchange with zeolites: Jour. Chem. Phys., v. 6, p. 429-438.

Thompson, F. C., and Rowlands, S., 1943, Dual decay of potassium: Nature, v. 152, p. 103.

Thomson, J. J., 1905, On the emission of negative corpuscles by the alkali metals: Phil. Mag., ser. 6, v. 10, p. 584-590.

Thomson, J. J., 1914, Rays of positive electricity: Proc. Roy. Soc. London, ser. A, v. 89, p. 1-20.

Thomson, J. J., 1921, *Rays of Positive Electricity and their Application to Chemical Analyses* (2nd ed.): London, Longmans, Green and Co., 237 p.

Tilley, D. R., and Madansky, L., 1959, Search for positron emission in K^{40}: Phys. Rev., v. 116, p. 413-415.

Turner, D. L., Potassium-argon dating of Pacific Coast Miocene Foraminiferal Stages, *in* Bandy, O. L., ed., *Paleontological Zonation and Radiometric Dating:* Geol. Soc. America Special Paper 124. (In press.)

Verbeek, A. A., and Schreiner, G. D. L., 1967, Variations in ^{39}K:^{41}K ratio and movement of potassium in a granite-amphibolite contact region: Geochim. et Cosmochim. Acta, v. 31, p. 2125-2133.

Vine, F. J., 1966, Spreading of the ocean floor—New evidence: Science, v. 154, p. 1405-1415.

Von Koenigswald, G. H. R., Gentner, W., and Lippolt, H. J., 1961, Age of the basalt flow at Olduvai, East Africa: Nature, v. 192, p. 720-721.

Von Weizsäcker, C. F., 1937, Über die Möglichkeit eines dualen β^- Zerfalls von Kalium: Physik. Zeitschr., v. 38, p. 623-624.

Wager, L. R., 1964, The history of attempts to establish a quantitative time-scale: p. 13-28 *in* Harland, W. B., Smith, A. G., and Wilcock, B., eds., *The Phanerozoic Time-scale:* Quart. Jour. Geol. Soc. London, v. 120s, 458 p.

Wanless, R. K., and Lowdon, J. A., 1961, Isotopic age measurements on coeval minerals and mineral pairs: Geol. Survey Canada Paper 61-17, p. 119-124.

Wanless, R. K., and Lowdon, J. A., 1963a, K-Ar age measurements on mineral pairs: Geol. Survey Canada Paper 62-17, p. 121-122.

Wanless, R. K., and Lowdon, J. A., 1963b, K-Ar age measurements on biotite-muscovite pairs: Geol. Survey Canada Paper 63-17, p. 122-124.

Wanless, R. K., Stevens, R. D., Lachance, G. R., and Rimsaite, R. Y. H., 1965, Age determinations and geological studies. Part I. Isotopic Ages, Report 5: Geol. Survey Canada Paper 64-17, 126 p.

Wasserburg, G. J., Hayden, R. J., and Jensen, K. J., 1956, A^{40}-K^{40} dating of igneous rocks and sediments: Geochim. et Cosmochim. Acta, v. 10, p. 153-165.

Wasserburg, G. J., and Lanphere, M. A., 1965, Age determinations in the Precambrian of Arizona and Nevada: Geol. Soc. America Bull., v. 76, p. 735-758.

Wasserburg, G. J., Mazor, E., and Zartman, R. E., 1963, Isotopic and chemical composition of some terrestrial natural gases: p. 219-240 *in* Geiss, J., and Goldberg, E. D., eds., *Earth Science and Meteoritics:* Amsterdam, North-Holland Publ. Co., 312 p.

Wasserburg, G. J., Wetherill, G. W., Silver, L. T., and Flawn, P. T., 1962, A study of the ages of the Precambrian of Texas: Jour. Geophys. Research, v. 67, p. 4021-4047.

Webb, A. W., and McDougall, Ian, 1967, A comparison of mineral and whole-rock potassium-argon ages of Tertiary volcanics from central Queensland, Australia: Earth Planet. Sci. Letters, v. 3, p. 41-47.

Weeks, M. E., 1956, *Discovery of the Elements* (6th ed.): Easton, Pa., Jour. Chem. Education, 910 p.

Westcott, M. R., 1966, Loss of argon from biotite in a thermal metamorphism: Nature, v. 210, p. 83-84.

Wetherill, G. W., 1957, Radioactivity of potassium and geologic time: Science, v. 126, p. 545-549.

Wetherill, G. W., 1966, Radioactive decay constants and energies: p. 513-519 *in* Clark, S. P., Jr., ed., *Handbook of Physical Constants*, Geol. Soc. America Memoir 97, 587 p.

Wetherill, G. W., Aldrich, L. T., and Davis, G. L., 1955, Ar^{40}/K^{40} ratios of feldspars and micas from the same rock: Geochim. et Cosmochim. Acta, v. 8, p. 171-172.

Wetherill, G. W., Bickford, M. E., Silver, L. T., and Tilton, G. R., 1965, Geochronology of North America: NAS-NRC Nuclear Sci. Ser., Report No. 41, 315 p.

Wilson, E. D., 1939, Pre-Cambrian Mazatzal revolution in Central Arizona: Geol. Soc. America Bull., v. 50, p. 1113-1164.

York, D., Macintyre, R. M., and Gittins, J., 1965, Excess Ar^{40} in sodalites (abs.): Trans. Am. Geophys. Union, v. 46, p. 177.

Zartman, R. E., 1964, A geochronologic study of the Lone Grove Pluton from the Llano Uplift, Texas: Jour. Petrology, v. 5, p. 359-408.

Zartman, R. E., Brock, M. R., Heyl, A. V., and Thomas, H. H., 1967, K-Ar and Rb-Sr ages of some alkalic intrusive rocks from central and eastern United States: Am. Jour. Sci., v. 265, p. 848-870.

Zartman, R. E., Wasserburg, G. J., and Reynolds, J. H., 1961, Helium, argon, and carbon in some natural gases: Jour. Geophys. Research, v. 66, p. 277-306.

Zussman, J., ed., 1967, *Physical methods in determinative mineralogy:* New York, Academic Press, 514 p.

APPENDICES

Appendix A

CONSTANTS AND CONVERSION FACTORS

CONSTANTS

Decay constants of K^{40}

$$\lambda = 5.305 \times 10^{-10}/\text{yr}$$

$$\lambda_\epsilon = 0.585 \times 10^{-10}/\text{yr}$$

$$\lambda_\beta = 4.72 \times 10^{-10}/\text{yr}$$

Branching ratio

$$R = 0.124$$

Half-life of K^{40}

$$t_{1/2} = 1.31 \times 10^9 \text{ yr}$$

Atomic abundance of K^{40}

$$K^{40}/K_{total} = 1.19 \times 10^{-4} \text{ mole/mole}$$

$$= 1.22 \times 10^{-4} \text{ gram/gram}$$

Composition of atmospheric argon

$Ar^{40} = 99.600$ percent
$Ar^{38} = 0.063$ percent
$Ar^{36} = 0.337$ percent
$Ar^{40}/Ar^{36} = 295.5$
$Ar^{40}/Ar^{38} = 1{,}581$
$Ar^{36}/Ar^{38} = 5.35$

CONVERSION FACTORS

To convert	To	Multiply by
weight percent	ppm	10^4
ppm	weight percent	10^{-4}
percent K	percent K_2O	$1.205 \ K_2O/K$
percent K_2O	percent K	$0.8301 \ K/K_2O$
moles Ar^{40}/gram	ppm Ar^{40}	4.000×10^7 gram ppm/mole
moles Ar	cc STP Ar	2.241×10^4 cc STP/mole
cc STP Ar	moles Ar	4.462×10^{-5} mole/cc STP
cc STP Ar^{40}/gram	ppm Ar^{40}	1.785×10^3 gram ppm/cc STP
ppm Ar^{40}	moles Ar^{40}/gram	2.500×10^{-8} mole/gram ppm
ppm Ar^{40}	cc STP Ar^{40}/gram	5.602×10^{-4} cc STP/gram ppm

NOMOGRAM FOR POTASSIUM-ARGON AGE CALCULATIONS

(pocket inside back cover)

The potassium-argon nomogram is a graphical device for finding potassium-argon ages from potassium and argon analytical data. Potassium data must be in weight percent, but may be expressed as either K_2O or K. The quantity of radiogenic Ar^{40} may be in units of either moles/gram or cc STP/gram. Age is in millions of years.

To use the nomogram, place the left end of a straightedge on the appropriate potassium value. If the value is in terms of K_2O, use the left side of the scale; if it is in terms of K, use the right side of the scale. Next, place the right end of the straightedge on the appropriate value for Ar_{rad}^{40}/gram. If the argon measurement is in moles, use the right side of the scale; if it is in cc STP, use the left side of the scale. The potassium-argon age, in millions of years, may be read at the point where the straightedge intersects the center scale. For example, using the data from the sample calculation in Appendix C ($K_2O = 0.720$ percent, Ar_{rad}^{40}/gram $= 1.122 \times 10^{-10}$ mole/gram), the potassium-argon age read from the nomogram is 103 million years.

Given any two quantities represented by the three scales, the third quantity can be determined with a straightedge. Thus the nomogram also can be used as an aid in estimating the quantity of argon to be expected from a sample, the appropriate sample weights, and so forth. In addition, it can be used to convert between mole Ar and cc STP Ar or between K and K_2O.

The nomogram can be read to an accuracy of about 2 percent. It was prepared using the decay and K^{40} abundance constants given in Appendix A.

SAMPLE POTASSIUM-ARGON AGE CALCULATION

This sample age calculation utilizes data from an actual age measurement for hornblende (sample 7G013) from the San Marcos Gabbro, a unit within the Southern California batholith. Potassium was measured by flame photometry using a lithium internal standard. Argon was analyzed by isotope dilution using a bulb-tracer system. The mass analyses were done with a Reynolds-type mass spectrometer operated in the static mode. One pair of "sweeps" from the spectrometer chart is shown in Figure 5-14. The extrapolation of the uncorrected argon ratios for the static analysis is shown in Figure 5-15. In addition to the information contained in these two figures and the constants from Appendix A, the following data are required to complete the age calculation:

Potassium Analysis

K_2O (duplicate analyses) $= \left. \begin{array}{l} 0.716\% \\ 0.725\% \end{array} \right\}$ 0.720%

Argon Analysis

W [sample weight] $= 3.1814$ grams

T_0 [initial tracer value] $= 3.086 \times 10^{-10}$ mole Ar^{38}

δ [tracer depletion constant] $= 0.826 \times 10^{-3}$

X [tracer number] $= 44$

$(Ar^{40}/Ar^{38})_T$ [Ar^{40}/Ar^{38} ratio for tracer] $= 0.0012$

$(Ar^{36}/Ar^{38})_T$ [Ar^{36}/Ar^{38} ratio for tracer] $= 2.67 \times 10^{-5}$

D [spectrometer discrimination correction factor for two mass units] $= 0.999$

In the example, data and calculated values appear in **boldface type,** constants in lightface type.

I. Calculation of K^{40}

   A. Calculate grams of K.

$$K = \frac{(\%K_2O)(\text{grams K}/\text{grams }K_2O)(W)}{100}$$

$$= \frac{(0.720)(0.8301)(3.1814\text{ grams})}{100} = 0.01901\text{ gram}$$

   B. Calculate moles of K^{40}.

$$K^{40} = \frac{(\text{atoms }K^{40}/\text{atoms K})(\text{grams K})}{(\text{grams K}/\text{mole K})} = \frac{(1.19 \times 10^{-4})(0.01901\text{ gram})}{39.10\text{ grams}/\text{mole}}$$

$$= 5.789 \times 10^{-8}\text{ mole}$$

II. Calculation of radiogenic Ar^{40}

   A. Calculate moles Ar^{38} in tracer using equation (5-8).

$$Ar_T^{38} = T_0 e^{-\delta X} = (3.086 \times 10^{-10}\text{ mole }Ar^{38})e^{-(0.826\times10^{-3})44}$$

$$= 2.976 \times 10^{-10}\text{ mole.}$$

   B. Calculate true Ar^{40}/Ar^{38} and Ar^{38}/Ar^{36} ratios in the gas mixture from the uncorrected values given in Figure 5-15,

$$Ar^{40}/Ar^{38} = 0.743, \qquad Ar^{38}/Ar^{36} = 1.012,$$

by using the spectrometer scale factors from Figure 5-14 and the discrimination correction, D.

$$(Ar^{40}/Ar^{38})_M = (Ar^{40}/Ar^{38})(D)\frac{(\text{Scale }40)}{(\text{Scale }38)} = (0.743)(0.999)\frac{(10\text{ volts})}{(5\text{ volts})}$$

$$= 1.485.$$

$$(Ar^{38}/Ar^{36})_M = (Ar^{38}/Ar^{36})(D)\frac{(\text{Scale }38)}{(\text{Scale }36)}$$

$$= (1.012)(0.999)\frac{(5\text{ volts})}{(0.005\text{ volts})} = 1011.$$

C. Calculate total Ar^{40}.

$$Ar_{total}^{40} = (Ar^{40}/Ar^{38})_M(Ar_T^{38}) = (1.485)(2.976 \times 10^{-10} \text{ mole})$$

$$= 4.419 \times 10^{-10} \text{ mole}.$$

D. Calculate Ar_{rad}^{40} using equation (5-6).

$$Ar_{rad}^{40} = Ar_T^{38}\Bigg\{(Ar^{40}/Ar^{38})_M - (Ar^{40}/Ar^{38})_T$$

$$- \left[\frac{1-(Ar^{38}/Ar^{36})_M(Ar^{36}/Ar^{38})_T}{(Ar^{38}/Ar^{36})_M(Ar^{36}/Ar^{38})_A - 1}\right]\left[(Ar^{40}/Ar^{38})_A - (Ar^{40}/Ar^{38})_M\right]\Bigg\}$$

$$= (2.976 \times 10^{-10} \text{ mole})\Bigg\{(1.485) - (0.0012)$$

$$- \left[\frac{1-(1011)(2.67 \times 10^{-5})}{(1011)(5.35)-1}\right]\left[(1581)-(1.485)\right]\Bigg\} = 3.570 \times 10^{-10} \text{ mole}.$$

E. Calculate percentage of Ar_{rad}^{40} in the analysis.

$$\text{Percent } Ar_{rad}^{40} = \frac{100 \ Ar_{rad}^{40}}{Ar_{total}^{40}} = \frac{(100)(3.570 \times 10^{-10} \text{ mole})}{4.419 \times 10^{-10} \text{ mole}} = 80.8\%.$$

III. Calculation of the apparent age using equation (4-3).

$$t = 1.885 \times 10^9 \ log_e\left[9.068\frac{Ar_{rad}^{40}}{K^{40}}+1\right]$$

$$= (1.885 \times 10^9) \ log_e\left[(9.068)\frac{(3.570 \times 10^{-10} \text{ mole})}{(5.789 \times 10^{-8} \text{ mole})}+1\right]$$

$$= 102.6 \times 10^6 \text{ years}.$$

DERIVATIONS OF FORMULAE

EQUATION (5-4). ISOTOPE-DILUTION FORMULA FOR AN ELEMENT WITH TWO STABLE ISOTOPES

Definitions

A_{1N} = atoms of isotope A_1 in sample

A_{2N} = atoms of isotope A_2 in sample

A_{1T} = atoms of isotope A_1 in tracer

A_{2T} = atoms of isotope A_2 in tracer

x = atoms of element A in sample

y = atoms of element A in tracer

$(A_1/A_2)_N$ = composition of sample

$(A_1/A_2)_T$ = composition of tracer

$(A_1/A_2)_M$ = composition of mixture

First we write

$$x = A_{1N} + A_{2N}.$$

Then divide both sides by A_{2N} and solve for A_{2N}:

(a) $$A_{2N} = \frac{x}{1 + (A_1/A_2)_N}.$$

Similarly,

(b) $$A_{2T} = \frac{y}{1 + (A_1/A_2)_T}.$$

Multiply both sides of (a) by A_{1N}/A_{2N} and solve for A_{1N}:

(c) $$A_{1N} = \frac{x(A_1/A_2)_N}{1 + (A_1/A_2)_N}.$$

Similarly,

(d) $\qquad A_{1T} = \dfrac{y(A_1/A_2)_T}{1+(A_1/A_2)_T}.$

Now

(e) $\qquad (A_1/A_2)_M = \dfrac{A_{1N}+A_{1T}}{A_{2N}+A_{2T}}.$

Substitute (a), (b), (c), and (d) into (e) and simplify:

$$(A_1/A_2)_M = \frac{x(A_1/A_2)_N[1+(A_1/A_2)_T]+y(A_1/A_2)_T[1+(A_1/A_2)_N]}{x[1+(A_1/A_2)_T]+y[1+(A_1/A_2)_N]}. \qquad (5\text{-}3)$$

Solve for x:

$$x = \frac{y[1+(A_1/A_2)_N][(A_1/A_2)_T-(A_1/A_2)_M]}{[1+(A_1/A_2)_T][(A_1/A_2)_M-(A_1/A_2)_N]}. \qquad (5\text{-}4)$$

EQUATION (5-6). ISOTOPE DILUTION FORMULA FOR RADIOGENIC ARGON

Definitions

Ar_{rad}^{40} = atoms of radiogenic Ar^{40} in sample

Ar_T^{i} = atoms of isotope i in tracer

Ar_A^{i} = atoms of isotope i in atmospheric contaminant

Ar_M^{i} = atoms of isotope i in mixture

The subscripts also apply to the isotope ratios.

Given equations (5-5),

(a) $Ar_M^{40} = Ar_{rad}^{40} + Ar_T^{40} + Ar_A^{40},$

(b) $Ar_M^{38} = Ar_T^{38} + Ar_A^{38},$

(c) $Ar_M^{36} = Ar_T^{36} + Ar_A^{36},$

we rewrite (a) and (c):

(d) $Ar_M^{40} = Ar_{rad}^{40} + (Ar^{40}/Ar^{38})_T \, Ar_T^{38} + (Ar^{40}/Ar^{38})_A \, Ar_A^{38}.$

(e) $Ar_M^{36} = (Ar^{36}/Ar^{38})_T \, Ar_T^{38} + (Ar^{36}/Ar^{38})_A \, Ar_A^{38}.$

Divide (b) by (e) and solve for Ar_A^{38}:

$$\text{(f)} \quad Ar_A^{38} = Ar_T^{38} \left[\frac{1 - (Ar^{38}/Ar^{36})_M (Ar^{36}/Ar^{38})_T}{(Ar^{38}/Ar^{36})_M (Ar^{36}/Ar^{38})_A - 1} \right].$$

Divide (d) by (b) and solve for Ar_{rad}^{40}:

$$\text{(g)} \quad Ar_{rad}^{40} = Ar_T^{38} (Ar^{40}/Ar^{38})_M - Ar_T^{38} (Ar^{40}/Ar^{38})_T$$
$$- Ar_A^{38} [(Ar^{40}/Ar^{38})_A - (Ar^{40}/Ar^{38})_M].$$

Substitute (f) into (g) and simplify:

$$Ar_{rad}^{40} = Ar_T^{38} \Bigg\{ (Ar^{40}/Ar^{38})_M - (Ar^{40}/Ar^{38})_T$$
$$- \left[\frac{1 - (Ar^{38}/Ar^{36})_M (Ar^{36}/Ar^{38})_T}{(Ar^{38}/Ar^{36})_M (Ar^{36}/Ar^{38})_A - 1} \right] \left[(Ar^{40}/Ar^{38})_A - (Ar^{40}/Ar^{38})_M \right] \Bigg\}.$$

$$(5\text{-}6)$$

INDEX